The Revolution of 1861

—— ● ● ● ——

CIVIL WAR AMERICA

Gary W. Gallagher, Peter S. Carmichael,
Caroline E. Janney, and
Aaron Sheehan-Dean, *editors*

The Revolution of 1861

• • •

The American Civil War in the Age of Nationalist Conflict

Andre M. Fleche

THE UNIVERSITY OF NORTH CAROLINA PRESS
Chapel Hill

This book was published with the assistance of
the Fred W. Morrison Fund for Southern Studies
of the University of North Carolina Press.

Designed and set in Miller by Rebecca Evans
Manufactured in the United States of America

The paper in this book meets the guidelines for permanence
and durability of the Committee on Production Guidelines for
Book Longevity of the Council on Library Resources.

The University of North Carolina Press has been a member
of the Green Press Initiative since 2003.

Library of Congress Cataloging-in-Publication Data
Fleche, Andre M.
The revolution of 1861 : the American Civil War in the
age of nationalist conflict / Andre M. Fleche.
p. cm. — (Civil War America)
Includes bibliographical references and index.
ISBN 978-0-8078-3523-4 (cloth : alk. paper)
1. United States—History—Civil War, 1861–1865—Causes. 2. Nationalism—
United States—History—19th century. 3. Nationalism—Southern States—
History—19th century. 4. Nationalism—Confederate States of America—History.
5. Self determination, National—United States—History—19th century. 6. Self
determination—Europe—History—19th century. 7. Europe—History—1848–1849.
8. Revolutions—Europe—History—19th century. I. Title.
E459.F54 2012   973.7—dc23   2011024071

16 15 14 13 12   5 4 3 2 1

for Meredith

Contents

Illustrations

Acknowledgments

ONE OF THE PLEASURES OF COMPLETING A PROJECT IS CALLING TO mind all of the people who have helped to bring it to fruition. The research for this book began at the University of Virginia, and many friends, colleagues, and mentors have influenced the book's development. First and foremost, I must thank Gary W. Gallagher for his instruction, advice, and professional example. He taught me much about history and scholarship, and raised my aspirations in countless ways. His influence truly made a difference in my life.

Many others at Virginia and beyond offered me feedback and advice. Peter Onuf took an early interest in this project, and his comments, questions, and timely interventions guided me as I formulated my arguments. I also benefited from the wisdom of Edward L. Ayers and Michael F. Holt, both of whom commented on portions of this book. Sophia Rosenfeld and Stephen Cushman read an early version of the manuscript in its entirety and offered suggestions and advice. Brian Owensby encouraged me to think beyond the borders of the United States, and Stanley Nadel provided commentary on my discussion of German forty-eighters. The dedicated staff at the Alderman and Harrison-Small special collections libraries aided me in many ways throughout the course of my research.

A vibrant and collegial community of talented scholars at the University of Virginia made studying in Charlottesville exciting. I especially enjoyed participating in the Civil War Era seminar, a group that met frequently to share works in progress. Its members, Keith Harris, Wayne Wei-Siang Hsieh, Caroline Janney, Jaime Martinez, John Mooney, Cynthia Nicoletti, Katherine Pierce, Aaron Sheehan-Dean, Matthew Speiser, and Kid Wong-srichanalai, all read drafts of my chapters, discussed my ideas, and challenged my thinking. Many other friends and colleagues with a wide variety of interests also influenced me and made my time at Virginia a happy one, including Carl Bon Tempo, Benjamin Carp, Kristin Celello, Peter Flora, Laurie Hochstetler, Derek Hoff, Kurt Hohenstein, Christopher P. Loss, Moritz Mälzer, Rob Parkinson, Chris Nehls, Brian Schoen, and Ethan Sribnick.

In 2006, I was fortunate enough to join the globally oriented and inter-disciplinary Department of History, Geography, Economics, and Politics at Castleton State College. I could not have asked for a more supportive group of colleagues. I thank Adam Chill, Melisse Pinto, Judy Robinson, Scott Roper, Jonathan Spiro, Trish van der Spuy, and Carrie Waara, all of whom encouraged my research and read portions of my manuscript. The excellent staff at the college's Calvin Coolidge Library assisted me in the final stages of my work, and Lauren Olewnik and Franny Ryan helped me track down some crucial interlibrary loan materials.

The editors and staff at the University of North Carolina Press have worked with skill and professionalism in bringing this project to print. I would like to thank David Perry in particular for his expertise and patience during the long process of turning a manuscript into a book. Zach Read and Paul Betz worked with me through the steps of submission and editing, and copyeditor Jeff Canaday skillfully helped polish the text. Two anonymous reviewers twice read drafts of the entire manuscript, and their suggestions and advice helped to make this a much better book than it would have otherwise been.

Above all, my family has been a source of strength, support, and inspiration. My parents, Timothy and Ellen Fleche, have always encouraged me in everything I have attempted. They fostered my interests, and their love and dedication gave me the courage to pursue my goals. My brothers, Justin and Alexandre, have stood by me in many endeavors and continue to play an important part in my life. I have also been blessed with a large and supportive extended family. My grandparents, Edwin and Virginia Fleche and Evelyn and the late Edgar Tomkin, along with all the members of the Fleche and Tomkin families, have been a source of comfort, guidance, and good cheer. My in-laws, the Petersons, and especially Gail Chapman and Steve Vogl, have touched me with their support, their generosity, and their interest in my studies. My wife, Meredith Chapman Fleche, has contributed to this project since the beginning. She has enthusiastically discussed ideas with me, served as editor and confidante, and, most recently, helped prepare images for the manuscript. She has shared many adventures with me and made many personal sacrifices to support this project. For these reasons, I have dedicated this book to her.

The Revolution of 1861

Introduction

The American Civil War and the Age of Revolution

ON JUNE 15, 1864, ERNEST DUVERGIER DE HAURANNE ARRIVED IN New York to observe the final act of what he would later call "five years of revolution, political turmoil and civil war" in the United States. The French liberal hoped to follow in the footsteps of Alexis de Tocqueville, a close family friend, by observing American democracy in action. While his illustrious predecessor had reported to French readers on the promise as well as the problems of a functioning republic, Duvergier de Hauranne would document how a democratic people dealt with the disintegration of their nation.[1]

Federal and Confederate partisans wasted little time in outlining their positions. One Union officer explained to the visitor that the abolition of slavery and the defeat of the rebellion would ensure the survival of the United States. Slavery and rebellion were inextricably linked in the soldier's mind. Slavery, he believed, posed a dire threat to America's experiment in modern nation-building. The uncompensated labor of enslaved human beings, he held, had led to the concentration of wealth in the hands of a select few. The class interests of rich planters ran counter to the development of a united polity based on the sovereignty of all the people, making true nationalism impossible. Slavery, he told the French visitor, threatened to lead to the emergence of "a military aristocracy." Destroying the institution would level the social hierarchy, thereby sustaining a nation based on representative government. "Give us a little more time," the officer concluded, "and that arrogant class that calls itself the aristocracy of the South will sink into the mass of the common people." Duvergier de Hauranne agreed. The newcomer to America immediately made connections between southern planters and the landed nobility that had so often resisted change in his native France. He became gradually convinced that "slavery in the South, bound up as it was with the ownership of land, was

1

giving birth to aristocratic vices that were eating out the heart of republican institutions."[2]

Duvergier de Hauranne's developing opinion did not go unchallenged for long. A French-Caribbean slaveholder and supporter of the Confederacy explained to him that the North's attempt to subjugate the South was doomed to fail. He believed that the South was exercising its legitimate right to national self-determination, and there was little the federal government could do to stop it. "The war will have served only to eternalize the division of the Republic," the Confederate supporter feared. He rejected any celebration of America's unique destiny in the world. Instead, he believed that North America, as Europe had, would fracture into a congeries of distinct, squabbling states. "In vain does this Republic boast that it has escaped the evils of the Old World," he told Duvergier de Hauranne. "Rather, it is entering an era of revolutions and civil wars, and God only knows when it will get out of it!" The United States, the observer from the Caribbean believed, would do better to accept the right of self-determination and break into two separate nations. "The Unionists are made to appear as alien despots," Duvergier de Hauranne reported, "while the Confederates are pictured as the true defenders of the nation and of liberty."[3]

Though in general Duvergier de Hauranne favored the North, no European needed to be reminded that the cause of national self-determination should be entitled to respectful consideration. The French liberal quickly became aware, as did many Americans, that America's Civil War was a struggle to resolve the great "nation question" that troubled the nineteenth-century world. During the decades that preceded the Battle of Fort Sumter, Europeans and North and South Americans had all taken up arms on at least one occasion to shape the character of the emerging international system of nation-states. The questions they addressed included the relationship between race and nation; the place of slavery, servitude, and class distinction in representative republics; and the legitimacy of the right of self-determination. When the Civil War broke out in the United States in 1861, Unionists and Confederates had a long history of precedents from which to draw ideas and inspiration.

Indeed, mid-nineteenth-century Americans believed they lived in what some historians have termed an "age of revolution." Ever since the American and French revolutions of the late eighteenth century established what Benedict Anderson has called "models" for "pirating" nationalist revolution, no monarch or imperialist in the Atlantic world sat easily upon his or her throne. Americans applauded every subsequent effort to overthrow the remnants of the ancien régime. They supported Latin America's independence in the first decades of the nineteenth century. Newspapers widely covered Greece's war for independence from the Ottoman Empire in the 1820s. In 1830, Americans argued that the revolutions in France and Poland challenged the doctrine of monarchical legitimacy and furthered American goals of spreading republican government across the globe.[4]

The pan-European revolutions of 1848 attracted the most attention. Although they failed to achieve their goals, they opened a transatlantic dialogue regarding nationalism, worker's rights, and the future of representative government at the precise moment Americans confronted the problems of sectionalism, slavery, and the expansion and later disintegration of the nation. The legacy of 1848 and the revolutions that had preceded it provided much more than a basis of comparison and analogy for Americans contemplating their own civil war. It directly influenced the competing nationalist ideologies both sides developed as they presented their cases to each other and to the world. Confederates argued that European nationalist movements provided models for their own efforts to establish a new nation-state. They seized on the "right of revolution" and the rhetoric of self-determination to make their case. Only voluntary communities, they argued, could become legitimate nations in the nineteenth century. Many Unionists, by contrast, built support for the war, and later for emancipation, by comparing southern slaveholders to the European aristocrats who had defeated progressive revolutionaries time and again in the past half-century. They increasingly argued that they could best defeat the southern aristocracy and preserve American nationality by confiscating large landed estates and liberating the South's peculiar form of human property. Nobility of either wealth or title, they argued, proved incompatible with the emergence of the nation in the modern world.[5]

The complicated legacy of the century's violent past also challenged the combatants of 1861–65 to explain to the world the universal relevance of their unique conception of the nation-form. When the federal government struck at slavery as the French had done during the 1790s and in 1848, Confederates were forced to develop an ideology of "white republicanism" that opposed both the "black republicanism" of the abolitionists and the "red republicanism" of radical European workers who had championed the socialist "right to work." Slavery, Confederates argued, made successful nationalist revolution possible by controlling the class conflict that had doomed European efforts. The U.S. government, while it fought to crush a rebellion against legitimate authority, risked alienating the victorious reactionary regimes of Europe by making explicit ideological appeals to Europe's workers and liberal middle class. Consequently, U.S. diplomatic efforts began by convincing heads of state that America's democratic republic would represent the principles of legitimacy and stability in international politics. In short, the fight over the future of republican government in America can also be seen as a fight over the legacy of 1848 and the meaning of nationalism and revolution in the Atlantic world.[6]

Historians have long sought to characterize the Civil War as a revolution. Charles and Mary Beard famously called the conflict "The Second American Revolution." The Beards have been joined by a host of ideological descendants who view the war as part of the process by which the Western world made the transition from a feudal and agrarian past to a modern capitalist economy. Such thinkers remain focused on forcing the war into a predetermined framework governed by dialectical economic change. Union victory, they argue, represents either the triumph of industry or the vindication of liberal-democratic values that enabled capitalist expansion. These models break down for several reasons. First, historians have increasingly made clear that plantation slavery proved perfectly compatible with early industrialization. Second, northern and southern society were in many ways as much alike as they were different. Both valued democracy and civil liberties for white men. Northern citizens often proved as hostile to including African Americans in political life as white southerners did. The market-oriented farmers and small producers of the antebellum North can hardly be said to resemble a "capitalist glacier" destined to engulf the backward South.[7]

Finally, teleological characterizations of the conflict ignore the historical context in which the war was fought. Southern revolutionaries believed they were joining the Poles, Italians, Irish, and Hungarians who had also acted in the tradition of liberal self-determination during the 1840s and 1850s. Slavery, Confederates argued, did not represent the principles of a dying past; rather, Confederates maintained that the peculiar institution could help usher in an era of progress characterized by prosperity and harmonious class relations between white men. The progressive thinkers in Europe and America who favored the North also offered interpretations of the war that differ widely from those of modern historians. The work of Karl Marx, which provides the theoretical basis for the Beard thesis and its variations, provides a case in point. Marx, in a way his more recent students do not, celebrated the American nation in the early 1860s for being "the highest form of popular self-government till now realized." He described the "present struggle between the South and the North" as a struggle not between agrarianism and capitalism but between "the system of slavery and the system of free labor." His views varied little from many engaged Unionists. Marx and like-minded Unionists believed that the defeat of the "slave-holding aristocracy" would enable the world's free workers to prosper as small landholders on America's endless frontier. Only the betrayal of the promises of Reconstruction and the economic developments of the late nineteenth century made it possible to speak of the triumph of industrial capitalism.[8]

Midcentury Americans naturally sought to explain the war by referring to recent world history and current events, as did Marx. They chose to describe the conflict using the term "revolution" as often as they employed the labels "civil war," "rebellion," or "war between the states." "We live in revolutionary times, & I say God bless the revolution," declared Horace White, noted Chicago journalist and editor, as he celebrated the election of Abraham Lincoln during the winter of 1861. Jonathan Worth, who would serve as governor of North Carolina, reacted to the secession of his home state in a similar fashion. "We are in the midst of war and revolution," he wrote from Asheboro in May 1861. "N.C. would have stood by the Union but for the conduct of the national administration which for folly and simplicity exceeds anything in modern history." A self-described neutral but worried Maryland physician and planter confided to his diary, "Our country is in a terrible excitement at this time—in a revolution, the result of which, no man can tell." Massachusetts woman of letters Lucy Larcom shared his fears that the "revolution" that had begun in 1861 would pit "brother . . . against brother." Committed southerner John Beauchamp Jones faced the conflict with less ambivalence but with an equal appreciation for the nature of the coming violence. He resolved, "At fifty-one, I can hardly follow the pursuit of arms; but I will write and preserve a Diary of the revolution." Jones had unwittingly echoed New York diarist George Templeton Strong, who spoke of "revolutionary times" and observed in January 1861, "Even the most insignificant memoranda of these revolutionary days may be worth preserving. We are making history just now fearfully fast."[9]

Historians of the Civil War have been content to explain these semantic choices by referring to the continuing importance of the American Revolution in popular culture. The legacy of 1776 had an undeniable impact on the intellectual predilections of the generation that fought the Civil War. Both sides claimed to be striving to preserve the government conceived by the founding fathers. Unionists and Confederates alike compared themselves to the patriots whose sacrifices established American independence. But the legacy of the revolution, while important, is not sufficient to describe the intellectual environment in which mid-nineteenth-century Americans thought and acted.[10]

The testimony of observers in the North and the South reveals that global events profoundly influenced American interpretations of the Civil War. The *New York Herald* asserted in 1861 that the conflict compared favorably with "the overthrow of dynasties in France, England and Italy." Charles Ingersoll, in his widely published *A Letter to a Friend in a Slave State*, immediately thought of the recent revolutions in Europe in explaining to his acquaintance the ideological importance of the coming war. He feared that the disintegration of the Union would afford Old World reactionaries the opportunity to take revenge on Americans for their long-standing support for representative government. Ingersoll recalled that "the sentiment of sympathy, in the United States, was loud and universal, when, in the eventful year of 1848, crowns seemed to be falling off the heads of the monarchs of Europe." He now warned his southern friend that Old World reactionaries would promote the destruction of the Union out of the "natural desire of aristocratically ruled countries, to witness the failure of [American] institutions."[11]

Americans recognized that the legacy of 1776 was insufficient to provide all the answers to the questions of nationality that troubled both sides of the Atlantic in the middle of the nineteenth century. The nationalist revolutions of the eighteenth century had left problems and ambiguities that statesmen and revolutionaries in the nineteenth century sought to resolve. The American Revolution of 1776 did not create an organic nation. It never decisively answered the question of the compatibility of slavery with republican institutions, or determined what citizenship rights landless laborers should enjoy. Instead, it left a conglomeration of states, each with individual institutions, interests, rights, responsibilities, and approaches regarding race and labor. Nineteenth-century Americans recognized as much. The federal constitution of 1787 had strived to create a "more perfect Union," and Abraham Lincoln believed his generation would have to finish the job. White southern revolutionaries offered an entirely different answer to the question of American national viability. They argued that sustainable nations could only be constructed out of sectional unions bound by common institutions and interests such as racial slavery.[12]

Mid-nineteenth-century thinkers in both the Old World and the New believed that they lived in an era in which the nation-state would take its final form. Unionists and Confederates alike strove to convince the world that their causes could improve upon past models and usher in an age in which nationalist strife gave way to consensus and harmony. The turmoil of revolution-torn Europe provided much for them to consider in their quest to establish an ideal state. The first French revolution introduced the equation of "people" and "nation" by establishing an administratively centralized state resting on an equal and sovereign citizenry. Napoleon's imperialism and the Congress of Vienna's restoration of old-regime governments betrayed that promise. The midcentury revolutions sought to redeem it. Revolutions in Hungary, Italy, and Ireland proclaimed the people's right to establish a nation by rebelling against foreign rule. Revolutionaries in France, Austria, and the German states sought to create unified nations by overturning the rule of titled nobility and by restoring the rights of suffrage, free speech, and free assembly to broad segments of the population. New innovations to the program of nationalist revolution also began in 1848. In France and Eastern Europe, reformers definitively declared the incompatibility of unfree labor and representative government by freeing, respectively, slaves and serfs. French workers also demanded that the state evolve to address problems of labor and unemployment by declaring the right to work and establishing government-funded "national workshops." Karl Marx began envisioning a new kind of nation in which class interests united workers across national borders.[13]

None of these alternatives came to fruition. Reactions in 1849 and 1850 succeeded in reestablishing monarchy and aristocracy as Europe's governing principles. The movements for self-determination failed to create independent nations. The events of the era, however, provided Americans with much to consider as they struggled to define the future of the nation-form in the wake of the collapse of their own united republic. Southern nationalists argued that they could improve upon European efforts at self-determination by keeping their working class enslaved and rejecting the communism that troubled Old World nations, a communism they called "red republicanism." Many Unionists argued that they could create a stronger nation by removing the aristocratic ruling class, and the slavery that sustained it, from the American republic. Patriots in both sections crafted an answer to the nation question that engaged the issues raised by Europeans in the years since the French Revolution.

Americans reacted to several other European events of international importance between 1848 and the outbreak of war in 1861. The Crimean War shaped the European balance of power and attracted American observers, including future Union general George B. McClellan. The unification of the Italian peninsula, attempted in 1848 and completed on the eve of the American Civil War, received more attention. The Risorgimento won support in the United States, even while prompting self-serving celebrations of American republicanism and condescending commentary on Italian fitness for self-government. In American imaginations, however, the revolutions of 1848 eclipsed more recent events for two important reasons. First, the revolutions represented the most recent "Europe-wide event" that promised to make the Old World more like the New. Even Italian unification appeared to Americans to be an outgrowth of the earlier conflagrations. Second, the dissemination of ideas through immigration gave 1848 outsized importance. Thousands of forty-eighters entered the United States during the 1850s, and many of them played key roles in the Civil War that followed.[14]

Our understanding of the Civil War has much to gain from a broader outlook. Much of the American public, and many scholars, except for a few recent exceptions, continue to hold a parochial vision of Civil War history, one most widely disseminated by such works as Ken Burns's popular television documentary *The Civil War*. The argument should be familiar: American brothers fought the war over uniquely American issues and in the process forged a unique American identity. The story of the origins of the war has been told and retold as a story of domestic political conflict over the peculiar issues of sectionalism and slavery in the republic. Few scholars dissent. As one historian noted: "We write about liberty without much reference to the French Revolution, about Jacksonian Democracy without reference to the democratic ferment of Europe in the 1830's and 1840's, about American reform without reference to the epic struggles in Britain to halt the slave trade, to free the slave, and to improve the lot of the industrial worker." One might add that we describe Confederate secession without mentioning the attempt of the Irish and Hungarians to secede, respectively, from the United Kingdom and the Austrian Empire in 1848; we discuss the Republican Party's free-labor ideology without reference to French laborers' demands in 1848 for the right to work; and we examine the formation of a united American nation in the mid-nineteenth century without considering contemporary efforts to unite Germany and Italy.[15]

Situating the Civil War in an "age of revolution" teaches us several things. First, it shows that Americans were engaged with the world around them. Global events shaped American ideology as much as any notion of

America's status as a "city upon a hill." Second, placing the debate over slavery alongside European efforts to struggle with the problems of class and labor explains why some northerners hostile to black equality could be convinced to back emancipation. Destruction of the slave-power aristocracy was essential for the rights of white workers, they believed. Finally, resituating the Civil War in a global context demonstrates the disturbing side of the rhetoric of nationalist self-determination. The fact that liberal arguments could justify racial subordination shows how easily Americans and Europeans could later embrace colonialism. In order to understand the complex ideological issues raised by the Civil War, historians must look at events on the other side of the Atlantic, just as mid-nineteenth-century Americans did.

The pages that follow explore the ways in which these Americans constructed their ideas about northern and southern nationalism as they contemplated the revolutionary changes that had swept the Atlantic world in the years before the Civil War. The first two chapters of this book focus on the development of American understandings in a domestic context. Chapter 1 examines American reactions to foreign revolutions and explores how European immigrants labored to keep a coherent memory of their causes alive in the United States, a task which grew more difficult during the divisive 1850s. The second chapter demonstrates just how contested the meaning of nationalist revolution had become by 1861. The chapter traces the ways European Americans applied competing conceptions of liberal nationalism as they chose sides and mobilized for war in the months after the Battle of Fort Sumter.

The remainder of the book shows how politicians, diplomats, soldiers, and intellectuals in the North and in the South reiterated and reinterpreted these ideas as they explained their respective causes to the world. Chapters 3 and 4 elucidate the theories of nationalism that northerners and southerners developed during the first two years of war. Union officials were forced to reconcile the principles of national legitimacy with their respect for the right of revolution, while most white southerners, by contrast, seized on the cause of national self-determination. The coming of emancipation in 1863 challenged both factions to reassess their positions. Chapters 5 and 6 explore how the abolition of slavery shaped the development of nationalist ideologies in the last three years of the war. Many northerners increasingly abandoned their more conservative rhetoric and embraced the destruction of a slaveholding aristocracy as a precondition of national unity. Confederates, nevertheless, continued to insist that only slavery could provide the stability that nations needed in an age of violent class conflict. Supporters of both these positions believed that victory for their respective causes held the key to a progressive future for the entire world.

1

World Revolutions and the Coming of the American Civil War

THE YEAR 1848 PROVED PARTICULARLY SIGNIFICANT FOR THE FUTURE of the American nation. On February second of that year, negotiators representing Mexico and the United States concluded the treaty of Guadalupe Hidalgo, which ended the Mexican War and extended America's boundaries to the Pacific Ocean. Several weeks later, revolutions broke out in Europe that promised to establish representative governments across the continent. It seemed to many observers that America's experiment in republican government had succeeded in establishing a model for successful nation-building that could be followed anywhere in the world. Some observers even suggested that the millennium had arrived. By applying their system to the world, Americans believed a peaceful and prosperous community of nation-states would emerge across the globe.

At the height of the Union's success, however, Americans came face to face with their nation's own mortality. The revolutionary movements in Europe collapsed in a wave of reaction. Monarchy and aristocracy emerged ascendant once again. At the same time, the American union appeared to be in danger of imploding. The rapid and dramatic expansion of the American nation threatened to disrupt the Union by reinvigorating the debate over the place of slavery in the territories. In this context, the memory of the revolutions that had rocked Europe during the past half-century proved especially relevant. The growing sectional crisis caused Americans to reflect on the meaning of the revolution of 1776, and at the same time take note of the ways in which thinking about democratic revolution had changed in the years since that event.

Americans in the North and the South remained profoundly influenced by the legacy of their own revolution. They especially celebrated their experiment in republican government, or "republicanism," by which they meant the rule of elected officials, not kings, queens, or princes. They believed that the example of the American patriots of the War for Independence could inspire people around the world to rise up and establish representative governments of their own. For the thinkers and statesmen that held these views, the spread of republican government and the expansion of the American nation became vitally important. Such a development would ensure the future of the fragile American union and, indeed, the world. Many Americans shared Thomas Jefferson's faith in the ability of representative republics to perpetuate global peace and prosperity. The success of America's federal system seemed to confirm that belief. In America, in the view of Jefferson and others, many sovereign republics had agreed to associate for the express purpose of promoting the good of the whole. The new United States, governed by the will and well-being of the people, appeared to have transcended the power politics and petty dynastic ambitions that had so often bathed Europe in blood. If the states of the Old World only followed America's lead in establishing republics, it seemed, world peace might reign indefinitely. In such a friendly international environment, America's young nation could endure forever.[1]

The "legacy of 1776," however, never remained static during the nineteenth century. Instead, the meaning of America's revolution changed in response to foreign events as well as domestic ones. The French and Haitian revolutions, the wars for independence in Latin America, and the mid-century revolutions in Europe engaged concepts and issues that the patriots of 1776 had not anticipated. These wars and revolutions seemed to present different models of republican nation-building and offer alternative definitions of what democratic revolution could entail. European nationalist movements, unlike the American Revolution, defined "oppressed nationalities" in ethnic or cultural, rather than voluntary, terms. Many of them also engaged questions Americans had not yet resolved. European nationalist movements confronted the problems of slavery and industrial and rural poverty that troubled societies on both sides of the Atlantic. Americans intent on celebrating and perpetuating their own revolutionary heritage would increasingly have to make clear exactly how they defined that heritage.

Mid-nineteenth-century Americans believed they lived in an age of revolutions. They tracked the progress of the ideals embodied in their revolution of 1776 by observing European struggles for freedom from monarchy, aristocracy, and despotic government. The successes and failures of Old World peoples served as a barometer of the strength and safety of America's experiment in republican government, as well as a reminder of the unique global role played by the United States. The French Revolution of 1789 promised to remake the map of Europe by introducing the principle of national self-determination to the continent's peoples. It also sparked the Haitian Revolution of 1792, which resulted in the creation of the Western Hemisphere's second independent republic. In the first decade of the nineteenth century, the people of Spanish America began a struggle to establish independent republics throughout South and Central America. Napoleon's final defeat in 1815 threatened to halt this proliferation of new nations and republics. The Congress of Vienna, which met from late 1814 to mid-1815 to decide Europe's political future, favored the restoration of monarchy and paid little heed to the nationalist aspirations of the people. Germany, Italy, and Eastern Europe remained a divided patchwork of kingdoms and princedoms. The Holy Alliance of Russia, Austria, and Prussia pledged to stamp out revolution wherever it might appear. The allied powers even discussed forcibly reintroducing monarchy and empire to the New World. During the 1820s, Thurlow Weed, the future Whig and later Republican editor and politician from New York, argued that the Alliance held "fell designs upon American freedom."[2]

Still, conservatives in Europe could not prevent nationalist conflict from erupting during the 1800s. By the mid-1820s, most of Spain's colonies in Central and South America had finally won independence after a series of long and bloody wars. The United States of America, newly confident in its power after surviving the War of 1812, issued the Monroe Doctrine, pledging to prevent the reestablishment of empire in the New World. In 1830, a series of fresh revolutions disturbed the peace of Europe. Russia had to brutally suppress a movement for independence in Poland. That same year, the French deposed their monarch and installed the constitutional regime of King Louis Philippe, and the Belgians began an ultimately successful effort to secede from Holland.

The spectacle of oppressed peoples on two continents rising up in the name of national rights excited and inspired Americans. The impact in the United States of the Polish uprising proved especially strong. Poland's failed rebellion against Russian authority produced a wave of exiles seeking haven in America's "model republic." These first nineteenth-century "refugees of revolution" reminded Americans of the worldwide impact of the American example of representative government. Major Gaspar Tochman, one of the leaders of the movement and a future supporter of the Confederacy, gave speeches throughout the 1830s and 1840s praising America's revolutionary example and calling attention to the heroism of Poland.

Tochman encouraged his followers to appreciate that the growing internationalism of the nineteenth-century world made political developments on one side of the Atlantic vitally important to communities on the other. He celebrated the "glorious achievements" of the American Revolution and maintained that American political movements were often "observed and considered in Europe" and had "a great weight in its political scale." Tochman believed that Americans held a historic mission to bequeath to the world the "blessings of liberty" enjoyed in the United States. If they failed, however, and Europe's "despotic rulers" defeated the people "still struggling for their liberties," he reasoned that America, "alone, unaided and single-handed," would "have to contend with the combined forces of all Europe" to maintain the "rights of man."[3]

Tochman's speeches created a sensation in the United States. Legislatures in New York, Massachusetts, New Hampshire, Vermont, Connecticut, Virginia, Ohio, Indiana, and Kentucky passed resolutions of support and appreciation. One lawmaker from New Hampshire resolved, "As Americans and as freemen, our feelings and best wishes are always with man in his contests against tyranny." The Vermont assembly professed "a deep interest in the establishment and maintenance of free and liberal principles of government throughout the world." Thomas Jefferson Randolph of Albemarle County told the Virginia legislature that "the cause of Poland is the cause of Liberty and of men against tyranny and power." Although Randolph conceded that the revolutionaries had been crushed by "despotism," he maintained that Poland's "patient magnanimity" and "invincible firmness" foreshadowed "the dawn of a brighter destiny." Americans, galvanized by such calls to arms, held more than seventy pro-Poland meetings up and down the East Coast between 1840 and 1843. The presence of the Light Artillery Blues at a demonstration in Norfolk, Virginia, in April 1843, highlighted the militarist side of the legacy of 1776 by calling to mind the duty of a free people to defend their liberties with force of arms.[4]

By the mid-1840s, U.S. citizens held great hopes and great fears for the future of Europe and America. The uprisings, upheavals, and rebellions they witnessed seemed to offer confirmation of mankind's desire for freedom and republican government. Some Americans professed themselves willing to fight to help others achieve that freedom. That militant self-confidence deteriorated, however, as events in Europe increasingly produced ambiguous outcomes. The revolutions of 1848 and 1849 offer a case in point. They surpassed all predecessors in magnitude, visibility, and impact on Americans intent on preserving republican liberty throughout the

Atlantic world. The spectacle of Europeans across the continent attempting to replace monarchical governments with representative polities reminded Americans of their own struggle for self-government. That legacy sowed the seeds for future conflict, however, as Europeans moved beyond general calls for liberty and freed serfs, slaves, and workers chained to the cycles of capitalism. What could have been a quickly forgotten series of events remained important in American memories as waves of revolutionary immigrants entered an America beginning to grapple with sectionalism, slavery, and the future of republican government at home.[5]

Europe's midcentury revolutions began in late February 1848, when crowds took to the streets of Paris in protest of King Louis Philippe's decision to forbid the assembly of a group of liberals and reformers planning to hold a political banquet coinciding with the birthday of George Washington. Clashes with troops followed, rioters erected barricades, and full-scale rebellion broke out in the national capital. Louis Philippe abdicated his throne the following day. In his place, the revolutionaries inaugurated a provisional government led by the poet Alphonse de Lamartine and the liberal Alexandre Auguste Ledru-Rollin. Radicals secured the inclusion of socialist Louis Blanc and the simple worker Alexandre Albert. France's new leadership enacted universal manhood suffrage and set the date for elections to a national assembly that would draw up a constitution for the second French republic.

News of the revolution in France spread quickly throughout Europe. Across the German states, students, liberals, workers, and peasants took to the streets demanding free speech and free suffrage. Crowds invaded palaces and estates and forced their owners to revoke all feudal laws. In the Austrian Empire, rioters in Vienna chased into exile Clemens von Metternich, the hated architect of the Congress of Vienna, which had restored monarchy to the European continent after the defeat of Napoleon in 1815. Even Pope Pius IX fled the Papal States, giving way to Joseph Mazzini, who took charge of the new "Roman Republic." Further to the south, the people of Naples, the capital of the Kingdom of the Two Sicilies, deposed the notoriously repressive King Ferdinand II, who had also faced a revolt on the island of Sicily earlier that year.

Like the French, revolutionaries across Europe demanded basic civil rights and the establishment of representative governments. In the German states, the Italian states, the Austrian Empire, and elsewhere, however, nationalism was at least as important a goal. Since the wars of Napoleon, German, Italian, and central European patriots dreamed of establishing great nations. They hoped to establish the right of all peoples who shared a common culture, language, or ethnicity to unite under a common government, a principle that was dubbed "national self-determination." In the German states, the forty-eighters won the right to hold elections to select representatives to meet at a parliament in Frankfurt, which was charged with writing a constitution for a united German nation. In Hungary, revolutionaries under the lead of Lajos "Louis" Kossuth declared Hungary's autonomy and then independence from Austria. The Italian peninsula exploded into violence as patriots in the provinces of Lombardy and Venetia fought for freedom from the Austrian Empire. Count Camillo Cavour of Piedmont and the nationalist Giuseppe Garibaldi pledged military support with the ultimate goal of establishing an independent and united kingdom of Italy. Even the British Isles did not escape disturbance in 1848. That spring, English authorities preemptively arrested John Mitchel, a key member of the Irish Confederation established to advocate home rule for Ireland. In July, William Smith O'Brien carried through with a planned uprising, which included men such as Thomas Francis Meagher, Michael Doheny, and John Dillon, men who would reappear in Civil War America. The English authorities put down the tiny revolt easily and also weathered a demonstration of Chartists inspired by the movements on the continent, but it was clear that change might come even to Great Britain.[6]

Americans, for their part, reacted with enthusiasm to the initial news from Europe. As historian Timothy Roberts has shown, 1848 "offered the prospect that a democratizing Europe would follow the example of an established U.S.A." Observers noted the providential coincidence of the revolution in France with the birthday of George Washington. New York City held a "Great Demonstration" in April 1848, in which marches, speeches, and resolutions supported the revolutionary effort to secure self-government. Southern cities such as Richmond and New Orleans also held parades and banquets. Citizens adopted the dress and emblems of the revolutionaries. Towns in Indiana, Mississippi, and Ohio named themselves after Louis Kossuth, and villages in Arkansas, Wisconsin, and Pennsylvania took the name of Alphonse de Lamartine. George Templeton Strong summed up the feelings of most Americans when he hailed revolutionary Europe as "the great battlefield of democracy against the institutions of the past age."[7]

The U.S. government also offered official gestures of goodwill. Richard Rush, minister to France, quickly recognized the provisional government, and President Polk appointed Andrew Donelson minister to the still theoretical "Federal Government of Germany." The Taylor administration later dispatched A. Dudley Mann to Hungary with the authority to recognize the new nation. One Mexican War veteran attempted to organize a legion to join the fight against the monarchs of Europe.[8]

As the "springtime of peoples" turned into a more radical revolutionary summer, however, American unity fractured. The new French republic abolished African slavery in its colonial possessions. Prussia completed the emancipation of serfs from feudal regulations. Hungary did the same. The French provisional government, following the lead of socialist Louis Blanc, responded to the cry of unemployed workers for the "right to work" by establishing National Workshops that would provide direct government employment. When the popularly elected but moderate legislature moved to end the scheme, workers took to the barricades in bloody defiance. During these so-called June Days, thousands died, as workers, inspired by dreams of socialism, clashed with the national army and the police. George Templeton Strong lamented the fact that European revolutionaries had degenerated into "cowardly and clamorous mobs" afflicted by "democratic influenza." "Democracy is epidemic now and even Austria has gone mad," he recorded in his diary. Government troops eventually suppressed the rioters and paved the way for Napoleon III's assumption of imperial power. The collapse of the revolution in France foreshadowed the defeat of progressives across Europe. By 1850, the titled nobility had reasserted its authority in Prussia, the Austrian Empire, and the Italian and German states.[9]

The failure of the 1848 revolutions, as well as the increasingly radical turn some of them had taken, posed problems for Americans contemplating the safety and longevity of their own national experiment. The meaning and scope of what a democratic revolution could entail changed as the legacy of 1848 spoke to the issues of slavery and sectionalism in the great model republic. Timothy Roberts argues that Americans reacted to 1848 in two ways. They initially celebrated America's "revolutionary origins" while considering "the prospect of a second revolution in U.S. society, erupting over the issue of slavery." Historian Michael Morrison agrees. He contends that sorrow over the failure of Europe's revolution accompanied "widespread fear in the North and South that Americans were increasingly unable to recapture the spirit of or, worse, agree on the essence of their Revolution."[10]

For abolitionists, the revolutions of 1848 suggested that the promise of the American Revolution, which had declared that "all men are created equal," might finally be fulfilled. Frederick Douglass, in a speech delivered in August 1848 at the West India emancipation celebration in Rochester, New York, celebrated the downfall of monarchy in the Old World and applauded the decision of the French provisional government to abolish slavery in its colonial possessions. Douglass asserted that the revolutions of 1848 held clear lessons for Americans. He believed that the downfall of monarchy in the Old World foretold "the downfall of slavery" in the New. "This act of justice to our race, on the part of the French people," he wrote, "has had a widespread effect upon the question of human freedom in our own land." The Massachusetts senator and abolitionist Charles Sumner shared Douglass's convictions, but not his optimism. He feared that the revolutions in Europe highlighted only the hypocrisy of the American republic: "In Europe they *mob* for Freedom, in Washington for *slavery*," he wrote to Joshua Giddings. For Sumner, the 1848 revolutions foretold conflict and discord in the American republic. In September 1849 he explained to John Pringle Nichol the connections between the struggle for freedom in Europe and the sectional crisis in the United States: "Our present struggle is not with a feudal aristocracy; but with a modern substitute, the Slave-Power, which for years has given a tone to our national Govt." A year later the passage of the Fugitive Slave Act caused Sumner to compare the failure of the revolutions of 1848 to the setback facing America's abolitionists: "The wave of re-action, which, during the last year, swept over Europe, has reached our shores."[11]

White southerners took away very different lessons regarding the changing meaning of democratic revolution. John C. Calhoun and other defenders of the institution of slavery distrusted revolutions that had resulted in slave emancipation in the French West Indies. Their fears were exacerbated by the emergence of the Free Soil Party in 1848, and radical democratic disturbances at home, such as Rhode Island's Dorr Rebellion, which sought to eliminate property qualifications for voting. As Timothy Roberts has noted, Calhoun even tempered his grudging admiration for German parliamentarians' efforts to construct a federal republic with warnings that they not give the central government too much power. Louisa S. McCord, a conservative South Carolinian and defender of slavery, feared that the "socialism" inherent in France's June Days confirmed the wisdom of Calhoun's warnings. She denounced the expansion of government power and the notion that it might help bring about economic equality and "uniformity of wages." "That the State should be able to give every thing to every body, yet require nothing from anybody, is certainly an unfathomable enigma," she declared. The prospect that communism and socialism would take root in America proved most frightening to McCord. In her estimation, these new social theories of the nineteenth century, given ample spectacle during France's June Days, threatened to plunge society into a violent conflict between the rich and the poor. McCord believed that the ideological attack on property begun by socialist revolutionaries had influenced the growth of northern reform movements. "In our own country," she wrote, "we see too plainly at every turn the insidious effect" of the "fearful fallacy" that "Property is Robbery." She pointed out, "Free-soilers, barn-burners, anti-renters, abolitionists stare us in the face at every turn."[12]

The majority of Americans responding to the revolutions of 1848 did not yet share the forebodings of McCord and Calhoun or the hopes of Douglass and Sumner. Politicians attempted to capture the enthusiasm of the voting public by loudly proclaiming the united American nation's mission to bring liberty and republican government to the world. Some members of the Democratic Party supported the Young America movement that modeled itself after the Young Italy, Young Germany, and Young Ireland clubs that had attempted to bring freedom and unity to their respective nations. Young America celebrated the destiny of the United States to spread liberty throughout North America and advocated direct diplomatic or military intervention in favor of freedom in Europe. The Whig Party, while balking at supporting an interventionist foreign policy, cast itself as a defender of the right of self-determination and freedom from monarchical government in America and the world. Daniel Webster forcibly articulated this vision in his famous "Hülsemann letter." Austrian diplomat J. G. Hülsemann had protested Zachary Taylor's decision to dispatch A. Dudley Mann to Hungary with the power to recognize the new nation fighting for independence in 1848 and 1849. Webster, in his response, declared sympathy for independence movements throughout the world and, in the words of historian Michael Holt, "rehearsed America's historic mission to advance freedom everywhere through its own republican example."[13]

Louis Kossuth's visit to the United States in 1851–52 best exemplifies both the nationalist fervor and growing discord with which Americans interpreted the legacy of 1848. In 1851, Congress dispatched an American navy ship to Turkey with orders to offer the exiled Kossuth asylum in America. The Hungarian hero arrived in New York Harbor on December 4, 1851, at which Americans greeted him with a thirty-one-gun salute, "one gun for each of the States of the Union." Kossuth enjoyed a reception on Staten Island at which "the European revolutionary flags were hoisted" and accompanied by further cannonading and celebration. Cities across the

East and the Midwest greeted him with equal enthusiasm, and the ensuing "Kossuth-mania" that swept the country served as a reminder of Europe's struggle for freedom and America's own revolutionary legacy. Kossuth encouraged such excitement by praising America's revolutionary example. In his speeches, Kossuth praised America's free press and asserted that American liberty would "go forth and achieve the freedom of the world."[14]

Although Kossuth's bid for independence in Europe had failed, he now hoped to interest Americans in helping him to rekindle the revolution. In speech after speech, Kossuth called for financial aid, extension of the Monroe Doctrine to include Europe, and armed assistance in the next revolution. He refused to believe, he told a cheering Philadelphia crowd, that "when the battle for mankind's liberty is fought" the "sword of Washington" would "rest in its scabbard." If it did, he argued, "the despots of the European continent" who "leagued against the freedom of the world" might snuff out liberty "even here."[15]

Kossuth stirred up controversy when he ventured beyond praising America's revolutionary legacy and began soliciting money, military aid, and a revamped foreign policy. Although the Hungarian freedom fighter purposely refrained from taking stands on American "party" or "interior affairs," defenders of slavery shied from supporting any representative of the European revolutions that had taken such a radical turn. Abolitionists left his speeches furious that he did not speak out on the moral injustice of slavery. Some Democrats embraced Kossuth's program for intervention on behalf of republican revolution, while southern members of the party remained suspicious. Whig Party leaders positioning themselves for the election of 1852 appealed to the immigrant vote by praising Kossuth. The strategy backfired when some southern congressmen held a "non-intervention" banquet to counter the congressional welcome dinner for the Hungarian. Daniel Webster found himself forced to vacillate on a resolution of welcome for Kossuth, and President Fillmore bluntly refused to make any change in American foreign policy. The Whig Party endured a final embarrassment when southern members voted against any congressional resolution praising the "Magnificent Magyar."[16]

American interpretation of the meaning of 1848 fractured as Europeans sought increasingly radical goals, as revolutions failed, and as exiles injected themselves into American domestic politics. Still, the celebrations surrounding the outbreak of revolution in Europe, and the disagreements occasioned by Kossuth's American visit, might have remained obscure and forgotten incidents. Waves of visitors and immigrants to the United States

"Grand Military Reception of Governor Kossuth in New York." Kossuth's
raucous welcome prefigured the treatment many heroes of forty-eight
would receive upon arrival in the United States. (Author's collection)

during the politically charged decade of the 1850s, however, kept alive the memories of 1848. Unlike Kossuth, the newcomers did not refrain from participating in the debates over sectionalism and slavery in the republic. Radical German immigrants in particular looked forward to a second revolution aimed at the southern "Slave Power." Others, such as Ireland's John Mitchel, perpetuated a nationalist interpretation of 1848 that would inspire Confederates in 1861.

Louis Kossuth was neither the first nor the last forty-eighter to arrive in the United States to great fanfare. Friedrich Hecker sailed into New York Harbor on October 5, 1848. His premature rebellion in the name of a German Republic met defeat before most of the revolutions had a chance to get off the ground. Hecker sought immediate exile in the United States, though he would return briefly to Europe to participate in the Baden revolt in 1849. A crowd of 20,000 admirers and an official delegation headed by the mayor met him upon debarkation in New York City. He later enjoyed raucous welcomes in Newark, Philadelphia, and Cincinnati, where city residents honored him with a torchlight parade. Gottfried Kinkel, the German revolutionary and man of letters renowned for his escape from Spandau Prison, toured the East Coast, as had Kossuth, in the early 1850s in search of funds with which to foment a second revolution in Europe.[17]

The leaders of Ireland's failed rising also sought asylum in the United States. Irish forty-eighter Thomas Francis Meagher entered the United States through the Port of San Francisco. He had been arrested by British authorities after participating in Ireland's failed nationalist rising and was shipped to a penal colony in Tasmania, then called Van Diemen's Land. He later made a daring escape from captivity, took refuge in America, and immediately embarked on a speaking tour. His revolutionary compatriot John Mitchel followed him shortly thereafter. After transferring from his escape vessel to an American passenger ship, Mitchel took off his "hat in homage to the stars and stripes." The admiring Americans aboard made him feel, he confessed, "almost a citizen." News of his escape must have preceded him because upon arrival in San Francisco he found himself "surrounded by troops of friends." The celebration continued for three weeks. "More than princely are the hospitalities of the Golden City," he recorded in his journal. "I have been feasted at the grandest of banquets, presided over by the Governor of the State." Before joining his Irish compatriots in New York, Mitchel received word of what newly arrived heroes of '48 could routinely expect: "I am going to be a demigod for two or three weeks—so my American friends warn me . . . going to have a reception and dinners."[18]

Unlike Kossuth, many of these exiles became permanent residents. As revolution universally failed and it became increasingly clear that even determined men working in safety in Switzerland or England could not foment a second armed conflict on the continent, an increasing number of revolutionaries resolved to seek liberty and freedom in the United States. Carl Schurz circulated for a time in the London exile community, where he met Kossuth, Giuseppe Mazzini, and Karl Marx. Louis Napoleon's coup d'état in 1851 finally convinced him that "the efforts connected with the revolution of 1848 were now hopeless" and that "further developments in the direction of liberal movements must necessarily have a new starting point." Schurz recalled the day he decided to leave Europe for America after meeting a dejected and defeated Louis Blanc in Hyde Park, London. "C'est fini, n'est-ce pas? C'est fini!" Blanc had remarked. In that moment, Schurz resolved to go to the United States. "The ideals of which I have dreamed and for which I have fought I shall find there," he wrote, "if not fully realized, but hopefully struggling for full realization. In that struggle I shall perhaps be able to take some part."[19]

Other revolutionary immigrants to America agreed with Schurz in viewing their new home as the embodiment of the republican ideals they had failed to achieve in Europe. Friedrich Kapp wrote that he came to New York "like so many others" in search of a state of "individual independence." John Mitchel praised America's freedom from the "landlordism" that weighed like a "mill-stone around the neck of the British Empire," making his "beautiful 'Erin of the Streams' what she is." He anticipated Louis Hartz by 100 years in celebrating America's blank slate that ensured fair negotiations between "landlord" and "tenant" and allowed for the natural development of liberal institutions. "In European nations legislators cannot begin at the beginning, for they have to deal with the existing interests of castes and classes," he wrote. He believed that only "bloody revolutions" could overthrow "the last strong-holds of ancient feudalism" and ensure that "the soil be distributed among the people." Ottilie Assing, the German feminist, reformer, and companion to Frederick Douglass, found it "a daily delight to know that I am living in a republic and to witness the happiness of the people." She marveled that America's poor displayed "nothing of the servile demeanor that they are made to adopt among us in early youth."[20]

Hundreds of thousands of like-minded immigrants found refuge in the United States during the 1850s. Historian Bruce Levine estimates that 130,000 Germans arrived in the United States each year during the 1850s. The foreign-born population as a whole increased 84.4 percent, and the new arrivals represented a 12 percent increase over the U.S. population of 1850, even when adjusted for departures. Ottilie Assing described the typical array of immigrants who accompanied her across the Atlantic aboard the *Indian Queen* in September 1852. "There were young scholars, sober farmers with wives and children who intended to buy a homestead in Wisconsin, craftsmen, an actor, and—political refugees, without whom hardly a ship sails for America these days."[21]

Historians have built on A. E. Zucker's estimate that at least 4,000 of the new German arrivals participated directly in the revolutions of 1848. Carl Wittke considers that number conservative, and points out that such estimates, influenced by the presence of well-known personalities, ignore anonymous revolutionaries and sympathizers, to say nothing of the groups of Hungarians, Irish, Italians, and French who sought refuge in the United States. Wittke and Levine both point out that the revolutions of 1848 certainly affected many of the hundreds of thousands who emigrated for economic or vaguely political reasons, regardless of their ability to claim status as revolutionary veterans. All agree that the forty-eighters achieved a level of visibility and importance out of proportion to their numbers. The average revolutionary was more educated, wealthier, and more politically engaged than his fellow immigrants. Many of the most important German-language newspapers in the 1850s boasted forty-eighter editors, and several Irish revolutionaries also established influential papers.[22]

Vocal forty-eighters kept the memory of their revolution and the worldwide importance of America's heritage of 1776 alive in the minds of U.S. citizens, officials, and immigrants. In February 1854, the members of a group calling themselves the Universal Democratic Republicans held a massive demonstration in New York to commemorate the anniversary of the February 24, 1848, French revolution. Marchers carried the American flag alongside the "European rouge or red flag of the Universal Democracy." Each of the revolutionary movements of 1848 received commemoration. "The Italian Republicans bore the first glorious tricolor that was hoisted over the barricades of Milan," reported one observer. The revelers adjourned to a supper room decorated with the names of cities and countries associated with republican revolution: Paris, Milan, Rouen, Baden, Hesse-Kassel, Messina, Lyons, Vienna, Hungary, Venice, Prussia, Berlin, Poland, and Rome.[23]

Speeches were delivered in several languages, praising America, republican government, and the struggle against tyranny. General Giuseppe Avezzana, the "heroic defender of Genoa in 1849," spoke on the importance of unity among "the martyrs of tyranny of different nations" for the "overthrow of despotism." Señor Rodrigues addressed the cheering crowd in French and declared war "in favor of the principle of democracy and the sovereignty of the people." Speakers in Polish and Magyar elicited "frequent patriotic shouts familiar to the revolutionary period of Hungarian and Polish history." Monsieur Boccarisse, the master of ceremonies, led the assembly in drinking toasts to the red flag, Washington, the American people, and American republican institutions. W. J. Rose of New York responded to the last toast with a message of universal solidarity: "On the ramparts of Rome, in 1849, Frenchmen, Italians, Poles, Englishmen, Spaniards and Americans fought together and . . . when the fires of liberty were lighted, Americans would be again found in the ranks of European Republicans."[24]

Saint Patrick's Day festivals in cities across the United States in the 1850s provided similar occasions to celebrate American republican exceptionalism and renew the call for liberty in Europe. Irish forty-eighters John Mitchel, John Dillon, and Richard O'Gorman presided over New York's celebration in 1854, while flanked by armed Irish militia companies. Mitchel's address lauded "the potent shelter of the American flag" and the "city where the exiles of all European lands meet as in a common house." The Irish community of Cincinnati toasted the American constitution and "the Patriots of '48," including O'Brien, Mitchel, and Meagher. "Hibernicus," a correspondent for the *Citizen*, reported that St. Patrick's celebrations in Kentucky also joined the benefits of American nationality with a resolve to "revisit" the "native land" with "a holy spirit of vengeance" toward "the blood stained Saxon."[25]

Militia companies and workers' organizations fostered an international outlook and kept the goals of 1848 alive in America. A delegation of working men in Fall River, Massachusetts, raised a subscription to aid "victims of British oppression" such as the "turnouts" in Preston, England, who fell victim to one of the first lockouts in labor history. The Gratton Guards, many of them old members of the Irish Confederation, formed in "gratitude for the protection afforded them by their adopted country," but also for "revenging the cause of their exile on their old enemy—England." The "Meagher Republican Grenadiers" met in full uniform at Hudson House in New York in 1854. The event attracted, one reporter testified, an "infusion of the young blood of Ireland and Young America." The ardent young men fortified their patriotism with numerous toasts. They tipped their glasses first to "Liberty, Equality, Fraternity, everywhere." Then they hailed "the

Universal Rights of Man, without distinction, the world over." The revelers went on to recognize "John Mitchel, Michael Doheny, and their comrades, still true to the hopes and purposes of 1848," and concluded by eagerly anticipating "the Downfall of all Tyranny, Civil and Ecclesiastical."[26]

Speaking tours in the mold of Kossuth's vied with public demonstrations to project the message of 1848 beyond a purely ethnic audience. Thomas Francis Meagher toured the West Coast and the southern states advocating the cause of Irish liberty. In New Orleans, Meagher avoided any sectional controversy by affirming his "oath of allegiance to the constitution, laws, and sovereignty of the Republic of the United States." In San Francisco he spoke at an Irish Republican gathering at the Music Hall and championed representative government and the separation of church and state. His address on Irish reformer Daniel O'Connell drew rave reviews in Boston.[27]

Meagher joined John Mitchel in an effort to disseminate their revolutionary message more widely by publishing a newspaper, the *Citizen*, which began publication in 1854. The new sheet attracted attention and garnered enthusiastic support because it dedicated itself to renewed revolution in Europe by spreading republicanism from America. The *London Daily News* commented on the new journal's boisterous reception in the streets of New York in 1854: "When the first number of this newspaper was to be issued, the crowd was so great and so pressing, that there was personal danger in attempting to get a copy."[28]

In the pages of the *Citizen*, John Mitchel called for the freedom of Ireland and the renewal of revolution in Europe. His editorials fostered a sense of solidarity between revolutionaries of any nation that fought against monarchy and oppression. Mitchel praised the "gallant Hungarians, Germans and Italians" who had risen against "foul tyranny." He hailed the revolution that fought the "Land Tenure in Austria," which he believed subjected peasants to "forced labor and other duties and services to their lords." Columns in the paper celebrated Irishmen who became Hungarian patriots "by choice" and fought alongside Kossuth. In many articles, Mitchel denounced the "devoted allies of European Monarchies" whom he believed to be the "determined enemies of European Republicanism." Mitchel argued that conservatives unfairly insisted on denouncing support for representative government as "Red Republicanism," a cause he defined as nothing more than support for a "Republic on the American pattern." In his adopted country, Mitchel supported a homestead bill that would provide "Free Homes for Free Men" and prevent European-style "landlordism" and "despotism." His paper also came out in favor of the rights of the laborer to "adequate support for himself and family."[29]

Like the Irish patriots, the German revolutionary community, led by the forty-eighters, achieved an unusual level of political and civic participation during the 1850s. The postrevolutionary immigrants, known as the "Greens," ridiculed the "Grays," Germans who had come to the United States before 1848, for their dearth of culture, lack of political engagement, and unwillingness to take stands on issues of moral importance. Like their Irish, French, Italian, and Hungarian comrades, the German revolutionaries embraced the American union as the perfect platform for launching renewed revolution in Europe. Zealous German Americans founded revolution societies, or *Revolutions-Vereine*, that would raise money to aid refugees and future revolutionaries in Europe. The German Revolutionary League went so far as to advocate the annexation of European states into the United States in order to form a world republic. A conference at Wheeling, Virginia, in 1852, and a book cowritten by forty-eighter Theodor Pösche, entitled *The New Rome: The United States of the World*, discussed putting the plan into practice.[30]

As the Germans resigned themselves to the failure of revolution in Europe, they focused on making the American nation everything they had hoped Germany would become. Under the leadership of forty-eighters such as Wilhelm Weitling, a growing ethnic working class organized unions, or *Arbeitervereine*, that supported strikes, fair wages, and the amelioration of working conditions. German forty-eighters also carried out self-designated missions to bring culture and learning to their countrymen in America. Eduard Schroeter established free-thinking clubs in New York and Milwaukee called *freie Gemeinde* that discussed radical democratic politics and religion. Chapters could soon be found throughout the East and Midwest. Friedrich Kapp founded a German American school in Baltimore, and Hans Balatka brought classical music to Wisconsin with his Milwaukee *Musikverein*.[31]

Friedrich Hecker, the hero of the republican revolution in Baden, established the first Turner Society in the United States in Cincinnati. These *Turnvereine*, first founded during the German resistance to Napoleon, aimed at producing mentally and physically fit republican citizens through the seemingly incongruent combination of gymnastic training and political indoctrination. Their mission statement championed the "cultivation of rational training, both intellectual and physical, in order that the members may become energetic, patriotic citizens of the Republic, who could and would represent and protect common human liberty by word and deed." The Turner movement spread through every major American city, including Charleston, New Orleans, and St. Louis. Revolutionary veterans such as Gustav Struve, August Willich, and Karl Heinzen opened chapters in New York, Milwaukee, and Boston.[32]

The newly politicized German American community's fierce devotion to upholding the true principles of republican government ensured engagement with the most controversial issues of the 1850s. The Turner clubs published journals, held lectures, and formed militia companies designed to protect America's free institutions. A gathering of Turners in Philadelphia in 1851 created a national organization that adopted the name *Sozialistischer Turnerbund*, or Socialist Turner Society. The new group's manifesto predicted that socialism would inspire the next revolution in Europe, and promised to promote the "final victory of the oppressed classes" over "the old aristocratic class." These typically politicized Turners declared, "Socialism of to-day, in which we Turners believe, aims to remove the pernicious antagonism between labor and capital. It endeavors to effect a reconciliation between these two, and to establish peace by which the rights of the former are fully protected against the encroachments of the latter." They considered slavery an obvious obstacle to these goals. The group urged its members to support the Free Soil Party "in every way possible."[33]

The radical forty-eighter Karl Heinzen, never one to be outdone in the realm of socialist politics, published his Kentucky Platform in Louisville in 1854. The document invoked the goals of both 1776 and 1848 and supported the goals of the Turnerian Socialists as a means of improving the American republic. Heinzen called for the direct election of senators, recall, women's rights legislation, and a foreign policy revamped along the lines drawn by Kossuth. He also demanded free land for settlement by small farmers in the West.[34]

In general, calls for social reform appealed to a broad cross-section of forty-eighters. Irishmen, Germans, Italians, and Hungarians alike could support calls for renewed revolution in Europe. They all supported aid to working men in America and celebrated the united front workers had presented in Europe. That camaraderie between European revolutionaries showed signs of strain, however, when the question of slavery and its expansion increasingly troubled American politics. On January 4, 1854, Senator Stephen A. Douglas of Illinois introduced in the Senate a bill for the organization of the Nebraska territory. Douglas's original bill, which was needed to begin construction of a transcontinental rail line, proposed to allow Congress to admit the new state of Nebraska "with or without slavery." In the weeks that followed, southern politicians successfully pushed Douglas to amend his bill so as to include an outright repeal of the Missouri Compromise, which had banned slavery from what would become the Kansas and Nebraska territories. Instead, the bill would allow the settlers themselves to decide whether or not to allow slavery there, a concept called "popular sovereignty." The so-called Kansas-Nebraska Bill forced all Americans to take a stand on the issues of slavery in the territories. For European radicals, the choice was just as divisive as for the native-born. For some revolutionaries, slavery represented a reactionary influence in American social and political life. As the debate over slavery in the West intensified, European radicals grew increasingly convinced that it had to be destroyed for the United States to reach its potential. Others, however, viewed the conflict over slavery as a distraction that took attention away from their true goals—the achievement of self-government for all white men. They feared that arguing over the "slave question" would lead to the breakup of the United States, which would make freedom in Europe impossible to achieve.[35]

The Irish, in particular, refused to embrace abolitionism. During the 1850s, hundreds of thousands of them fled to America in an effort to escape the Potato Famine and the poverty they endured as renters and tenants on estates in their homeland. Once in the United States, they took up residence in dilapidated city neighborhoods like New York's notorious Five Points, where they lived and worked alongside other immigrants and free blacks. Like African Americans, they faced scorn and discrimination from the native-born white majority. This did not, however, foster solidarity between them. Most Irish feared that the prospect of racial equality would serve as a barrier to their full acceptance as white Americans. The Catholic press often pointed out that most abolitionists were also Protestants hostile to Irish Catholics and their traditions. Indeed, many supporters of antislavery also advocated temperance laws and opposed providing Catholic schools with public funding.[36]

As a result, most Irish in America embraced the Democratic Party, which protected slavery, held out the promise of democracy for all white men, and opposed Whig and later Republican moralism. The agitation of the slavery issue, Democrats argued, would lead only to the division of the republic, which would discredit the cause of representative government in the eyes of the world, thereby threatening the prospect of freedom in Europe. There was much irony and tension in this stance. Many nationalists in Ireland had long attacked the political "slavery" of whites as well as the actual slavery of blacks. In 1841, Daniel O'Connell, the famous "liberator" of the Irish who led the movement for repeal of the Act of Union binding Ireland to Britain, issued an appeal to his countrymen in America urging them to support the cause of abolition. The address provoked outrage in the United States. Many Irish and American supporters of repeal in the North and in the South, including John Hughes, archbishop of New York, denounced O'Connell's missive as a dangerous intrusion into American affairs that would disrupt the Union, threaten Irish acceptance in the Democratic Party, and ultimately distract the world from the true cause of home rule for Ireland. When O'Connell's movement failed to achieve its goals, many blamed the disappointment on his quixotic quest to end African slavery.[37]

In the years that followed, few Irish nationalists in America made the same mistake. They held that the existence of a strong and unified United States would do the most to promote Irish freedom, and they refused to link the causes of political self-determination for Ireland with emancipation for African Americans. John Mitchel, for one, touched off a firestorm of controversy when he remarked in the midst of the debate over Kansas and Nebraska in 1854 that he did not oppose slavery. The man who Frederick Douglass had once argued "sanctified" the cause of Ireland through "martyrdom" in pursuit of liberty stated that he even wished to own "a good plantation, well stocked with healthy negroes, in Alabama." Mitchel shockingly denied that it was a "crime," a "wrong," or "even a peccadillo" to "hold slaves" or "keep slaves to their work by flogging or other needful coercion."[38]

American abolitionists reacted with anger and disbelief to the heresy proclaimed by one of their heroes of '48. A stunned Henry Ward Beecher assured audiences that he did not believe that "Dillon and O'Gorman, O'Brien and hosts of memorable others, [were] so sordid and so selfish in their conception of human rights and liberty" to join Mitchel in taking the motto "My liberty everything; Man's liberty nothing." Wendell Phillips, in a speech at the Tabernacle in New York, lamented the fall of "a great man," a "fugitive" from "bondage," and an exile "for liberty." Theodore Parker predicted that the doctrines of "John Mitchel will go under," as the true lessons and legacies of 1848 reached the public.[39]

White southerners, on the other hand, rushed to praise the Irish revolutionary who proved that one could remain true to the principles of 1776 and 1848 while defending the right of free white citizens to hold slaves. The *New Orleans Crescent* commented on the growing sectionalism in America that made it impossible for a man to "make himself acceptable" at one end of the country "unless at the cost of becoming detestable at the other end." Mitchel's pronouncements made him in the South "on the instant, everything he [had] ceased to be in the North." The appreciative literary societies of the University of Virginia invited Mitchel to deliver an address in which he discussed the possibility of national improvement and "elevation" at the expense of the "decay and degradation of some other race." The *Globe* of Portsmouth, Virginia, denounced Beecher and those who did not "appreciate the difference between being an Irishman, the political slave of England, and an African, the social municipal slave of the white man." The editor explained, "Mitchel has been trying to beat it into the fanatic head of Beecher that there is both a distinction and a difference."[40]

The legislature of Louisiana passed official resolutions of praise for Mitchel and explicitly linked his defense of slavery with the legacies of 1848, 1776, and the causes of nationalism and self-government. The members of the state house and senate praised Mitchel for his actions in Europe. "We cherish the warmest sympathy for all who have made patriotic sacrifices for the emancipation of a nation from political tyranny and oppression," they declared. In taking on the slave question, the legislators argued, Mitchel now defended America's "great constitutional rights." Mitchel, in his response, denounced abolitionists who, in his opinion, threatened the unity of the United States, which he considered to be "the completest, grandest, achievement and movement of the wit and courage of man in modern times."[41]

At the same time, politically engaged Germans grappled with the slave question. For many Germans, the Kansas-Nebraska Act threatened to allow the expansion of slavery throughout the Midwest. Dreams of escaping European despotism and wage labor on free western farms evaporated in an instant. Anti-Nebraska rallies erupted in German communities on the East Coast and across the Midwest. Speakers invoked the principles of 1848 and warned of slaveholding aristocrats intent on usurping the western land, land which, to them, represented an escape from poverty, industrial labor, and European degradation. They urged their followers to respond as they had in 1848. At one such meeting in Washington Hall, New York, a Dr. Försch declared, "In this country as well as in the Old World, we have to start the cry, 'Revolution!'" The crowd erupted in cheers. Carl Schurz, who had recently taught himself English by reading newspapers, novels, and

Shakespeare, traveled to Washington in 1854 to sit in on Congress's debates over the bill. The experience energized the revolutionary veteran and gave him a new cause to pursue in the New World. "When I come in touch with this atmosphere of political activity, I feel the old fire of 1848 coursing in my veins," he wrote to his wife from the nation's capital. Despite his setback in Europe, he assured her he would continue the struggle. "Although the reaction in Europe has thrown me out of my course," he wrote, "you may still see your husband coming to his own." After hearing Congress debate the future of the West, Schurz had no doubt about the cause he would now take up: "The great fight against slavery, the only blot that sullied the escutcheon of the Republic, and the only malign influence . . . that threatened the fulfillment of its great mission in the world!" Success in this struggle, he believed, would depend on applying the revolutionary program of 1848. As in Europe, he explained to Gottfried Kinkel, success depended on "breaking up the country-gentry party."[42]

Despite fierce opposition from abolitionists, Germans, and northern free-soilers, the Kansas-Nebraska Act passed Congress in late May 1854. The Kansas-Nebraska Act raised the prospect of conflict between North and South, and exacerbated divisions of opinion among forty-eighters. Even German unity fractured. The National Turner Convention, led by forty-eighters and held in Buffalo, New York, in 1855, announced its opposition to slavery. The decision forced the secession of chapters in Charleston, Savannah, Mobile, and other cities in the Deep South. Turners from cities such as St. Louis, Baltimore, Wheeling, and Louisville ratified the decision and ensured that antislavery voices would remain in the border slave states. Irish and Germans alike interpreted every subsequent incident in the sectional crisis by referring to the goals they had fought for in 1848. Indeed, the sectional crisis raised the prospect that they would again have to take up arms and fight for their beliefs in a new revolution in America.[43]

To most German forty-eighters, the institution of slavery seemed to replicate the social structure dominated by large landholders and privileged aristocrats that revolutionaries had sought to supplant in almost every revolution since 1789. After witnessing defeat in Europe in 1848, progressive immigrants felt that the forces of reaction now threatened the nation they hoped would redeem the world. "The problem of slavery is not the problem of the Negro," argued Friedrich Kapp, "it is the eternal conflict between a small and privileged class and the great mass of the non-privileged, the eternal struggle between aristocracy and democracy." Carl Schurz wrote his

Carl Schurz, as he appeared in the 1850s. (Author's collection)

friend, mentor, and fellow revolutionary Gottfried Kinkel in 1855 to complain about the "indirect effect" the slave system had upon the government of the United States. He singled out "the aristocratic character of Southern society," and southern society's opposition to all "political ideas of justice." Progressives, he believed, would have to abolish slavery in the United States if they ever hoped to see the country lead the world in fulfilling the goals of 1848. He told Kinkel that the United States would never "interfere practically in the interest of the freedom of the peoples of the world" until the power of the slaveholders was destroyed.[44]

While German forty-eighters railed against the Kansas-Nebraska Act, John Mitchel offered a very different take on the new law. He was not disturbed that it had repealed the Missouri Compromise and opened the territories to settlement and possibly slavery. Instead, he praised its provisions allowing white settlers to decide the issue for themselves. He hailed the passage of the bill as a victory for "self-government," a cause he supported for both "the whites of Nebraska" and those downtrodden by European oppression. Mitchel believed that popular sovereignty upheld "the first principle of this Republic—the right of the people to govern themselves." On that principle, Mitchel believed, the United States had cemented its "national honor" and world mission. He now argued that preoccupation with what he termed "the destiny of the negroes" would jeopardize the cause he believed would transform Ireland and the world.[45]

By late 1854, the conflict over slavery had erupted in violence. As rival free-state and slave-state settlers determined to shape Kansas's institutions streamed into the territory, they took up arms in support of their respective causes. Americans and Europeans alike placed the growing conflict in a revolutionary framework established in 1848. As Timothy Roberts has shown, the fighting in Kansas prompted many Americans to recall the revolutions that had rocked Europe less than a decade earlier. To cite one example, Sarah Tappan Doolittle Robinson, a New England settler on the Kansas prairie, reacted with shock and surprise that one of her neighbors, "a Hungarian Doctor" who claimed he "fought for Hungary by the side of Louis Kossuth," violently supported the slave-state cause. She expressed dismay that the revolutionary who had fought oppression in Europe now deigned to openly support "the side of the oppressor here." The "sack of Lawrence" and the destruction of an antislavery printing press by supporters of slavery in the spring of 1856 confirmed Robinson's belief that the southern "Slave Power," like the European despots of 1848, planned to snuff out the liberties of a free people. Such brazen acts, in her opinion, surpassed even the most determined European reactionaries. Louis Napoleon, she observed, "gave three distinct and formal warnings, in the last French revolution, before dealing the fatal blow," while in America the reaction had arrived suddenly.[46]

Many German veterans of the revolutions of 1848 viewed the violence in Kansas as a second call to arms in the cause of liberty. As early as 1851, Friedrich Kapp had foreseen the separation of North and South "owing to the slavery question," a separation that would result in a "struggle" that could only be solved with "blood." Carl Schurz wrote to alert his old revolutionary companion Gottfried Kinkel to the exciting prospect of carrying on in America the struggle they had begun in 1848. "There is a struggle going on in this country in which we should all take part," he wrote during the Kansas crisis in 1856. The former revolutionary had lost none of his willingness to employ violence in the battle between slavery and freedom: "I am not sure that this fight can be decided without powder. I doubt it." Karl Heinzen bluntly explained how the new struggle in America would influence the cause of liberty in the Old World. "Opposition to the politics of slavery in America is a battle against reaction in Europe," he wrote.[47]

The elections of 1856 and 1860 brought these arguments to a wide audience. During the mid-1850s, many radical Germans joined the new Republican Party, which committed itself to stopping the spread of slavery into the western territories. In 1856, Carl Schurz campaigned for the party's first presidential candidate, John C. Frémont. He described to Henry Meyer his happiness at once again struggling for a cause, as he had in 1848–49. "It is the first time in seven years that I have taken part in politics—in a time which arouses even the sleepiest and in a cause which is second to none in the world in reach and greatness," he wrote. Schurz later recalled how Frémont's defeat in 1856 had discouraged his fondest hopes formed in Europe and America. "Was not this like the disastrous breakdown of the great movement for popular government on the European continent in 1848?" he exclaimed. "Was the democratic principle to collapse in America too?" he asked apprehensively.[48]

During the campaign of 1860, Schurz redoubled his efforts to make others see the question the way he did. On the campaign stump, he linked slavery, threats to republican government, the legacy of 1776, and the failure of 1848. His self-described leitmotif lauded the American Republic as the only force capable of leading "mankind toward democratic government." He avoided appealing to the "sentimental sympathies" of his audiences regarding the treatment of slaves. Instead, he stressed the "incompatibility of slavery with free institutions of government," and attacked white southerners for "living upon the forced labor of others" and finding "their pride in being gentlemen of leisure." Schurz insisted that the "laboring classes" alone furthered the "progress," the "enterprise," and, above all, the "liberty," that would make America a great nation.[49]

Some Republicans in the North, both native and foreign-born, picked up Schurz's message that denounced an aristocratic Slave Power and invoked the legacies of 1776 and 1848 in defense of free labor. One student of Schurz's speeches remarked that "after twelve years, the Revolution of 1848–49 is bearing fruit in America." A reader of Cleveland's *Wächter am Erie* compared the Republican convention of 1860 to the Frankfurt Parliament and asserted that both demonstrated "how precious liberty is." Ottilie Assing declared that Germans should be "naturally opposed to slavery" because of their hatred of "aristocracy," "tyranny," "laziness," and "any unproductive waste of time." Charles Sumner, writing to Salmon P. Chase from his convalescence in Europe, agreed that the Republican cause held worldwide significance: "Looking at our cause from this distance I see its grandeur more than ever. I also see more clearly than ever its certain success. . . . Slavery seems more hateful; for I see now better than before how it degrades us in the family of nations and prevents our example from acting as it should in Europe. Liberty every where suffers through us."[50]

The Republican vision did not go unchallenged, however. Democrats in the North and South reacted with alarm to the willingness of foreign revolutionaries to champion a "European style" democracy in the United States. In the minds of such patriots, it became increasingly clear that 1848 had introduced disturbing amendments to the legacy of 1776. If democratic revolution now entailed threats to private property in the form of collectivization of workers and the abolition of slavery, then movements in the name of liberty and self-government had gone terribly wrong. Thomas R. Whitney of New York echoed Louisa McCord in warning about the dangerous "Red Republicans, agrarians, and infidels" that the European revolutions had bequeathed to the U.S. in the form of refugees. The *Cleveland Plain Dealer* also denounced "Red Republicans" as "a lawless, reckless set of impostors" who, the editor feared, would "get up riots and carry on revolutions" in their adopted country.[51]

Most Irishmen, revolutionaries included, retained their loyalty to the Democratic Party, where they found acceptance as white Americans. As Democrats, they feared that the agitation of the slavery issue would only divide and destroy the American republic. As revolutionaries, they worried that the radicalism of their German friends would lead to ruin, as it had in Europe. John Mitchel declared he was "no socialist" and insisted that the growing assault on slavery would only distract the world from the nationalist goals of 1848. During the mid-1850s he moved to Tennessee, where he continued to promote freedom for Ireland and what he regarded as true republicanism in the United States. His new newspaper, the *Southern Citizen*, argued that northern Republicanism and fanaticism threatened the true legacy of 1776. It seemed increasingly clear to him that white southerners were the true defenders of republican self-government, which he defined as democracy for white men.[52]

Many of his southern neighbors reached the same conclusion as the turbulent decade of the 1850s drew to a close. In October 1859, the radical abolitionist John Brown led his dramatic raid on Harpers Ferry, Virginia. He hoped to foment a slave rebellion that might lead to the establishment of a free state in the mountains of the South. Brown believed he was acting the part of the heroic nineteenth-century revolutionary and was most certainly influenced by the dramatic events of 1848. In the midst of the fighting in Kansas, Brown had hired Hugh Forbes, an Englishman who had fought alongside Garibaldi in Italy and who had participated in the defense of the Roman Republic in 1849, to help him drill his men. Forbes taught from his *Manual of the Patriotic Volunteer*, written to instruct the people in the art of fighting against oppression. When news of Brown's raid reached Europe, Victor Hugo lauded him as a "hero and a martyr" who had attracted "the eyes of the whole of Europe." White southerners, on the other hand, recoiled in horror. When Abraham Lincoln was elected the following year, they prepared to leave the Union to establish their own independent nation.[53]

By the time of the secession crisis of 1860–61, both northerners and southerners could draw on conflicting articulations of the meaning of nineteenth-century democratic revolution as they girded for a violent upheaval of their own. Supporters of the North could draw on a vision that emphasized freedom for all human beings from an oppressive slave aristocracy. Many white southerners became convinced, however, that they could point with equal determination to European revolution as a precedent for their experiment in nationalism, self-government, and freedom from an oppressive central power. When violence erupted in April 1861, observers on both sides would argue that they led the latest democratic revolution to break out in the nineteenth-century Atlantic world.

2

●

The Revolution of 1861

DURING THE EARLY MORNING HOURS OF APRIL 12, 1861, CONFEDERATE cannon opened fire on a federal fort guarding the approaches to Charleston Harbor. The sectional tension that had plagued the Union for decades erupted into war between two self-proclaimed nation-states. Fort Sumter surrendered after a thirty-three-hour bombardment, and the world quickly took note. On April 16, William Howard Russell of the London *Times* arrived in Charleston to report on the outbreak of war in America. The British journalist found the citizens of the "cradle of secession" seized by a revolutionary frenzy. Russell reported that "crowds of armed men" filled the streets with what he called "battle-blood running through their veins." The sanguinary scene immediately reminded Russell of the disturbances that had swept Europe thirteen years before. "The streets of Charleston present some such aspect of those of Paris in the last revolution," he exclaimed. Upon returning to New York in July, Russell found that the "revolutionary furor" he had witnessed in the Carolinas had spread to the North. He described flag-raisings in every city square, flag-raisings he compared to the "planting of the tree of liberty in France in 1848." The Revolution of 1861 had begun.[1]

European Americans across the country, like their native-born counterparts, took up arms and joined the struggle. During the 1850s they had drawn on the legacy of revolutions in their home countries as they defined the nature of America's national experiment in self-government. The secession of South Carolina in 1861 compelled them to once again act on their convictions. They could choose to side with the South in what Confederates proclaimed was a struggle for national independence that would affirm the rights of self-determination for all peoples; or, they could fight a slaveholding aristocracy dangerous to the civil liberties of all mankind. Success in this new revolution, they believed, would prove crucial to constructing a nation that would embody all that they had failed to achieve in Europe.

In early 1861, the citizens of the states on the border of the Confederacy faced the highest stakes. In the wake of the Battle of Fort Sumter, Virginia, North Carolina, Tennessee, and Arkansas elected to join the new Confederate nation. The people of Missouri, Maryland, Kentucky, and Delaware would likewise have to choose to cast their lot with one nation or the other. The conflict between Unionists and Secessionists in these states proved particularly contentious and violent. The willingness of the foreign-born to act on their convictions might well have affected the balance of power in their state and ultimately determined the fate of the Union.

A close look at the secession crisis in St. Louis, Missouri, perfectly demonstrates how the legacy of revolution influenced European Americans to choose sides and mobilize for war in 1861. St. Louis held an important position as a large urban center in a slave state with a diverse ethnic population, a population including a powerful contingent of European revolutionary refugees of 1848. Heinrich Boernstein and Carl Ludwig Bernays, who had edited a radical Paris journal that published the work of Karl Marx and Heinrich Heine, owned the leading German-language newspaper in the city. Carl Daenzer and Theodore Olshausen, who had also participated in the revolutions of 1848, rounded out the St. Louis German community's team of editors. The city's Irish, on the other hand, looked with suspicion on the vocal anticlericalism and radicalism of the German forty-eighters, even though they sympathized with antimonarchical nationalist movements in Europe.[2]

The election of Abraham Lincoln in 1860 brought tensions to a head. The ensuing secession crisis threatened to remove Missouri from the Union. European Americans who had lived through democratic revolution in the Old Country now faced a strikingly similar conflict in the New World. The warnings that outspoken leaders had developed in the 1850s now seemed to be coming true. The future of the adopted nation of European Americans and the fate of republican government once again seemed to be in jeopardy. The hopes and fears they had developed for the American Union during the 1850s influenced their response. Germans in St. Louis faced the long-predicted prospect of domination by a "Slave Power" that in their eyes resembled the landed aristocracy that spearheaded reaction in Europe in 1848. Thousands of them took up arms to defend the model republic in this *Zweite Freiheitskampf,* or "Second Freedom Struggle," as forty-eighter Fritz Anneke referred to this new revolution in America.

Many Irish, however, offered an alternative interpretation of 1848 and its legacy. The Irish Catholic priest John Bannon denounced the tyrannical central government that threatened to destroy the prosperous American republic and trample the rights of the people with radical German mercenaries. Bannon had not participated directly in the revolutions of 1848 but sympathized with Irish nationalism while a seminarian in Ireland. Now, thousands of his parishioners and countrymen joined the First Missouri Confederate Brigade and embraced a new Confederate nationalism that upheld the rights of oppressed national minorities to rise and fight in the name of self-government, as Washington had done in 1776, and as the Irish and Europeans had done in 1848. These two competing visions of the revolutionary legacy inspired European Americans who chose sides and took up arms as the Revolution of 1861 engulfed the American republic.[3]

The German forty-eighters in St. Louis, like their counterparts in cities throughout the country during the 1850s, supported a variety of reform movements aimed at perfecting the model American republic to which they had fled. These editors advocated a mixture of utopian socialism, anticlericalism, and abolitionism in the pages of the German American press. They advocated aid to the poor, high wages, better working conditions for laborers, and public works for the unemployed. The inaugural edition of Karl Daenzer's *Westliche Post* promised in September 1857 to represent the "principles of freedom and the well-being of the people against every form of injustice, oppression, monopoly, and aristocracy."[4]

The institution of slavery represented the gravest concern of German forty-eighters. Ownership of human beings, they believed, created a powerful landed aristocracy that violated the civil liberties of workers and nonslaveholders, threatened the future freedom and existence of the republic, and behaved in all respects like the despots and reactionaries of Europe. A self-described "working man" named "Paul Plato" wrote one Republican newspaper to warn readers that in the proposed Confederacy "the rights of the working man will be no more regarded than they are now in the empire of Austria." He compared secessionists to "monarchists, usurpers, human blood suckers, and tyrannical aristocrats." Heinrich Boernstein's *Anzeiger des Westens* argued that the struggle to prevent the spread of slavery into the western territories pitted those who valued "small property in land" against those who would foster "aristocratic exploitation." The paper argued that Germans supported the principles of antislavery since abolitionists shared the same goals for which the forty-eighters had "fought in their homeland." The enemies of slavery, the editor asserted, "want the territories given to the free white man and not to the slaveowning baron of the South."[5]

The political behavior of the planters who dominated Missouri's Democratic Party only confirmed the fears of the revolutionaries that slavery produced an oppressive, aristocratic government unfriendly to freedom, national development, and civil liberty. As historian Adam Arenson has shown, progressive Missourians hoped that St. Louis would play a leading role in developing the American West. They fought to make their city the hub of a great transcontinental rail line and supported the opening of the territories to white labor. Slaveholding Democrats, fearful that a flood of abolition-minded northeasterners would descend on Missouri and neighboring Kansas, opposed those efforts. Like their counterparts throughout the South, they passed a number of acts designed to defend the institution of slavery. In 1849, future governor Claiborne Fox Jackson sponsored a series of resolutions in the Missouri legislature that would have made it more difficult to pass any new laws restricting the institution. The subsequent failure of a bill in the Missouri legislature to incorporate a town founded by Germans convinced forty-eighter editors that planter politicians targeted Europeans for discrimination because of their liberal views. Alarmed German editors argued that proslavery politicians threatened to establish a European-style despotism in the United States that violated the rights of free speech, association, and expression. When slaveholders proposed outlawing abolitionist mailings, the *Mississippi Blätter* reacted with horror. "Accepting and carrying out this act would put an end to freedom of the press in Missouri," the editor argued, "and in its place there would rule censorship and inquisition by postmasters and justices of the peace."[6]

The involvement of the forty-eighter community in Republican Party politics spread these views to an English-speaking audience. B. Gratz Brown, an ally of the Republican Blair family of St. Louis, brought the arguments of the forty-eighters to English readers through his newspaper, the *Daily Missouri Democrat*. The *Democrat* charged that secessionists conspired to establish a monarchy, or worse yet, an empire or a despotism similar to "the reign of some Louis Napoleon." One article asserted that southern society was "essentially aristocratic," and that the "penchant for monarchical institutions" had been recently growing among "the large plantation proprietors." The editor pointed out that a planter who owned "an extensive tract of country" and lorded over "a thousand of his fellow human beings" naturally desired "to be a duke or a count—to wear the insignia of an order, and strut in the court of a monarch." Secession, the paper warned, would make such a dream possible and "introduce into the New World the crimes and miseries of the old." The "aristocratic idea," the editor argued, would manifest itself in new "gradations of rank and class established by law." Foreigners and poor white laborers would be disfranchised. Southern society, he believed, would make "property and birth" the basis of "political rights and social privileges."[7]

The articles in the *Democrat* singled out South Carolina for condemnation. That state had led the secession movement and had lagged behind others in introducing nineteenth-century democratic reforms. Most egregiously, the state's legislature, not the people, continued to choose presidential electors. The editors of the *Democrat* believed these facts represented more than innocent coincidence. They asserted that the planters who ruled South Carolina favored monarchy and curtailed the rights of suffrage. "To all material intents," one article explained, "the non-property holder is disfranchised, and though he may vote, he must vote for the governing class, the slaveholders, or he cannot vote at all." The editor made sure to stress the comparison with reactionary, post-revolutionary Europe: "This is precisely the kind of voting the people of France were allowed to do after the coup d'état of Louis Napoleon in 1851–2." The editor declared that the "government of that State is a mean and exacting aristocracy, and the common people enjoy less real liberty than they do in Great Britain or Germany." He believed that in South Carolina the press "is subsidized and trammeled as much as it is in Austria, and the liberty of speech is smothered with worse than French despotism." Another alarmed editorialist asserted that the desire of southern agents to win support from Louis Napoleon proved that Confederates, led by the reactionary state of South Carolina, wished to establish a monarchy in the New World.[8]

The prospect of belonging to a new nation founded on such principles frightened many Germans in St. Louis. Encouraged by Republican politicians, they had linked the presidential campaign of 1860 to European politics and their own fight for liberty in 1848. Toasts to Giuseppe Garibaldi, who had organized the defense of the Roman Republic in 1849, and in 1860 and 1861 struggled for Italian unity and freedom, "excited the greatest enthusiasm" at Republican rallies in the state of Missouri during the autumn of 1860. Friedrich Münch, author and future Missouri state senator, argued that American politics could be understood in comparison with the European ideological categories of far left, center left, center right, and far right. The abolitionists represented the far left, which, on both sides of the Atlantic, demanded "rapid progress and reckless upheaval." In America,

Münch argued, the abolitionists had made temporary allies with the center left Republicans who advocated reform and rejected revolution except as a last resort. Whigs and Know Nothings, he asserted, could be thought of as part of the center right, which worked to uphold the status quo. Münch believed that the extreme right in Europe and America formed the "party of reaction" and included "despots," "obscurantists," and slaveholders who aspired to become "owner[s] and lord[s] of hundreds of people in servitude." Münch's audience needed little prompting to link these slaveholders to the despots and aristocrats of Europe and the secessionists of 1861. "The extreme Right triumphed in Germany in the reaction of 1849," he reminded his readers.[9]

By early 1861, Germans had developed an intellectual framework that prepared them to interpret the sectional struggle and the ensuing Civil War as an outgrowth of the revolutionary conflicts that had wracked Europe. The efforts of Missouri's governor, Claiborne Fox Jackson, to join the secession movement convinced Germans that they stood to lose all the rights they cherished in the New World. In January 1861, Governor Jackson removed control of the police and local militia from the hands of St. Louis's Republican mayor. The move seemed disturbingly familiar to observers of reaction in Europe. One Republican Party newspaper sounded the alarm: "The throne of the despot is to be raised up in the ruins of citizen self-government. Henceforth the citizens of St. Louis are to be subject to the will of a dictator." Pro-Union sheets branded Governor Jackson a "military dictator" who aimed to establish a "despotism" that would prove "more tyrannical" than that of "France, Austria, or Russia." One observer bluntly stated that if the governor's new armed forces took action against the city's Unionists, the guilty parties would "stop being an American, and become an Austrian or a Neapolitan." When the secessionist-controlled police board cracked down on German businesses open on Sunday, Republicans made the analogy between secession and reaction explicit: "Soon we shall lose the freedom of the press. Austria and South Carolina will be at home in Missouri."[10]

The outbreak of violence at the hands of secessionists in South Carolina offered Germans further confirmation that slaveholders conspired to proscribe civil liberties and republican freedom as European aristocrats had done in 1848 and 1849. One Republican paper asserted that the behavior of secessionists proved that slaveholders "loved to rule, but they would rather rule by force than by persuasion." The editor considered the rebellion "an inevitable development of the philosophy of slavery" that in-

cluded a "passion for a new form of society, divided into castes and orders, and culminating in a feudal aristocracy." The "plantation aristocracy,"
he asserted, entertained "profound contempt" for "greasy mechanics" and
"hard-fisted farmers," and threatened their rights of "suffrage," "majority
rule," and "freedom of expression." Germans in St. Louis consequently believed they had a duty to strike against slavery, secession, and the governor
of Missouri. The forty-eighters had already demonstrated their willingness
to fight for their principles, and they would do so again. One editor warned
that Germans held an "inborn and instinctive . . . hostility against the heap-
ing up of capital and aristocratic trifles. This hatred of aristocracy, whether
of birth or wealth, has already toppled thrones and inspired revolutions
that are immortally inscribed in the annals of world history."[11]

Despite their failure in Europe, the revolutionaries retained a firm faith
in their ability to perfect the republic and to change the world for the better. Still, the disintegration of the American nation, they believed, would
lead to international disaster by finally extinguishing the hopes of 1848.
One former revolutionary declared that, even after the failure of 1848, "the
whole European world" in 1861 stood poised to cast off "its old chains"
through "an elemental upheaval." He believed that victory over slavery in the American Civil War would help speed that process in the Old
World. German forty-eighters in America argued that the growing internationalism of the nineteenth century world connected peoples, ideas, and
continents. One St. Louis citizen wrote a Republican editor and asserted
that America "shines like a beacon light in the dark of struggling human-
ity," bringing hope to the "serf and the peasant." But the influence could
also go the other way. One observer noted that just as the American Revolution of 1776 preceded and influenced the French Revolution of 1789,
so too would the revolutions of 1848 anticipate and affect the Civil War.
An enthusiastic editor summed up the situation by declaring, "This is the
American 1848!"[12]

The Germans in St. Louis responded forcefully to their editors' call for
revolution. In late April, U.S. Army captain Nathaniel Lyon, acting with
authority from the War Department, began the direct enrollment into
Federal service of German "home guard" units, Turner companies, and
"committees of safety." The revolutionary excitement steadily increased as
bands of men, often under the command of forty-eighters, marched to the
U.S. arsenal in St. Louis to receive their weapons and commissions. A delegation of ladies assembled to present the Turner companies and Major
Nicholas Schüttner's men with a U.S. flag. The ladies declared the stars

and stripes "the symbol of the freedom of a great people." One Republican paper praised those European immigrants who left "the tyranny and oppression of aristocracy and crowns behind," and now fought to protect "a government of the people." Observers who remembered the struggle for liberty in Europe reacted with emotion to this latest confirmation of German willingness to defend civil rights and representative government. "When the columns marched along the wall," one revolutionary recounted, "we felt ourselves set back into the days of 1848 and 1849, and the dried-up milk of enthusiasm seemed in fact to flow again."[13]

Franz Sigel's regiment received its flag during the first week of May. The Women's Union presented the colors to the dashing hero of the 1848 Baden rebellion while urging the men to "cut a path for freedom through the poisonous mists" and, as in Germany, fight for a "united, great, free Fatherland." Sigel spoke for many forty-eighters as he praised the "great republic" as "the last refuge for liberty" that welcomed the "free men of Europe." He asserted that the defense of the Union embodied the "same great principles" to which he had "devoted" his "past life." For Sigel, defeat of the Slave Power would ensure that the spirit of 1776 and 1848 would continue to live in America.[14]

While Germans mobilized to defend the Union, members of the Democratic Party and supporters of slavery and southern rights looked with alarm upon the Republican movement that threatened to bring antislavery politics to ascendancy in Missouri. They denounced the St. Louis Republicans' radical, European-style socialism that attacked property rights, economic privilege, and, by extension, slavery. Democrats began conflating "Black and Red Republicans" and comparing the German unionist platform to the most radical ideologies of "Mazzini, Kossuth, Ledru Rollin, and Louis Blanc." One Democratic state senator, during the debate over the secession of Missouri, "denounced the German population bitterly" and applied to them the terms "Red and Black Republicans." Democratic newspapers warned that conservative Americans should be wary of "scarlet red speakers." The year 1848, one paper claimed, had introduced to America "Pure red republicans! People rotten from the ground up, red all the way through to their kidneys." These "pure desperate wreckers," the paper claimed, threatened the property rights of slaveholders and capitalists alike.[15]

Southern-rights Democrats used these arguments to exacerbate divisions between the Germans and the Irish in St. Louis. Democratic politicians told the Irish that if they remained in the Union they would have to submit to "Dutch rule" and endure "Dutch infidelity." The Irish voted heavily for Daniel G. Taylor, an anti-Republican and a conditional Unionist, in the April mayoral election. Father John Bannon, worried in 1861 about the radicalism and anticlericalism of his German fellow citizens, would later return to his homeland to further Confederate diplomacy by enlisting to the cause prominent Irish forty-eighters such as William Smith O'Brien. Even if slavery mattered little to Bannon as a concrete interest, he and many of his Irish compatriots in St. Louis could not allow their city and the American republic to be threatened by ideological Germans they believed to be as oppressive as the English. In the coming struggle, Bannon and a significant portion of the Irish in St. Louis would cast their lot with the Confederacy, which they viewed as another downtrodden nation struggling for autonomy.[16]

The tension between German Unionists and Irish Confederates intent on preserving the legacy of 1848 exploded at the so-called Battle of Camp Jackson. When militia companies loyal to Missouri's secessionist governor gathered on the outskirts of St. Louis, Father Bannon and many of his parishioners and countrymen joined them. They expressed a determination to defend Missouri from subjection by an abusive central authority. One member of the Missouri Confederate Brigade, which would include Bannon and many of the men at Camp Jackson, compared "Ireland in her struggle for self-government" to the Confederacy in its bid for independence. He acknowledged that "Irish blood asserted itself" through service in the Missouri Brigade and the Confederate armed forces. Southern patriots believed that they followed in the tradition of the Irish in 1848 and Washington in the "Great Rebellion," both of whom had fought "the worst of all tyrannies" and "raised a cry for liberty."[17]

Nathaniel Lyon, now in control at the arsenal, had no intention of watching while secessionists gathered strength in an attempt to take Missouri out of the Union. On May 10, he launched a preemptive strike on the troops assembled at Camp Jackson. Four regiments of new U.S. volunteers marched from the arsenal to encircle and capture the militia encampment. Politician Frank P. Blair commanded the first regiment, while forty-eighters Heinrich Boernstein, Franz Sigel, and Nicholas Schüttner headed the other three. The German community reacted with electric excitement. As a body of troops passed the local Turner hall, one observer reported, "everyone rushed to the windows in wild haste." The hall erupted in "a great shout of jubilation" when "it was known for certain that a blow was being directed against the camp." The ensuing wave of emotion exceeded even the excitement accompanying the outbreak of revolution in Europe. "We saw old men weeping tears of joy, and everyone gripped his weapon tightly," reported the *Westliche Post*. "We saw few scenes of this sort in 1848 or 1849, either in Paris or in the Baden-Palatine Revolution," continued the editor. "It was one of those splendid moments when emotion glowing deep in the heart of the masses suddenly breaks into wild flames."[18]

The outnumbered Missouri militia surrendered immediately. Violence erupted, however, as hostile civilian crowds gathered to watch Union troops escort their prisoners through the streets of St. Louis. Hecklers began harassing the inexperienced soldiers as the volunteers crossed the boundaries of Bannon's heavily Irish St. John's Parish on their way to German strongholds at the arsenal and the Turner hall. Nervous troops fired into the air and armed civilians responded. Before officers could calm the ensuing mayhem, several civilians and soldiers lay dead, including Captain Constantin Blandowski, Polish patriot and veteran of the Hungarian Revolution.[19]

Partisans on both sides moved to claim the legacy of 1848 as they attacked those they regarded as the enemies of liberty and freedom. One editorial denounced Union general William S. Harney's promise to suspend hostilities in an attempt at compromise as "a product of the American political style, not of the European revolutionary style." Franz Sigel's regiment presided over a funeral ceremony at the Turner hall to honor Blandowski as the first martyr in this latest struggle for liberty. The *Anzeiger des Westens*, satisfied with the raid on Camp Jackson, remarked, "It is generally known that the year 1848 still causes European despots indigestion, but we would have hardly have expected it to sit like a cobblestone in the belly of the despots here as well."[20]

In the meantime, Irish and American secessionists denounced the "Camp Jackson Massacre," which they attributed to the influence of European radicalism. "These reds and Forty-eighters are to blame for everything," exclaimed one editorial. Released from captivity, Bannon preached prosouthern sermons before joining the Confederate service as a chaplain. Archbishop Peter Richard Kenrick of St. Louis endorsed the choices of the city's Catholic secessionists and attacked the many Irish joining the Union army throughout the North. He ridiculed New York's unionist archbishop John Hughes, who, in Kenrick's view, had vacillated in defense of liberty in Europe in 1848 and in America in 1861.[21]

Unionists acted to contain the damage their cause sustained among the Irish in St. Louis. Thomas O'Reilly, an Irish doctor loyal to the Union, addressed a series of missives to his fellow countrymen in an attempt to dissuade those who favored secession. The city's Republican newspaper printed an address delivered by William Howard Russell of the London *Times* arguing that the Irish could strike a blow for liberty by preserving the Union. These efforts bore some fruit. Unionists in St. Louis attempted to recruit an "Irish brigade" of their own by appealing to many of the same themes that attracted Germans to the Union fold. The frantic appeals that appeared in the paper attested to the extent of the damage that had been done. One citizen apologetically explained, "If the Irish vote the secession ticket in this State, it is because they will be misled in the matter." Dr. O'Reilly denounced the "pseudo friends" and "low trickery and reckless audacity of the political gamblers" who led many of his countrymen to become "tools of the faction who have plunged our country into rebellion and secession." St. Louis's Republican newspaper apologized for the "political differences" that prevented the city's Irish that did fight for the Union from being "the first in the field." In the end, Ella Lonn, in her seminal studies on foreigners in the Union and Confederate armies, could only identify one Irish Union regiment from Missouri, while she found two Irish Confederate regiments from St. Louis, and a battery and another regiment from all of Missouri.[22]

Like their fellow-citizens in Missouri, European Americans across the country chose to uphold the legacy of 1848 as Confederate nationalists or liberal Unionists. The Germans, Irish, Poles, and Hungarians who joined the Union and Confederate war efforts echoed the themes articulated by St. Louis's ethnic communities. Forty-eighters, revolutionaries, and likeminded Europeans who supported the Confederacy's bid for independence stressed the self-determination of peoples and the rights of national minorities to self-government. Their Unionist counterparts fought for liberty and civil rights threatened by a despotic, landed, slaveholding aristocracy.

News of the Battles of Fort Sumter and Camp Jackson spread the revolutionary enthusiasm throughout the North's forty-eighter communities. In New York, a multinational group of revolutionary veterans joined the "Garibaldi Guards" commanded by Colonel Frederick George Utassy, who had served with Kossuth in Hungary. The city held a public ceremony for the regiment, at which the soldiers received an American flag, a Hungarian flag, and a "tricolor standard" allegedly carried by Garibaldi's men during the campaigns of 1848 and 1849. A reporter asserted that Garibaldi had, "with his own hand," planted the tricolor "on the battlements of one of the castles of the Eternal City—a triumphant emblem of liberty and power."

The Garibaldi Guards would now carry it into battle in America. Lieutenant Colonel Repetti accepted the tricolor for his men and expounded upon its meaning for the regiment: "It is with very great pleasure that I accept the duty of presenting to you this memorable flag—a flag which Garibaldi himself has consecrated to the cause of liberty." Repetti described the flag as a gift and urged his men, who included Hungarians, Germans, Italians, Frenchmen, and Spaniards, to "defend it through every peril." The regiment erupted in cheers and the band struck up "La Marseillaise."[23]

Other veterans of 1848 also prepared for war. Alexander Asboth, the Hungarian officer and future Union general who had fought alongside Kossuth in Hungary, issued a call to his countrymen, published in the *New York Times*, that urged them to congregate at Astor House to enlist. In his appeal, he reminded Hungarians that Kossuth and Washington had fought for the same principles, and asserted that while they awaited a movement on behalf of independence in their old homeland, they could not sit idly by while their adopted country lay "upon the verge of dissolution, the realization of which would be a triumph for all despots and the doom of self-government." Alexander von Schimmelfennig, one of the military leaders of the Baden rebellion, advertised in the *Baltimore Wecker* of April 19 for recruits to fight alongside him in another struggle for liberty. Friedrich Kapp offered to organize a regiment of scythe-men, who he asserted had served admirably during the Polish rebellion. Friedrich Hecker organized the Illinois 24th Infantry, which would be known as "Hecker's Regiment" throughout the war. Scores of regiments commanded by forty-eighters entered Union service in 1861, including Peter Joseph Osterhaus's 12th Missouri, Friedrich Salomon's 9th Wisconsin, Hans Böbel's 26th Wisconsin, Eduard Siber's 37th Ohio, Gustaf Tafel's 106th Ohio, Adolf Engelmann's 43rd Illinois, and August Willich's 32nd Indiana. The *New Yorker Criminal Zeitung und Belletristisches Journal* summed up the situation: "In the conflict between liberty and slavery, civilization and barbarism, loyalty and treason, the Germans will play, not a subordinate, but a leading role. The spirit of 1848 is abroad again."[24]

Carl Schurz agreed. The veteran of the European revolutions had been predicting throughout the 1850s that a conflict with the Slave Power would erupt, and he now seized the opportunity to spring into action. "It is a time for men of decision and resource," he wrote to his wife during the secession crisis. "I should not be surprised if your husband would be called into service again." He speculated that he might not "carry the sword again," but believed it "very possible that I may be active about organization and

"Presentation of Colors to the Garibaldi Zouaves, New York, May 1861." (Courtesy of Prints and Photographs Division, Library of Congress, Washington, D.C., LC-USZ62-119789)

such like in connection with the preparations for this decisive struggle." Schurz believed that the Civil War was the most recent and cataclysmic manifestation of the nineteenth century's revolutionary mission. "We live in a wonderful time," he wrote. "It is not merely an age of the adventurer and upstart whom cleverness and favoring circumstances have raised up; it is likewise the age of conscience-ruled men who dominate affairs by the force of honesty and shatter all opposing obstacles."[25]

Schurz, of course, classed himself among those men. He had often looked back with regret at his limited role in the failed revolutions of 1848. In retrospect, he believed he had been too young in 1848 to play a key role in the drama. The outbreak of war in America convinced him, however, that fate had deposited him in the right place at "precisely . . . the right age." It seemed to Schurz that events in Europe and America in 1861 promised to fulfill the principles for which he had struggled in 1848. He spoke with admiration of the success of the Risorgimento that was forging a nation out of the long-oppressed Italian states. In Europe, he marveled that "Garibaldi comes forth as knight errant, fighting for an ideal" against the reactionary forces that "measured their development by centuries." At precisely the same moment in America, he observed that the "honest will-power" of Abraham Lincoln attempted to thwart "the rise of a tyrannical party and the lawless attempts of an antisocial element." "If things do not deceive me," he wrote, "the end of the political slave power draws near." The once-defeated revolutionary displayed nothing but faith for the future. For Schurz, such an outcome would take on world-historic importance. "The Republican Party," he wrote, "needs only to understand its might in order to carry through with one single stroke a reform which will be among the most notable of our day."[26]

Eager to take part in the unfolding revolution, Schurz started immediately for Washington, D.C. He packed into his handbag the two pistols he had carried in the aftermath of the 1848 revolutions while rescuing his university professor and mentor, Gottfried Kinkel, from Spandau Prison in Berlin. He learned upon arrival in the capital that he had been appointed American minister to Spain, but in meeting with Lincoln he made it clear he desired a military position. He argued that his experience in 1848 qualified him for a leadership role in the coming armed struggle. He told the president that he had "seen some little field service in the revolutionary conflicts of my native country, and had ever since made military matters a favorite subject of study." Schurz endeavored to prove his martial worth while waiting for confirmation of his diplomatic appointment. He traveled to New York to put his experience and reputation to use by recruiting Europeans to fight in the Union army. Schurz found several of his old revolutionary acquaintances already at work in the city. Max Weber, who had served as an officer in the army of the Grand Duchy of Baden but defected and joined the revolutionaries in 1848, had already assembled the 20th New York. Other Germans joined the 8th New York, led by Ludwig Blenker, who had commanded revolutionary units in 1848. Colonel Leopold von Gilsa, a Prussian officer who had joined the revolution, aided efforts in the Empire State, and Franz Mahler, who served in Baden, led recruiting in Pennsylvania. Schurz managed to recruit several companies for the 1st New York—the "Lincoln Cavalry"—and review Blenker's regiment before leaving for Madrid.[27]

Irish Americans in New York, New England, and the Upper Midwest also girded for conflict. Their decision to cast their lot with the Union appears to represent a decisive break with their countrymen in Missouri who had joined the secessionists. Their experience, however, provides the exception that proves the rule. While they declined to support Confederate nationalism, these men also justified their decisions by invoking the goals of 1848. The revolutionary veteran Thomas Francis Meagher raised the Union's famous Irish brigade despite acknowledging the similarities between the ambitions of Ireland and the cause of the Confederacy. "In this controversy, my sympathies are entirely with the South!" he had declared upon hearing news of Fort Sumter. "You cannot call eight millions of white freemen '*rebels*,'" he explained to his Republican father-in-law. "You may call them '*revolutionists*' if you will." Still, he made the difficult decision to fight for the Union because he believed a reunited American nation would pose a stronger challenge to monarchical England. "We could not hope to succeed in our effort to make Ireland a Republic," he reasoned, "without the moral and material aid of the liberty-loving citizens of these United States." From the perspective of Irishmen in the North, the freedom of their native land could best be secured with the aid of a strong Union. A contemporary chronicler of the Irish Brigade echoed the German forty-eighters in describing why many of Meagher's men agreed to confront the Slave Power: "The Irish felt that not only was the safety of the great Republic, the home of their exiled race, at stake, but also, the great principles of democracy were at issue with the aristocratic doctrines of monarchism. Should the latter prevail, there was no longer any hope for the struggling nationalists of the old world." An article in *Harper's Weekly* explained the motivations of the Irishmen who fought for the Union under Michael Corcoran by comparing the "Southern aristocracy" to the "British aristocracy," both of which believed they were "born to rule other men."[28]

Not every European immigrant in America heeded these calls to arms. Many conservative Germans and Irishmen in the North had no quarrel with slavery and supported peaceful compromise with the South. Still, some of them also joined their more radical countrymen in making the link between 1848 and 1861 as they justified their position. The radicals they had opposed in their homelands, they feared, now threatened to disturb the peace of the American republic. Josef Dünnebacke, a German settler in Dallas, Minnesota, argued that "abolitionists" and "*European forty-eighters*" had "helped hatch the war" by refusing to compromise over slavery. One devout German Catholic immigrant agreed. "The source of this war," he argued sarcastically, could be found in the "beautiful European gift that the dear forty-eighters, the heroes of freedom who have broken with God and their respective monarchs, have brought to this beautiful land." Their support for military conflict with the Confederacy carried ironic unintended consequences, he believed. War would only weaken the

United States and allow what he called "European despots" a free hand in Europe and the New World. A distracted United States would be powerless to enforce the Monroe Doctrine, let alone aid the cause of liberty in Europe.[29]

Significant evidence suggests that many of the Union's foreign-born rank and file embraced an interpretation of the war that linked the fighting in America to the promise of freedom in Europe. Though many of these soldiers were too young to have participated directly in the revolutions of 1848, they echoed the forty-eighter editors and leaders in equating antislavery with opposition to aristocracy and support for republican government. Albert Krause, a young New York sergeant, refused ever to consider returning to Europe. "I have tasted freedom and it tastes too good," he declared. Krause proved happy to fight to preserve a "free land" where "the subordination to superiors is nothing like that in a European monarchy." Carl Hermanns, who left Europe to become a teacher in America, did not fight in the war but shared the views of many of his countrymen who joined the army. He wrote from Philadelphia in 1862 to his family in Germany to assure them that the wars of the mid-nineteenth century foreshadowed the defeat of "princely and papal authority" the world over. Adolph Frick, an immigrant and a Turner who served as a Unionist first lieutenant from Missouri, directly linked the defeat of princes to victory for the Union in the American Civil War. "America's free republic," he asserted, represented a "thorn in the eye" of "European princes." Victory for the Confederacy would allow them to "bring tyranny" to the New World. Both he and forty-eighter Dietrich Gerstein, who settled in Michigan and joined the Union army as a private, believed that freedom for Germany depended upon the outcome of the struggle. "Should this republic really be lost," Gerstein feared, "then the struggle of mankind for freedom will be in vain." Peter Welsh, a member of the Union's famous Irish Brigade, saw the question in exactly the same way. "This war," he declared, "is a war in which the people of all nations have a vital interest." He believed that if the Union failed, then "the old cry will be sent forth from the aristocrats of europe [*sic*] that such is the common end of all republics." August Horstmann of the 45th New York explained to acquaintances that the "North's free working people struggled here against the lazy, haughty Junker-spirit of the South." He summed up the feelings of many Europeans who fought for the Union: "For us this war is a sacred struggle of principles." He concluded that the war would "forever" destroy slavery and break the "neck of the southern aristocracy."[30]

It is important to note that some Europeans who fought for the Union had never been particularly opposed to slavery. Still, they found motivation for war in the prospect of fighting to overthrow a powerful planter-aristocracy. Such men often drew easy comparisons between southern slaveholders and the European ruling class and committed themselves to defeating both. John Henry Otto, after marching into Oxford, Georgia, felt he had entered "the abode of the aristocracy." Otto, a captain of a regiment from Wisconsin, believed that the vast wealth of the planters displayed in "stately mansions" fostered antidemocratic feelings of class superiority hostile to "personal liberty." Forty-eighter Marcus Spiegel enlisted in the Union army with no intentions of freeing the slaves. "It is not necessary to fight for the darkies, nor are they worth fighting for," he declared. His impressions of the Virginia countryside, which he compared to a "settlement of Aristocracy," quickly soured him on the character of southern society. His hatred for despotic ruling classes led him to embrace war policies at odds with his beloved Democratic Party. He admitted to his wife that "if the Democrats are not in favor of whipping these Aristocratic Rebels until they consider they are whipped, I am not with the Democrats." By the end of the war, he declared himself a "strong abolitionist" out of his desire to look out for "the best Interest of the white man in the south and the black man anywheres." Magnus Brucker, a U.S. army surgeon and veteran of 1848, shared Spiegel's belief that "*slavery* is the ruin of free white workers."[31]

Though the forty-eighters who joined northern armies included some of the Union's most committed supporters, the ambivalence of many about the morality of slavery demonstrated the extent to which the meaning of democratic revolution had fractured in the years since 1848. Like John Bannon, some supporters of freedom in Europe compared the North, not the South, to the despots of the Old Country. Confederates, they argued, fought for self-government and freedom from an oppressive central authority. In this conception, the revolutions of 1848 had established the right of self-determination in which oppressed peoples rose and claimed a place in the international "family of nations." The Confederate experiment in nationalism and regional independence seemed to follow the European revolutionary example, while northern efforts to conquer the fledgling nation resembled conservative reaction.

South of the Mason-Dixon Line, some European revolutionaries and their followers invoked this legacy of revolution as they mobilized for the Confederacy. Gaspar Tochman, the Polish freedom fighter of 1830 who had spent two decades advocating renewed struggle in Europe, left Washington,

D.C., for Richmond, Virginia, after war broke out in April 1861. Although he had long admired America's revolutionary example, Tochman objected to the decision of the U.S. government to forcibly suppress the South's bid for national independence. He arrived in the Confederacy determined to recruit fellow European revolutionaries to join what he considered to be the Atlantic world's latest nationalist struggle. Tochman's appeal "to the Refugees in America from Foreign Lands" appeared in the June 4 issue of the *Richmond Enquirer*. He addressed his letter to his "fellow countrymen of the Old World" who had sought the freedom and liberty in America that they had failed to achieve in Europe: "Whether driven from the homes of our birth by the oppressors of our native land, or revolting from the tyrannic despotisms and the pretended constitutional monarchies of Europe, we have sought and found new homes and safe asylums in these far-famed, prosperous and hitherto happy States of the American Union." In Tochman's opinion, the United States had afforded refugees the opportunity to enjoy "constitutional liberty" and participate in a political life "founded upon . . . self-government and State sovereignty."[32]

Tochman believed that Lincoln's decision to use armed force against the South threatened that happy heritage. War prompted Tochman to declare that the U.S. government was "not now the standard of human liberty, but the symbol of a despotic tyranny." He opposed the consolidation of all power in the Federal Government, a consolidation he believed placed in jeopardy what he called "the individual liberty of man." Revolutionary refugees who had witnessed reaction in the Old World might once again have lost the freedoms for which they had fought in 1848. Northern armies, according to Tochman, stood poised to establish "a despotism precisely similar to those of Europe."[33]

Tochman offered his services to the Confederate States of America and looked for soldiers to follow him. "I now most earnestly invoke and call upon you, my fellow exiles from the despotisms of Europe," he wrote, "to unite with me in defense of those cherished principles of self-government, constitutional liberty, and state sovereignty." White southerners, for their part, respected Tochman for his revolutionary credentials. They praised the "veteran officer so distinguished . . . in the glorious revolution of Poland." Confederate supporters believed that his "well known and well deserved popularity" promised to attract "thousands of foreigners" to the Confederate cause. He only needed to explain to them the "grievous mistake" Unionists made "in fighting for despotism against constitutional liberty."[34]

Tochman's efforts immediately bore fruit. His recruiting efforts in Virginia and later in Louisiana yielded a "Polish Brigade," which included German and Hungarian troops. In fewer than six weeks after he had issued his proclamation, 1,415 foreigners enlisted in his brigade, and he recruited 1,700 Confederate soldiers in all. On June 20, 1861, Tochman wrote Secretary of War Leroy P. Walker from his headquarters in Louisiana to report on his progress: "Twenty companies are already raised, uniformed and drilling, here, and some in Mississippi; seven mustered into service and encamped at Amite. Six were to be mustered in today, and the rest on Saturday." He asserted that the formation of his brigade even elicited a "favorable reaction among the foreigners" in "Missouri and the North."[35]

Gaspar Tochman hoped that his success would secure him a leadership role in the new Confederate military. He dreamed of being commissioned a general and once again leading the troops of a fledgling nation into battle. His ambitions were never realized. When his units mustered into service, the War Department appointed American-trained officers to lead the men. A bitterly disappointed Tochman stepped aside, but refused to give up easily. He embarked on an ultimately unsuccessful two-year effort to assuage his wounded ego by petitioning the secretary of war and the Confederate congress for reinstatement with general's rank. Still, his revolutionary reputation endured undiminished among Confederates. Congress passed a resolution in 1863 praising his "devotion to sound principles and free government." For his part, Tochman retained his belief in the international significance of the Confederacy's fight for independence. In the midst of the Civil War, he returned to Poland to take part in the rebellion against Russian rule that began in 1863. While in Europe, he promised Secretary of State Judah P. Benjamin that he would "elucidate, develope [sic], and defend the principles which have induced me to take part in this war with the Confederate States."[36]

John Mitchel, the Irish forty-eighter and southern nationalist, also led efforts to enlist his countrymen in the Confederate cause. He was in Paris when he heard news of Fort Sumter and made immediate plans to join the Confederacy in its war for independence. Upon arrival in Richmond, Virginia, Mitchel secured a position on the *Richmond Enquirer*'s editorial staff while his two sons enlisted in the Confederate army. The paper's opinion page immediately displayed Mitchel's influence. In early 1863, the paper published a letter from Mitchel's revolutionary companion John Martin arguing that all Irish nationalists had an ideological duty to support the Confederacy. Martin, whom the paper called "one of the ablest and best of the 'Irish Exiles' of 1848," declared unequivocally that his sympathies lay with the South. The people of the Confederacy, Martin argued, provided a ringing endorsement for the right of national self-determination: "A most noble people has there to take its place among the nations," he declared.[37]

Under Mitchel's direction, the *Enquirer*'s editorials immediately linked Irish and Confederate struggles for independence. The paper cast "shame" upon the Irish federal regiments that "prostituted the emblems of their country's ancient glory" by carrying the harp and sunburst into battle at the head of an "invading and plundering horde." Those symbols had been borne by what Mitchel called "Ireland's noblest exiles" against "all the chivalry of Europe." He believed they should only be used in support of the cause of national independence. Another editorial denounced the treachery and hypocrisy of "Irish Yankees" who fought "to make an Ireland of these Confederate States." William Smith O'Brien, another Irish hero of 1848, contributed a letter to the *Enquirer* in which he took issue with his fellow forty-eighter Thomas Francis Meagher's support for the Union. Anyone who contended that Ireland had a right to withdraw from domination by England, he argued, must support the Confederacy's bid for independence. The significance of the Civil War for O'Brien lay in determining whether or not political entities had "a natural and indefeasible right to determine what form of government is most conducive to their interests."[38]

The Confederate army also attracted some Germans and Hungarians to its ranks. Although most of the Germans in Texas's large forty-eighter communities remained loyal to the Union, some joined the South's bid for independence. Francis Richard Lubbock, Confederate wartime governor of Texas, remembered that many of his state's Germans had left the land of their birth "to escape political persecution" and were connected to those "who had participated in the struggle for German freedom in 1848." While his assertion was certainly false that "all such heartily sympathized with the South in the defensive war she was waging," his claim that "not a few enlisted in the Confederate army and did valiant service in the field" may not be far off the mark. Carl Coreth, son of German immigrant settlers near New Braunfels, enlisted in the Confederate service out of a feeling of obligation toward what he considered his family's adopted country. "There are people here who say they would not leave [for the army], they had not started the thing, etc. I feel duty bound to do it though," he wrote his brother Rudolph in May 1861. The Coreth family had left the Austrian Tyrol in 1846 only to return in 1848 and 1849. The extent of their participation in the revolutions is not known, but their republican sympathies were no secret. Most of their neighbors considered them to be forty-eighters when they returned to Texas in 1850. Rudolph, who joined Carl in the Confederate army, remained influenced by the legacy of 1848. Although he admitted to not always feeling "enthusiastic about our cause" he considered "our winning . . . as a matter of life and death," though he confessed he would attempt to get out of the army if the Confederacy ever adopted a monarchical form of government.[39]

Other free-thinking Germans proved less ambivalent. Dr. Adelbert J. Volck, a forty-eighter who settled in Baltimore, supported secession and served the Confederacy by drawing political cartoons ridiculing Lincoln and other Union officials. Kate Stone, daughter of a Louisiana slave owner, praised Mr. Kaiser and Mr. Hornwasher, two Hungarian "refugees" and "political exiles," who spoke of enlisting in the Confederate army. Their patriotism, she suggested, stemmed from the grandeur of the Confederate national cause. The two Hungarians, she believed, stood in admirable contrast to those who could not "appreciate the earnestness and grandness of this great national upheaval, the throes of a Nation's birth." Turner clubs in New Orleans and Houston also raised companies for the Confederate army. Captain Robert Voigt, a member of the Houston Turner Society and a Confederate soldier, enthusiastically embraced the war effort. He spoke proudly of his "duty" and "our cause" in his private letters.[40]

Voigt never clearly explained what he meant by those terms. Many of his fellow Europeans who fought on both sides did, however. By the end of 1861, thousands of them had joined the Union and Confederate armies to take part in this new revolution in America. Some of the individual issues for which they fought surely seemed alien to them, but the conflict's general principles proved startlingly familiar. Soldiers from a wide range of national backgrounds, who held a variety of political opinions, agreed that the war in America was of worldwide importance. Recent history had taught them to equate civil wars with revolutions fought in the name of the people. The desire for individual rights, human freedom, and national self-determination caused civil conflict in both Europe and America. The dilemma lay in determining how best to achieve those goals.

While European Americans loudly articulated their hopes during the first year of war, it would be left to native-born politicians and policymakers to give them tangible shape. As a result, northern and southern officials would have to make their case for Union or independence not only to themselves and their supporters, but also to the world. To do so, they would have to think in global terms and grapple with the troubling questions raised by the recent past. As they attempted to answer those questions, diplomats and statesmen would at times draw on and at times challenge the arguments of Europeans and forty-eighters, but at all times they would engage those arguments. In the process they would develop definitions of nationalism as deep and complex as any the nineteenth-century world had produced.

3

•

The Problem of Northern Nationalism

THE SPECTACLE OF EUROPEAN REVOLUTIONARIES TAKING UP ARMS
in America excited many northern patriots who had cheered movements
for freedom in Europe in the years before the Civil War. The willingness of
Old World liberals to embrace their adopted republic seemed to prove that
the North stood for liberty, progress, and freedom. For the nation's leaders,
however, the issues at stake did not appear so simple. In the months after
the Battle of Fort Sumter, they found themselves in an ironic position. They
would have to justify a war for reunion to observers at home and abroad,
some of whom rejected the radical policies favored by the most enthusiastic revolutionaries. As a result, northern thinkers, diplomats, politicians,
and policymakers had to construct a definition of American nationalism
that would appeal to a wide variety of constituencies. To do so, they strove
to articulate the Union cause in a way that balanced the liberal principles
of freedom with more conservative ideals of order and authority. Those
choices put them on a collision course with their most radical followers, as
events in Missouri quickly demonstrated.

In the summer of 1861, General John C. Frémont arrived to take command of the city of St. Louis. Frémont was a well-known and ambitious
adventurer and politician. In the 1830s and 1840s he had won fame as
an explorer of the American West, and in 1856 he ran for the presidency
as the first candidate of the Republican Party. The dashing "Pathfinder,"
as he was nicknamed, had attracted and fired the imaginations of many
liberal romantics. Frémont became especially popular among the European revolutionaries who were eagerly joining the Union war effort. Ernest
Duvergier de Hauranne reported, "Frémont has many followers among the
German settlers of the West, who have recently arrived from the mother
country." He surrounded himself with revolutionary refugees of 1848. The
gallant Charles Zagonyi, a veteran of Hungary's war for independence,

commanded Frémont's personal bodyguard. Alexander Asboth and John Fiala, who had also fought with Kossuth, served on the Pathfinder's general staff. In St. Louis, Duvergier de Hauranne asserted, the general was regarded "as a sort of revolutionary."[1]

Frémont's followers brought with them from Europe clear ideas and expectations about how a war should be conducted. Duvergier de Hauranne reported that they were more responsive to "doctrinaire ideas" than "practical" politics, and Frémont evidently felt the same way. On August 14, the general declared martial law in St. Louis. Radical opponents of the state's planter aristocracy now had clearance to strike directly at their enemy's property, power, and material interests. Frémont's men detained dissenters and shut down secessionist newspapers. They arrested citizens and opened military courts. Later that month, they rejoiced when Frémont ordered his soldiers to confiscate the property of southern sympathizers and free their slaves. Duvergier de Hauranne described the radical outlook of the general's supporters: "They have brought to the New World the instincts of European democracy, together with its radical attitudes and all-or-nothing doctrines. They aren't afraid of revolution: to destroy a barbarous institution they would, if necessary, take an axe to the foundations of society."[2]

Although revolutionaries like these brought much-needed zeal to the northern war effort, their most radical initiatives could also pose political problems for the national leadership. The actions of revolutionaries in St. Louis and elsewhere forced President Lincoln and his advisors to make tough choices about the type of war they would fight. Were they to strike at slavery and the property of secessionists in order to reestablish national authority? In the first year and a half of war, Lincoln offered a firm answer. He was not yet prepared to move in such a revolutionary direction. Upon hearing news of the unfolding events in Missouri, he immediately wrote to Frémont and ordered him to comply with Congress's First Confiscation Act, which had authorized seizure of only those slaves working directly in support of the Confederate war effort. Frémont refused, and Lincoln fired the intransigent general just over one month later. German Americans in St. Louis urged the president to change his mind. Radicals in St. Louis believed striking against property in land and slaves would weaken the southern "aristocracy" and preserve equal rights for all white men. The revolutionaries who staffed the editorial department of the *Anzeiger des Westens* explained the importance of attacking slavery. "The leading conspirators are slaveowners," they cried, "and as such form an oligarchy which is a conscious enemy of all free institutions." The administration's refusal to embrace abolition and confiscation confused and frustrated them. Their bitter disappointment and seeming isolation prompted B. Gratz Brown to speak for all those loyal to the legacy of 1848 by defiantly declaring, "*We* are the Revolution."[3]

Lincoln's handling of the Frémont episode underscored the dilemma that U.S. policymakers faced as revolution exploded into war during the summer of 1861. The most radical defenders of the Union eagerly anticipated a revolutionary struggle in which northern armies would attack secession, slavery, and the wealth and power of a southern plantation "aristocracy." Many moderates and conservatives in the North and in the Border States called for a much more limited conflict. They could condone a war to defend the Union, but would not fight to free slaves or infringe upon the property rights of their former fellow citizens. Their support, Lincoln knew, would be needed in order for the North to subdue the South.

Lincoln and his diplomats would also have to consider the positions and opinions of rulers throughout the world. As armies gathered in America, soldiers on both sides hoped that the conflict would be brief. If neither the Union nor the Confederacy could, with force of arms, successfully defend its claim to nationhood, however, then foreign interference and assistance might prove decisive. Consequently, as the first battles were fought, a war for public and world opinion began in earnest. During the spring and summer of 1861, supporters of the federal government took steps to prove to the world that the North and the South remained a single, viable, and legitimate national entity. The representatives of the Union would have to justify their war against the South in terms that statesmen and thinkers in Europe would understand. They found themselves in an awkward and contradictory position. American citizens, North and South, had often applauded revolutions in Europe and had always supported national self-determination. Now, northerners found themselves forced to uphold established authority. The arguments that they advanced would need to be couched in terms that could easily be embraced by the heads of state who had triumphed during Europe's midcentury revolutions.

During the first year and a half of war, Abraham Lincoln and his advisors committed themselves to a position that sought to reconcile liberalism with conservatism and liberty with order. In his first annual message to Congress, he explained to the American people that he had rebuked Frémont because he had wished to avoid plunging the nation into a "violent and remorseless revolutionary struggle." He stressed his conviction that "the Union must be preserved," but rejected the impulse to immediately employ "radical and extreme measures." He defended his order overruling the radical hero by appealing to stability and the rule of law. Lincoln held that a responsible nation could not undermine the rights of private property. "Can it be pretended that it is any longer the Government of the U. S.—any government of Constitution and laws,—wherein a General, or a President, may make permanent rules of property by proclamation?" he asked. He explained to Illinois lawyer Orville H. Browning that he, for one, could not "assume this reckless position. It is itself the surrender of the government."[4]

In 1861 and much of 1862, Lincoln refused to cultivate radical public opinion at the expense of the United States' reputation as a responsible nation-state. As he had with the conduct of the war, Lincoln learned to approach foreign policy in ways that balanced liberal principles with disciplined conservatism. He faced some of his toughest choices in filling the Union's vacant diplomatic posts. Forty-eighters, Lincoln well knew, formed an important part of the Republican political coalition and lent ideological fervor to the growing war effort. As a result, he named a significant number of German revolutionaries to positions in the foreign service of the United States. Carl Schurz, as we have seen, received the important post of American ambassador to Spain despite that fact that he was still considered a wanted man in Germany. The radical editors Heinrich Boernstein and Carl Bernays served as consuls in Bremen and Zurich.[5]

European leaders, however, did not always welcome these revolutionary refugees. The exasperated leaders of the Thuringian states rejected Gustav Struve as ambassador of the New World republic. Even some Americans commented on the appointments with skepticism. An article in *Vanity Fair* took a jaundiced view of the Schurz appointment. While the author conceded that his adventures in Europe had been carried out "all For Liberty—or rather *Freiheit*," he suggested with irony that it might be better "to send some gentleman out among the princes and potentates who hasn't got a rope around his neck." While Lincoln remained committed to Schurz, he proved perfectly willing to sacrifice principle for the sake of practicality in other instances. The president, for example, backed down when the Austrian government objected to the appointment of Ambassador Anson Burlingame, who had allegedly supported the revolutions of 1848.[6]

Perhaps the best-publicized of these episodes involved the Italian patriot Giuseppe Garibaldi. In 1861, ardent Unionists attempted to enlist the Italian hero in the federal armed services, once again forcing the Lincoln administration to reconcile enthusiasm for universal human liberty with the need for national stability. Garibaldi had become an international celebrity through his improbable success in helping to forge an Italian nation with the aid of an army of peasants and adventurers. Many Americans in the North and in the South believed he epitomized the nineteenth-century man—brave, altruistic, and devoted to national progress, self-determination, and human liberty. When the war broke out, many Americans in the North believed the veteran of 1848 and hero of Italian unification would make the ideal symbol to lead the Union's armies. After all, he had succeeded in uniting Italy. Why couldn't he now protect the Union of the states? Theodore Canisius, forty-eighter and U.S. consul in Vienna, wondered the same thing. Canisius, along with Henry S. Sanford, U.S. minister in Belgium, developed a plan to bring their hero to the United States. During the summer of 1861, Sanford traveled to Italy to sound Garibaldi out. The Italian revolutionary agreed to fight for the Union but demanded supreme command of the U.S. Army. Administration officials were not prepared to make such an offer and negotiations reached an impasse. Canisius, determined to keep the deal from failing, offered Garibaldi a command on his own authority. Garibaldi then demanded a further concession before joining the war in America. He stipulated that he would fight to save the Union only if he could guarantee the freedom of the slaves. "I will go thither with my friends," Garibaldi declared, "and we will make an appeal to all the democrats of Europe to join us." He held, however, that his appeal would need to uphold the "principle" he believed animated all revolutionaries—"the enfranchisement of the slaves, the triumph of universal reason."[7]

Canisius's offer caused a sensation in the United States. The prospect of Garibaldi's joining the struggle excited the American public. The *New York Herald* reported in September 1861 that an American minister "had renewed the offer of a commission in the U.S. Army to General Garibaldi, and that he had accepted it on certain conditions." The editors speculated that Frémont's proclamation freeing the slaves had prompted the general to accept the offer. The usually conservative *Herald* responded with excitement: "The liberator of Italy would prove a brilliant addition to our list of Union generals." The London *Times* took a less sanguine view. The paper asserted with irony that the hero of Italian independence now hoped to subjugate "a nation wishing to be free." Still, the *Times* could not dampen American enthusiasm. The mania for Garibaldi stirred northern eagerness for the services of other European revolutionaries. The fever raged unabated in early 1862 when the *Herald* reported a rumor that Colonel

Giuseppe Garibaldi. Many Americans believed Garibaldi epitomized enlightened nineteenth-century masculinity. (Author's collection)

Jean-Baptiste Adolphe Charras, minister of war in France under the republic of 1848, had received the latest offer of a Union command.[8]

The growing revolutionary fervor in America put Union diplomats in a difficult position. Policymakers worried about the damage the wild rumors would do to the North's image. William Dayton explained to the administration the problem in allowing revolutionary sympathies to impeach national credibility. "[Canisius's] sentiments may be all right," he conceded, "but just at this point of time, when Austria and Italy and France are so sensitive, it was scarcely worth while for our consul to throw them in the face of these powers." The State Department agreed. It rebuked the renegade diplomat when rumors of Garibaldi's impending arrival reached America. Canisius's attempt to enlist his revolutionary compatriots in the U.S. Army had been quashed. The United States, the message went, would remain a world power that reconciled liberty with order.[9]

Lincoln's handling of the Garibaldi episode preserved America's national standing in the eyes of world leaders. The president had refused to act rashly and side with persons and policies that many observers considered the essence of anarchy. Lincoln's position rested directly on his conception of the meaning of nationalism in the mid-nineteenth-century world. The federal government, he was keenly aware, was not the first government to deal with revolts, rebellions, revolutions, and violent challenges to national legitimacy. For the past century, he realized, people in Europe and the Americas had been asking questions about nationalism: What shape should nations take in the future? When was a nation legitimate, and when was it not? The answers to these questions would have to be developed in an international context, as diplomats, politicians, writers, and journalists in Europe and America engaged in a conversation about the nature of nationalism in the modern world. In the process, they would have to develop and articulate a definition of American nationality that considered questions that no Americans had ever yet directly answered. It would not be enough to insist that the United States was a nation. Instead, they would have to explain, in universal terms, precisely what it meant to be a nation. They would need to define the relationship between citizens and the state, and explain how they would balance the "right of revolution," which the United States had always advocated, with the necessity of national self-preservation that the country now faced. In order to do so, they took a position that upheld national order, integrity, and unity.

The task of explaining this position to the world fell, first and foremost, to the secretary of state, William Henry Seward. When Seward joined the Lincoln administration during the spring of 1861, he brought with him an extensive record of public service. He had served two terms as governor of New York and was elected to the Senate in 1848. In 1860, he had been widely regarded as the frontrunner for the Republican presidential nomination. Although he ultimately lost to Abraham Lincoln, many still considered him to be the leader of his party when he joined the cabinet in 1861.

During the 1850s, Seward had developed a reputation as a sectional firebrand. His suggestions that an "irrepressible conflict" existed between the North and the South and that a "higher law" should supersede the Constitution on questions regarding slavery had outraged white southerners as well as those northerners devoted to the peaceful coexistence of a union founded on the rights of the states. In truth, however, Seward was a committed American nationalist. During the secession crisis, he favored compromise at all costs, and even tried to engineer a reconciliation by offering unauthorized assurances to the South that the new administration would abandon Fort Sumter. In April, he suggested that the United States declare war on the European powers in the hopes that a foreign conflict would prompt the departing southern people to return to the fold and rally around the stars and stripes.

Lincoln immediately rejected Seward's proposals and made it clear that the president, not the secretary of state, would have the final say on all matters, foreign and domestic. Still, Lincoln would rely on Seward's expertise in crafting foreign policy. Despite his momentary lapse in reason, Seward was in no way ignorant of world politics. He had observed and commented on European developments throughout his political career. While in the Senate, he had welcomed Louis Kossuth to America and delivered speeches in favor of the freedom of Europe and Ireland. In 1860, while campaigning for Abraham Lincoln, he gave an address entitled "The National Idea; It's Perils and Triumphs." In it, he expounded upon ideas he had developed in the "irrepressible conflict" speech. He asserted that the principles of free labor, free soil, free speech, equal rights, and universal suffrage embodied in Republican definitions of American nationalism were also revolutionizing western and southern Europe.[10]

By the time war broke out in April 1861, Seward had thought long and hard about the relationship between nationalism, liberalism, war, and revolution. His engagement with current events taught him, above all, the critical importance of recognition in conferring legitimacy. To be a nation, a political entity had to be accepted as one by its fellow nations. As a result, Seward correctly predicted that Confederate officials would immediately dispatch representatives abroad to seek European favor and support. "It is a cardinal point with the seditious in modern revolutions to gain aid, or at least sympathy, in foreign countries," he warned George G. Fogg, the U.S. representative to Switzerland, in May 1861.[11]

To counteract those moves, Seward would have to act in kind. He would have to send representatives to Europe who could convince heads of state that the United States, both North and South, was one nation. Northern diplomats wasted no time. In May 1861, Cassius M. Clay, U.S. minister to Russia, stopped in Liverpool before hurrying on to St. Petersburg to take up his commission. While in Britain, he published an open letter to the English people insisting that the entire United States remained an indivisible nation. "'We the people of the United States of America,'" he explained, "are fighting to maintain our *nationality*." That same year, John Lothrop Motely, the American man of letters known for his monumental history of the Dutch Republic, published his own opinion piece in the London *Times*. Motely's exegesis on *The Causes of the American Civil War*, which northern sympathizers immediately reprinted for circulation at home, explained that the Constitution of 1787 had made the United States a "nation," forever distinguishing the Union from a league, a commercial alliance, or even a confederation. A subsequent article by an anonymous author in the *Continental Monthly* summed up the developing northern position by proclaiming, "WE ARE A NATION, not 'a tenant-at-will sort of confederacy.'"[12]

Clay, Motely, and their disciples believed that the permanent right to exercise sovereignty distinguished genuine nations from confederacies. Motely explained that the constitution of the United States was an organic law, ratified by the whole people; therefore, the document bound all citizens to offer allegiance to the government. Cassius Clay argued that secession amounted to nothing less than treason, which threatened freedom by undermining the legitimate authority that protected it. "Without *law* there is no liberty," he maintained. In conclusion, he encouraged the English people to adopt the Union cause as the cause of "real conservatism." Henry Adams, who along with his father, Charles Francis Adams, accompanied Clay to Great Britain, later remarked on the irony of the situation. For the first time on the international stage, he wryly observed in his famous autobiography, America posed as "the champion of legitimacy and order."[13]

As northern officials made their case to the world, they would be guided, first and foremost, by their interpretation of the Congress of Vienna. Although the statesmen at the Congress had denied nationality to some European ethnic and cultural groups, some northern thinkers argued that they had made progress in establishing an international family of great powers. True nationality, they reasoned, could not be maintained without stability. As a result, they believed that 1815 had set precedents in favor of the maintenance of existing political entities. One contributor to the *Continental Monthly* explained that the expansion of trade and commerce during the nineteenth century confirmed their wisdom. "The whole world," he asserted, "was to fraternize. It was to be an Arcadia in a ring-fence, an Arcadia solidly based upon heavy profits."[14]

Northern nationalists did go beyond the Congress of Vienna in some ways. They acknowledged that new nations could join this "charmed circle," but only after they had demonstrated the strength and power needed to maintain national authority and unity. Nineteenth-century thinkers in Europe and America believed that the trend of history ran toward stronger governments and a more unified citizenry. They called this concept "centralization." The French had achieved the supremacy of the government in Paris over the provinces in their revolution of 1789. The people of both the German and Italian states had, beginning in 1848, attempted to create a unified state out of divided polities. By the time the American Civil War broke out, it appeared that the Italians would be successful in achieving unity. A treatise on "American Nationality" that appeared in the *Princeton Review* in the autumn of 1861 declared that "a reviving civilization always manifests itself in a striving after national unity." The journal praised, as a result, the "strenuous efforts" to reconstruct "shattered" nationalities that could be witnessed "in Italy at the present time."[15]

For northern nationalists, the particularizing cause of secession stood in sharp contrast to the unifying cause of national consolidation. The Reverend Joseph P. Thompson, in an article that appeared in the pages of the *New Englander and Yale Review*, explained that secession threatened the principle of nationality itself. "The rebellion," he wrote, "puts in jeopardy *the political unity of a nation, historically and territorially one.*" John Lothrop Motely equated "disintegration" with "barbarism" and explained to his English readers that secession threatened to return Western civilization to the "chaos from which we emerged three quarters of a century since." An editorial in the *Chicago Daily Tribune* warned that successful southern secession would prove that the Union was "not a *Nation*," but "only a Confederation of petty states, like Germany." One correspondent of the *Continental Monthly* mocked the "vile and mean" men of the South who had "lost all national pride" because of their "small-minded provincial attachment to a State." He concluded that "the question whether [the U.S.] shall form one great nation or a collection of smaller states, is one of fearful importance."[16]

This question was important because many of the revolutions of the 1800s had contested the legitimacy of large unions. Centralization had been resisted on a number of occasions on both sides of the Atlantic by groups devoted to ethnicity or local self-interest. The Poles, the Irish, the Belgians, and now the Confederate states of the American South had all taken up arms to strike against constituted governments. In their place, they proposed to substitute smaller polities organized around ethnic identity or regional institutions and economic interests like slavery. These new political entities might join larger leagues or confederations for the sake of peace and safety as the American colonies had done in 1776 and as the southern states attempted to do in 1861; or they might fracture into warring fiefdoms. William Henry Seward wanted to avoid that possibility at all costs. He believed that such an alternative already existed in Latin America. There, without a unifying national force, large confederations, like Simón Bolívar's Gran Colombia, had broken down into warring states. If the United States could not exert its claim to nationhood, then two confederacies would emerge that might go the same way. Seward explained to his ambassador in France that "the success of [the Confederate] revolution" would be "not only a practical overthrow of the entire system of government, but the first stage by each confederacy in the road to anarchy, such as so widely prevails in Spanish America." His opinion was shared by a Kansas paper that feared the rebellion would reduce the United States to the "anarchical condition of Mexico and the South American republics."[17]

Such a prospect frightened most patriotic citizens of the United States. Thinkers like Seward assumed that the development of the nation-state was the most important of the many innovations of the nineteenth century. The emergence of nations across the globe distinguished the progressive present from the stagnant past. "The modern world," observed a contributor to the *Atlantic Monthly* in 1861, "differs from the world of antiquity in nothing more than in the existence of a brotherhood of nations." The author asserted that such an arrangement "was unknown to the ancients," who, he marveled, "seem to have been incapable of understanding" the concept. These convictions underscored the faith that nineteenth-century theorists held in the superiority of modern political philosophy. Enlightenment thinkers had glorified the institutions of the classical world, but nineteenth-century men would improve and perfect them. An 1861 article in the *Princeton Review* maintained that the growing popularity of the idea of nationality demonstrated "the constant tendency of civilization to realize . . . more and more perfect forms."[18]

By the 1860s, many patriotic thinkers in the United States believed that their country had made great progress in joining this brotherhood of powerful states. Indeed, the American republic had reached a crossroads by the middle of the nineteenth century. The founders had imagined a union of semisovereign states, held together by mutual self-interest. This conception of the country appeared outdated to many thinkers in the North by the time of the Civil War. Instead, they began speaking of an organic "nation," that could share with powers like Britain and France all the trappings of a modern, unified state. Thinkers increasingly equated national prestige with national power. Governments were judged by their ability to command the allegiance of their citizens and marshal the resources of the entire state. A correspondent of the *Continental Monthly* explained that "he who belongs to a *great* nation is thereby great of himself."[19]

Secession, then, called into question American greatness and threatened the nation's place among the powers of the world. Democratic lawyer and politician Robert McClelland, who had served in Congress, as governor of Michigan, and as secretary of the interior under Franklin Pierce, worried that the rupture of the Union would cast the Republic "from her pre-eminence in the family of nations." Gertrude de Vingut, a northern author and contributor to the *New Englander and Yale Review*, shared his fears. She explained that American greatness depended on national unity. "We have been," she wrote "a great, proud people, springing into existence with almost magical rapidity; able to take our place among the nations of the world, and make our flag respected wherever it might wave." Now she worried about enduring "the loss of prestige which will reduce [the United States] to a second rate power."[20]

The correspondence of Theodore Heard of Boston illustrates the dismay and personal dejection an ordinary citizen of the era might feel at the loss of national prestige. Heard was traveling through Europe during the secession winter of 1861 and received frequent updates from his parents on the crisis in America. His father wrote him in exasperation on the anniversary of George Washington's birthday: "The bells were rung and cannon fired this morning & again this evening, in honor, of whom? Of the 'father of his country!' What country?" The frustrated patriot feared that the inability of the nation to maintain its integrity disgraced the United States in the eyes of European powers. Theodore's mother likewise worried in February 1861 that "one half of the pleasure of going abroad" must be "destroyed in the feeling that we shall now be unable to repel the taunts and sneers thrown at us by foreigners." She had already heard that Americans in Europe "see themselves looked upon with less consideration than formerly." National identity, she believed, rested upon national order and integrity in the world of European power-politics. "Our ministers must feel cheap to go abroad as the agents of a ruptured union," she lamented. For her, secession called into question American national existence before the entire world. "I don't feel," she confessed "that I can ever have *pride* in my country again."[21]

Still, many northerners took comfort from their belief that the actions of the leading powers of Europe had set precedents in favor of established nationalities. William Henry Seward pointed this out to Charles Francis Adams, U.S. ambassador to Great Britain. He noted to Adams that many governments in Europe had recently faced revolutions in their own countries. In each instance, they had acted to suppress them in the name of national authority, usually with the approval of European heads of state. One Kansas newspaper, though it distrusted alliance with autocratic powers, nevertheless noted that Russia supported the Union out of fear of *"revolts and rebellions"* and respect for *"established* governments." This observation became the central point in the northern diplomatic effort. In the first year and a half of war, northern diplomats sought to make common cause with European statesmen, and to keep them out of America's conflict. To do so, William Henry Seward insisted upon comparing Confederates to revolutionaries in writing his instructions to the diplomats of the United States. Southern secessionists, he told U.S. ambassador to Prussia Norman B. Judd, had inaugurated a "rash and perilous revolution." In his letter to Charles Francis Adams, Seward referred to secession as a "revolutionary movement." The Confederacy's supporters represented a "revolutionary party," and the leaders of the self-proclaimed nation acted as "revolutionary authorities." Seward referred in similar fashion to the "revolutionary government" of the South in his dispatch to Henry S. Sanford, representative to Belgium.[22]

These comparisons were not merely rhetorical. Indeed, they relied on the real events of the recent past. Even the least-known European conflicts garnered the attention of American diplomats. To secure Dutch neutrality, Henry C. Murphy, ambassador to the Netherlands, dredged up the memory of Belgium's secession from Holland in 1830. He compared the Dutch experience with separatism to America's trials in the Civil War. Murphy suggested that the ordeal had tempered Dutch willingness to intervene in another nation's conflict. He wrote Seward that "the Netherlands has had a bitter lesson of experience under similar circumstances."[23]

Northern nationalists also took comfort that the British government had been slow to interfere on behalf of the Greek revolt against the Turks during the 1820s, the Polish revolution of 1830, and Hungary's and Italy's bids for independence in 1848. In each instance, the general public had expressed widespread sympathy for the cause of the rebels; nevertheless, the British government acted with caution and deliberation, as more than one northern observer attested. August Belmont, the northern financier and Democratic politician, spoke for many when he reminded a friend in Europe that "when Hungary . . . made an heroic effort to reconquer her nationality and independence, England did not cease to consider her as a revolted province, although the sympathies of the majority of the English people were on the side of the rebels." As for Italy, William Henry Seward instructed Rufus King, minister to the Papal States, to remind the Pope that unbridled nationalism had threatened the Vatican in 1848 and more recently during the Risorgimento. "His government is surrounded by the elements of a political revolution," Seward thundered.[24]

Of all the revolutions of 1848, northerners paid the most attention to the precedent that Britain had set in Ireland. Early in the war, Seward urged

Charles Francis Adams to compare the Confederacy's struggle with the attempts of Ireland to part ways with England. If Britain intervened in the war, it would only acknowledge the right of self-determination. "Would it be wise for her Majesty's government, on this occasion, to set a dangerous precedent?" he asked. Both Cassius Clay and John Lothrop Motely pointed out to their English readers that if the South could secede from the United States, then Scotland or Ireland could surely secede from the United Kingdom. At home, the northern press constantly echoed Seward's pointed questions and observations on this issue. *Harper's Weekly* pointed out that Great Britain would have certainly gone to war in April 1848 if "the Chartists had appeared in arms" or if the Irish nationalist Feargus O'Connor "had called upon the Queen to surrender Ireland." An article in the *Atlantic Monthly* chided British gentlemen who believed that the Civil War represented the "bursting of the bubble of Democracy" by pointing out that recent rebellions in Ireland and elsewhere could just as easily foreshadow the "bursting of the bubble of Monarchy."[25]

William Henry Seward believed that the issues at stake in the American war involved more than just precedent in international law. He insisted that the outcome of the Civil War held in the balance the fate of the Western system of established nation-states. Seward was convinced that in the event of a Confederate victory, fresh revolutions would break out across Western Europe. "Revolutions are epidemical," Seward wrote William L. Dayton, American minister to France, in 1862. He believed that any radical change in the national system on the American continent would be followed by moral convulsions of incalculable magnitude that, in his words, would "threaten the stability of society throughout the world." He predicted that the upheavals that would follow would exceed those of 1848 in scope and impact. These "more general" cataclysms, he held, promised to transform the map of Europe. Monarchy, he believed, would be swept away once the right of revolution against constituted authority had been established on both sides of the Atlantic. In a letter to John Bigelow, U.S. consul in Paris, he noted with irony that should the masses of the Old World indeed rise in revolt, they would naturally "espouse our cause," meaning republicanism and the rights of suffrage, speech, and press. Given the position of the Union, however, the United States could not "sympathize" with them in good conscience. Still, just the threat of a wider war, he hoped, would keep the powers of Europe out of the conflict. "It does not seem to me that England could engage in hostilities with us now even aided by France . . . without a revolution in both countries," Bigelow wrote.[26]

Evidence suggests that European leaders took this prospect seriously. George Perkins Marsh, U.S. minister to Italy, reported that European ministers desired international stability. He believed that continental statesmen favored the Union because the United States fought to sustain the causes "of constitutional authority, of the entirety of nationalities and of established order against causeless rebellion." The Prussian minister of foreign affairs told a member of the U.S. legation in Berlin that Prussia favored the Union because of "the principles of unrelenting opposition to all revolutionary movements." His Austrian counterpart stated that he "was not inclined to recognize de facto governments anywhere," and Pope Pius IX assured an American representative that the Vatican supported "law and order everywhere." The U.S. ambassador in Switzerland likewise reported that a member of the Swiss Federal Council asserted that the Swiss "had always opposed rebellion and revolution." History had proved as much. The ambassador wrote, "He [the Swiss statesman] alluded, I presume, to the days of 1848, during which this republic acted with equal liberality and wisdom."[27]

As Union policymakers labored to hold the United States together in 1861 and 1862, they believed that they had historical precedent on their side. They argued that they had a right to expect that European powers would continue to treat the warring states as a single, legitimate national entity. Their study of the recent past, however, yielded more than convenient precedents. It also taught them lessons about the meaning of nationalism in the modern world. Statesmen, diplomats, and thinkers in the North found themselves forced to develop and articulate their own definition of nationalism. In the process, they thought through some of the most troubling questions of the era. By the end of the war, they had created a complete definition of American nationalism that had implications for would-be nation-builders around the world.

Americans in the North identified the tension between local rights and central authority as one of the most fundamental questions of the era. The Civil War proved as much. Americans in the North and in the South received orders from their respective governments to mobilize for war, and in that moment had to choose between loyalty to a state and loyalty to a nation. European revolutionaries had had to do the same. The conflicts of the 1800s forced them to choose between loyalties to region, culture, and ethnicity, and loyalties to sovereign rulers. An article in *Harper's Weekly* asserted that the war in America would offer clear answers to this universal question: "How much country must a man love to be a genuine patriot?"[28]

Not surprisingly, the author concluded that a true patriot must love his whole country. He made his case by referring to Europe's recent history of conflict. He argued that parochial attachment to region had dashed the hopes of Italian nationalists in 1848. When fighting broke out that year, the paper insisted, would-be patriots took to the field as self-conscious representatives of city-states like Rome, Venice, Naples, Parma, Tuscany, and Sicily, and not as representatives of nations. "Lo," he exclaimed, "there were no Italians in all Italy." As a result, the national cause had withered, Austria triumphed, and "for thirteen years more Italy groveled in chains."[29]

The cause of secession threatened to inflict the same result on the citizens of the United States. If small groups representing narrow interests could overthrow constituted governments anywhere at any time, then the carefully constructed world community might descend into chaos. Abraham Lincoln considered secession "the essence of anarchy," as he stated in his first inaugural address. An anonymous journalist writing for the *Continental Monthly* agreed. "The application of this principle," he wrote, "ends society by destroying the order based on authority, and placing the State above the Nation, and the individual above the State." Border State intellectual John Pendleton Kennedy and contributors to both the *Princeton Review* and the *North American Review* took Lincoln's lead in denouncing secession as a "retrograde" movement toward anarchy, as did diplomat Henry Sanford in discussions with the Belgian foreign minister. The French liberal and intellectual Agénor de Gasparin worried that the southern cause was the symptom of a wider sickness that had infected the foundations of Western civilization itself. He classed secession among the numerous "anarchical doctrines" that had been "hatched" during the modern age. The propensity of hot-headed pseudovisionaries to challenge authority, he implied, threatened true nationalism throughout the world.[30]

Defending order based on authority was a difficult position for any supporter of the American republic to take. Americans had always valued the rights of revolution and self-determination. Now, northerners found themselves fighting to uphold centralized authority. Any honest defense of the northern cause would need to reconcile these two positions. The British philosopher John Stuart Mill noticed the problem as early as anyone. Mill was respected on both sides of the Atlantic as one of the leading political philosophers of the era. His support for nationalist movements on the European continent had made him one of the leading advocates of the rights of self-determination. As a liberal, however, he disapproved of slavery and generally favored the North in the Civil War. In 1862, he mused on his conundrum in a pamphlet that Unionists in America reprinted for domestic consumption. Mill conceded that, in general, he looked with favor on struggles for national self-determination. "I do not scruple to say," he admitted, "that I have sympathized more or less ardently with most of the rebellions, successful and unsuccessful, which have taken place in my time." He refused, however, to make his support for past revolutionary movements the basis of a universal rule. "The mere fact of being a rebel," he reasoned, did not give one "sufficient title" to sympathy. Instead, he argued, a people would have to present a moral claim to nationhood in addition to demonstrating the will and means to fight for it.[31]

The northern intellectual Orestes Brownson believed that the distinctions proposed by Mill pointed the way for northerners to solve their dilemma. Like Mill, he admitted that Americans had supported revolutions abroad as recently as 1848. He feared that his countrymen could not be rallied to fight with much enthusiasm under the banner of "Law and Order." Brownson proposed instead that northern nationalists might seize upon "another battle-cry." He argued that the Union effort linked the maintenance of national order to the maintenance of liberty. Patriots had to fight to preserve the government so that the United States could bring liberty to the globe.[32]

Brownson struck a chord. In countless articles and speeches, supporters of the Union followed him in reconciling support for what the *Chicago Daily Tribune* called "established authority" with support for freedom. The key lay in distinguishing between illegal rebellion and legitimate resistance to oppression. To cite one example, an article in *Harper's Weekly* explained that the world approved of the "late risings in Italy" not because "they were movements against established governments," but only because they were "struggles against intolerable oppressions." The Reverend Joseph P. Thompson warned those who automatically equated rebellion with freedom that the 1848 revolutions in Rome and France had succeeded only in reestablishing despotism. A contributor to the *North American Review* echoed Mill in holding that "revolution is a necessity rather than a right" and that "the right of revolution does not exist in all cases where the power of revolution is found." Edward Ingersoll succinctly summed up the new orthodoxy: "Conservatism is our only chance of safety. Conservatism of our own American institutions. . . . Liberty of speech, liberty of the press, liberty of the person."[33]

Abraham Lincoln, like Edward Ingersoll, most often sought to explain the war in conservative terms during the first year and a half of fighting.

Early in the war, Lincoln's interpretation of the conflict most often stressed stability, unity, and the rule of law in a global framework. On July 4, 1861, in a special message to Congress, Lincoln proudly proclaimed the North's mission "to demonstrate to the world that those who can fairly carry an election can also suppress a rebellion." While he feared that governments often erred on the side of being "too *strong* for the liberties" of the people, he also conceded that they might prove "too *weak* to maintain" their existence. In this, he was clearly responding to contemporary political thought in Europe and the Americas. As the *Chicago Daily Tribune* pointed out, many nineteenth-century Europeans assumed that monarchies alone would prove strong enough to uphold national authority, and that republics were doomed to disintegration. Lincoln sought to refute these notions. He admitted that America's "popular government" had often been termed an "experiment." It now struggled to prove itself capable of "successful *maintenance* against a formidable internal attempt to overthrow it." While the representatives of Europe's established order may have been hostile to Lincoln's faith in democracy and republicanism, they surely could understand and appreciate the broader implications of the goals Lincoln laid out in his speech. "It presents the question," he explained, "whether discontented individuals, too few in numbers to control administration, according to organic law, in any case, can always . . . without any pretense, break up their Government."[34]

Still, by the summer of 1862, the president faced a problem that could not be solved with rhetoric alone. It would take more than statesmanship to defend the authority of the government. It would also take force. In late July 1861, Lincoln, in the hopes of swiftly vindicating American nationalism, urged his generals to attack and disperse a Confederate army gathering at Manassas Junction, Virginia. The ensuing Battle of Bull Run resulted in an embarrassing rout of federal forces. Union officials could not restore order in the national capital for days. On the evening of the 23rd, William Howard Russell joined the French ambassador Henri Mercier at his residence on Georgetown Heights, which afforded views of the national flag flying above Fort Corcoran and the Arlington House across the Potomac. Defeated soldiers sat sullenly beneath the walls while President Lincoln and Secretary of State Seward passed among what Russell described as "the wreck of the army." He reported that none of the soldiers took any notice of their commander in chief. It seemed to Russell and his companions that all the symbols of American national sovereignty had lost their ability to command allegiance, authority, and respect. A member of the French legation remarked, "The Union is utterly gone—as dead as the Achaian League."[35]

Though the Frenchman's comments invoked ancient history, the recent past taught observers of the Civil War one final lesson about nationalism in the modern world. War, everyone now knew, was the final arbiter of the fate of nations. Conflict, above all else, demonstrated national viability, tested the strength of national institutions, and guaranteed national existence. Despite early federal defeats, the Reverend J. M. Sturtevant reassured his readers that all great nations were born out of blood and violence. No nation, he wrote, "can fulfill a great destiny without passing . . . through a baptism of suffering." The *Princeton Review* reflected that no people had "attained a nationality since history began" without undergoing "convulsive struggles and throes." The increasing carnage on the battlefield did little to shake their convictions. Indeed, it strengthened them. The Reverend Joseph P. Thompson explained in April 1862, in the aftermath of the bloody battle of Shiloh, that one of the "crowning mercies" of the war was its tendency to invigorate nationalist feelings. "It has evoked," he observed, "the sentiment of national unity with a life and power never before witnessed here, and without parallel except in the enthusiasm of France for her first Napoleon." He believed that the antebellum republic had been "drifting toward moral if not political disintegration." The outspoken sectionalism of the South, he maintained, had prompted the North to develop an unhealthy sectionalism of its own. The outbreak of war had broken the cycle. Northern citizens were now attempting to secure America's national destiny on the field of battle.[36]

As northern and southern armies met on those battlefields in 1861 and 1862, northern thinkers believed they had answered some of the most important questions of their age. They confidently constructed a definition of American nationalism that stressed the achievement of liberty through order. The stirring events of the past century, they explained, had established precedents in favor of the maintenance of existing governments. They did not feel, however, that in order to accept such a precedent they needed to abandon their prior support for the principles of nationalist self-determination. Revolution against established authority might indeed be legitimate, but could only be invoked as a last resort against indisputable oppression. Only stable governments, they argued, could protect true freedom. For that reason, committed Unionists believed that the maintenance of the United States would prove critical to the progress of the Western system of nation-states.

By the summer of 1862, however, the war had succeeded only in calling into question the future of the United States. Confederate soldiers had dealt Union hopes a grievous blow at Bull Run, and they continued to remain in the field. The carnage at Shiloh in April 1862 and General George B. McClellan's failure to capture Richmond that summer suggested that the Civil War was destined to become much larger and bloodier than any had imagined. At the same time, Confederate statesmen also went to work. Like their northern counterparts, southern intellectuals, editors, and diplomats labored to construct an intellectual justification for their experiment in nation-building. Their task would prove challenging, but they believed as wholeheartedly as their adversaries that they had history on their side. World events of the nineteenth century, southern intellectuals were about to argue, had laid the groundwork for the white South to assert its right to an independent existence.

4

•

The South and the
Principle of Self-Determination

ON APRIL 15, 1861, AMBROSE DUDLEY MANN OF VIRGINIA ARRIVED IN London, becoming the first official representative of the Confederate States of America to set foot in Europe. Mann had been there before, but as a diplomat in the service of the United States. In 1849, he had been dispatched to the revolutionary government of Hungary with authorization to recognize the new republic's independence from Austria. Now the makers of Confederate foreign policy sent him to win the same for the southern nation.[1]

Mann was joined two weeks later by William Lowndes Yancey, the famed fire-eater from Alabama, and Pierre Rost, a French-born Louisianan who had served in the armies of Napoleon. The three commissioners carried instructions designed to allow them to take advantage of their familiarity with the recent history of Europe. On March 16, 1861, Robert Toombs, the Confederacy's first secretary of state, reminded them that "the recent course which the British Government pursued in relation to the recognition of the right of the Italian people to change their form of government and choose their own rulers encourages this Government to hope that they will pursue a similar policy in regard to the Confederate States." He wanted his envoys to argue that the same "grave and valid" reasons that prompted "the people of Sicily and Naples to cast off a government not of their choice, and detrimental to their interests," impelled the people of the Confederate states to dissolve their ties to the Union. As historian Emory Thomas has pointed out, Toombs's directive "formed the basis of Confederate diplomacy throughout the nation's brief life."[2]

Confederate diplomats, politicians, and policymakers moved quickly in 1861 and 1862 to secure their claim to a separate national identity. While Union policymakers struggled to balance order, stability, and liberty, southern nationalists embraced the rights of self-determination. They used the arguments of their European American supporters and the example of the recent past to appeal to Europe's "family of nations." European revolutionaries, they argued, had established that any people could justifiably overturn an oppressive authority that stood in the way of legitimate national self-expression. Confederates now argued that they acted in the same tradition. Confederate officials, like their northern counterparts, realized that the success of their revolution depended on the recognition of the new southern nation by foreign powers. In order to achieve these goals, Confederate officials would have to convince observers in Europe that the Confederacy had a right to a separate national existence.

In order to do so, the southern nation's supporters developed a thorough and sophisticated view of world history that placed their revolution of 1861 at the end of a chain of events inspired by 1776. Confederate diplomats claimed that they fought as revolutionary nationalists, and compared themselves to the European freedom fighters of the past. They contrasted themselves with a North that they claimed infringed upon the rights of self-government, rights all liberals held dear, and insisted that their war would vindicate the principle of self-determination. In so doing, they developed a complex definition of the South's nationalist project.[3]

Their task would not be easy. The governments of Britain and France, Europe's two greatest powers, proved notoriously difficult to prod into action. Although their industrializing economies depended heavily on American cotton, both nations had outlawed slavery throughout their empires. Public opinion in Britain and on the continent balked at recognizing any government whose "cornerstone" rested on the institution of chattel slavery. The outbreak of open war in America in April complicated the situation further. Premature recognition of the Confederacy might result in unwanted hostilities with the United States. The government of British prime minister Palmerston determined to wait to assess the verdict of arms.[4]

On May 3, British foreign secretary Lord John Russell granted Yancey, Mann, and Rost an audience, but remained noncommittal on the possibility of recognition. The caution of the British government frustrated the Confederate commissioners. Yancey, suffering from poor health, resigned his post during late summer 1861. Rost and Mann continued on to the continent, but did not succeed in winning immediate recognition there either.[5]

Still, the Confederate government, now at Richmond, abandoned neither its efforts nor its philosophical position. While the Yancey-Rost-Mann mission struggled, Robert Mercer Taliaferro Hunter, who replaced Toombs as secretary of state in late July, prepared to mount a more focused effort. In September 1861, he named James M. Mason of Virginia and John Slidell of Louisiana envoys to Britain and France respectively. The pair was well qualified to pick up where Yancey, Rost, and Mann had left off. John Slidell, who had served in the U.S. House and Senate, held extensive experience as a diplomat. During the 1840s, he had been dispatched to serve as minister plenipotentiary to Mexico prior to the outbreak of war in 1846. James Mason also had experience with foreign affairs, having chaired the U.S. Senate's Foreign Relations Committee during the 1850s.

In the years since their appointment, many historians and some contemporaries questioned the skill and suitability of the two most important diplomats ever sent abroad by the Confederacy. Mary Chesnut, for one, worried that the studiously plebeian Mason would offend genteel British sensibilities. "He will say 'chaw' for 'chew,' . . . call himself 'Jeems,'" and "wear a dress coat to breakfast," she scoffed. Mason's defiantly rough-hewn ways may have indeed ruffled some feathers in England. There can be no doubt, however, that the southern statesman came prepared to argue the Confederacy's case on the merits. Mason had clearly thought long and hard about the politics of national identity in the nineteenth-century world. When he heard the news of Abraham Lincoln's election to the presidency in November 1860, he had immediately drawn connections between the position of the South and the plight of oppressed nationalities in Europe. "The people of the North," he lamented in a letter to the *Richmond Enquirer*, "have separated themselves from the people of the South, and the government they thus inaugurate will be to us the government of a foreign power. We shall stand to such power as Italy to Austria, and Poland to Russia. It will be one people governed by another people."[6]

R. M. T. Hunter hoped that Mason and Slidell, while in Europe, would continue to develop this conception of the southern nation's place in the world. He instructed Mason to point out to the British government that recognizing the Confederacy would be "precisely and entirely within the principles" established by British action on behalf of nationalist movements in Greece, Belgium, and Latin America. Hunter, as had Toombs, also invoked the struggle the Italian states had been waging since 1848 against Austrian domination. He went so far as to encourage Mason to quote Foreign Secretary Russell's own words supporting the Italian national cause. "We at least are convinced," Russell had written in reference to events in Italy, that Britain could never recognize an "authority" imposed "by force of arms" if it ran against "the national wishes." Hunter suggested that his agents remind Russell of his doctrine by asking an emphatic question: "Is not this sentiment still more applicable to the contest now being waged between the United States and the Confederate States?" He demanded to know whether the states of Florence, Parma, Modena, and Bologna had any more right to decide issues touching their "happiness" and "internal government" than "the people of the eleven sovereign States now confederated together."[7]

Mason and Slidell traveled an unexpectedly long and difficult road before reaching Europe and carrying out their instructions. On November 8, 1862, Union sailors found the two men aboard a mail steamer, the *Trent*, as they sailed for British territory. They were taken into custody and languished for weeks in a Boston prison. The ensuing *Trent* affair, as it became known, dramatically raised the issues of recognition and national sovereignty. The English people interpreted U.S. actions as an affront to national honor. Two presumably innocent civilians, it seemed, had been snatched while under the protection of the British flag. The Palmerston government demanded an explanation and an apology. After several tense months, Lincoln complied. He released Mason and Slidell, who promptly proceeded to Europe to carry out their mission.

They never succeeded in winning recognition. Ironically, they had come closest to precipitating armed foreign intervention in the Civil War while they sat in prison, and the United States and the United Kingdom argued over the rights of neutrals and belligerents. In the years since the resolution of the crisis in 1862, historians have dismissed the possibility that Mason and Slidell could otherwise have succeeded. Privileged with the knowledge that their mission ultimately failed, scholars of the Civil War have assumed that it never had a chance in the first place. But the mission did not look like a sure failure at the time. Lincoln and his advisors worked so hard to prevent the departure of Mason and Slidell because they feared what they might ultimately be able to accomplish. While northern officials hoped that their own appeal to national legitimacy would work to keep Britain and France from recognizing the Confederacy, they knew that the southern nation had favorable historical precedents of their own to draw upon.[8]

In the decades preceding the Civil War, other insurgent nationalists, not to mention the United States itself in 1778, had benefited from recognition abroad. Indeed, many northern liberals believed before the war that support for the rights of self-determination held the key to the coming world order. They now knew that the South would have a compelling case to make in the court of world opinion. To cite just one example, the northern intellectual Paul Ambrose, who wrote a series of letters on the war that was published in 1865, feared during the conflict that southern whites would "appeal to the sympathies of mankind as a people oppressed by unlawful force, and assume the part of patriots contending for their dearest rights." Such a strategy, he worried, would allow them to "present themselves to the tribunal of public judgment as legitimate, independent States, having a claim, by the law of nations, to immediate recognition by all other Powers."[9]

Ambrose proved remarkably prescient. While Mason, Slidell, Mann, Yancey, Rost, and others used many arguments to win the Confederacy friends abroad, including appeals to economic self-interest, their faith in the right of the South to independent nationhood made up the heart of their efforts. Confederate diplomacy depended as much on drawing inspiration and justification from a half-century's worth of revolution in Europe as it did upon the coercive power of cotton. Yet the Confederate use of the European example represented much more than just a simple set of talking-points for use by ambassadors of recognition. It was also tied to questions surrounding the meaning and legitimacy of nationalism in the Western world. The need to convince foreign governments that the new southern nation enjoyed as much right to a separate and equal standing in the world as any people at any time prompted Confederate thinkers to formulate one of the most complete definitions of the South's nationalist project that the Confederacy ever produced.

The diplomatic directives penned by Toombs and Hunter rested upon a growing body of thought that offered a theoretical basis for southern nationhood. The outlines of this worldview were sketched primarily by editors, journalists, and thinkers in newspapers and periodicals published at home and abroad, and resembled the arguments of John Mitchel, John Bannon, Gaspar Tochman, and the many other European radicals who had taken up the Confederate cause. While diplomats searched for convenient legal precedents and offered arguments designed to appeal to national self-interest, intellectuals sought to offer diplomats a past that could be used to explicate the Confederate cause and situate the new southern nation in modern world history.

The most complete, coherent articulation of this strategy can be found in the work of Henry Hotze. Hotze ranks among the most enigmatic figures in Confederate history. He was born in Switzerland in 1834 and emigrated to Alabama, where he became a naturalized U.S. citizen. During the 1850s, he worked as a journalist in Mobile, where he enthusiastically embraced the southern social system. At the age of twenty-two, he secured a reputation in the South for ideological soundness on the slavery question with his English translation of Count Arthur de Gobineau's seminal work on scientific racism, *Essai sur l'inégalité des races humaines*. He later insisted that his Swiss heritage disposed him to share his adopted countrymen's commitment to states' rights and self-government. Switzerland, he explained in 1860 to readers of the *Mobile Daily Register*, was the "oldest republic in the world" that "never knew king or feudal ruler," and shared with the United States a "system of confederated government." "States Rights and Federal powers," he wrote, had been "discussed over his cradle" as often as they had over the cradle of any native-born white southerner.[10]

When the war broke out, Hotze embraced what he referred to as the "great Revolution of '61." He marched to war with the Mobile Cadets, a militia company later incorporated into the Third Regiment, Alabama Volunteers. After several months' service in Virginia, he applied for an officer's commission. He did not receive a position in the army; instead, Secretary of War Leroy P. Walker found a more important use for his knowledge and talents. In September 1861, Walker sent Hotze on a quick trip to his native Europe as a Confederate purchasing agent.[11]

While in England on his mission, Hotze found his true calling. He became convinced that he could best serve what he often called his beloved "young republic" by explaining the principles of Confederate nationalism to an Old World audience. That fall, he won over R. M. T. Hunter and his eventual successor as secretary of state, Judah P. Benjamin. On November 14, 1861, R. M. T. Hunter sent Hotze back to England to establish contact with the Confederate commissioners abroad, report on British public opinion, and "impress upon the public mind" the key tenets of the Confederate cause. Early the next year, Hotze explained his ambition to carefully construct a justification for the Confederate effort at nation-building that engaged the most important issues and ideas of the recent past. "My pen can be useful to our cause and country only when it is controlled by an imperturbably calm temper and from what might be termed a historic point of view," he reported to Hunter in a letter from London dated February 28, 1862. Under his direction, the Confederate propaganda effort in Europe would take full advantage of Hotze's reading of history, by placing the Confederacy's nation-building project in the framework of nineteenth-century European revolution.[12]

To disseminate his message, Hotze began publishing a paper in London during the spring of 1862, which he named the *Index*. Throughout his tenure as editor, he worked hard to craft the paper's arguments and expand its reach. He faced a complicated task. As historian R. J. M. Blackett has shown, British public opinion diverged widely on the American question. While conservatives in the upper classes tended to favor the Confederacy because of its hierarchical social structure, the opinions of workers and members of the middle class could exert tremendous influence on British policies. Many of them supported the Union as an opponent of slavery and an embodiment of democratic political ideals. Still, liberal merchants, workers, and textile manufacturers depended on trade with the American South and might have been tempted to find reasons to support the Confederacy. As a result, Hotze crafted a range of arguments aimed at securing broad-based support. He appealed to economic self-interest, racism, and Anglo-Saxon solidarity. Most importantly, he stressed the principles of national sovereignty, a cause that could excite liberal proponents of self-determination without frightening conservative admirers of stability and legality.[13]

Consequently, Hotze recruited lead writers who he felt could best articulate the nationalist aspirations of the Confederacy. Hotze selected one of his English writers for what he termed his "minute acquaintance with American affairs coupled with . . . devotion to the cause of national independence." Hotze praised his Italian correspondent, Fillip Manetta, for his ability to "impress upon others the signs of the times as reflected in public opinion." The editor welcomed Edward Lucas to his staff by heralding his support for "Southern Independence" and noting that "the *Index* has obtained a historic position in this great American revolution." Such noted Confederates as Albert Taylor Bledsoe and John Reuben Thompson, prewar editor of the *Southern Literary Messenger*, also wrote for the paper. Bledsoe explained that he journeyed to England to promote "correct opinions . . . among the good and intelligent of the old Mother Country, of our young, heroic nation."[14]

In the pages of the *Index*, the theoretical basis for southern nationhood received its fullest expression. Hotze sounded the argument's keynote when he proclaimed that Confederates acted in an "age of liberal thought." Though white southerners proposed to establish a nation of slaveholders, they had to explain their cause in terms that modern thinkers in Great Britain and throughout the world would understand. To do so, Hotze's paper stressed the importance of the progressive emergence of nations in the development of Western civilization. The Confederacy's advocates, like those of the Union, believed that nationalism constituted the most important principle of the age, even if some current trends seemed to run against it.

The *Index* conceded that the defeat of the revolutions of 1848 and the civil war in America called into question the strength of nationalist movements. "It has been the fashion of late years to ridicule the idea of nationality, and to treat it as a chimera," mused one editorialist. "But nationality is, in fact, to the aggregate of a human society what liberty is to each of the individuals in the aggregate."[15]

This belief in the centrality of the "nation question" prompted the Confederacy's advocates to define their concept of nationalism. One editorial in the *Index*, from which the remarks above were taken, posed the question, "What Constitutes a Nation?" twenty years before the French philosopher Ernest Renan famously echoed the abbé Sieyès by asking "Qu'est-ce qu'une nation?" The answer proved so seminal in germinating Confederate ideas that it merits detailed examination. The answer to the question of nationhood began with a review of recent history. Like some northerners, the author of the editorial in the *Index* argued that the Congress of Vienna had established the blueprint for nationalist development in the modern world. Where northern nationalists saw an incipient society of happy and peaceful nation-states, however, the Confederate editorialist could only make out a jumble of aggrieved peoples and oppressed nations. The peacemakers who met at Vienna to reconstruct the map of Europe, he argued, ignored nationalism in favor of conservative reaction, and ended up destroying the political progress that the world had made during the last quarter of the eighteenth century.[16]

The American Revolution and the Wars of Napoleon had brought international attention to the problem of the self-determination of peoples. Though Washington and Napoleon had done much to establish the right of a discontented population to achieve self-government through force of arms, the verdict of Waterloo appeared, to the Confederate editorialist, to call that principle into question. He argued that the decisions made at Vienna to restore legitimate monarchies and the prewar balance of power by reconstituting continental empires violated the wishes of the people. The writer contended that "scarcely a government was constituted by the Congress of Vienna that did not receive under its sway fragmentary nationalities, whose traditions, prejudices, and tendencies were in conflict with its own." In the opinion of the author, Europeans committed a grave error by restoring traditional kingdoms and monarchies. "Instead of boundaries which the Creator had traced on the face of nature, and in the hearts of men," he charged, "they invented an artificial system, which, however skillfully devised as a balance of power, was in violation of natural laws, and therefore perishable." Consequently, Hotze's editorialist believed, "the peace of Europe was to be secured not by consulting the instincts of nationality, but by deliberately repressing and crushing them."[17]

As a result, the Congress of Vienna did not bring 100 years of peace, but instead sowed the seeds for future violence and discord by creating the conditions for revolution and bloodshed throughout Europe. Blatant disregard for the spirit of nationalism set the stage for a century troubled by nationalist conflicts. "In every instance where the peace of Europe has been seriously endangered since," the author reminded his readers, "it has been from this cause." He pointed to recent history to make his case. The Belgians and the Dutch had been united under one government by the peacemakers at Vienna. That regrettable decision had inevitably resulted in Belgian revolution and independence in 1830. "The Netherlands, North and South of the Scheldt, differing in race and religion, could not co-exist under the same governmental head," the editorial concluded. The revolutions of 1848–49 taught similar lessons. Those uprisings, the editorialist argued, showed that "Germany [was] haunted in its sleep by the dream of unity," and demonstrated that "Italy could no longer brook her German masters."[18]

The lessons of the recent past, the editorialist for the *Index* argued, proved that nineteenth-century wars and revolutions shared common causes. "Conflicts of nationality are the source of European discord," he wrote. The outcome of the conflict promised to erase the mistakes of the past and lead the world to a newer and better era. The spirit of nationalism, the writer believed, "whether burning with a peaceful light, or blazing up in a lurid flame of revolution, is consuming, one after the other, the artificial barriers set by the treaties of Vienna." The Civil War proved that the same held true in America. Confederates, he believed, deserved to be counted among those revolutionaries infused with the spirit of nationality. "We have just witnessed in the New World the sublime spectacle of the birth and fiery baptism of a nation," he concluded.[19]

Supporters of the Confederacy in Europe and America believed that their young nation held great promise for the world. Southern statesmen could begin with a blank slate and redraw the balance of power in the Western hemisphere by avoiding the pitfalls that had doomed the peace at Vienna. Like Hegel rhapsodizing on the perfection of the Prussian state, the Confederacy's advocates believed that their ascendant nation represented the pinnacle of political progress. Their new republic, the editors of the *Index* argued, represented "a government which it would have been deemed the sublimest consummation of European statesmanship to have created." One unidentified Confederate citizen in America agreed. In an open letter to William Howard Russell, printed for American readers in the *Richmond Enquirer*, he expressed his belief that the defense of the southern nation would prove "of vital consequence to the whole civilized world."[20]

Confederate spokespersons at home and abroad argued that their new government combined three of the most important political principles of the age: the notion of a confederated republic, the principle of national self-determination, and the right of self-government. Russell's anonymous correspondent argued that southern whites fought for a principle "always recognized" by the United States. "Every people," he wrote, has "a right to judge of the kind of government, (whether monarchical, autocratic or republican) which could best advance their happiness and progress." Editorials in the *Enquirer* and the *Index* argued that the Confederacy defended "liberty," which had always rested on the right of "national independence" and the "universally admitted principle of the *sovereignty of the people*." Even John Ruskin, the internationally famous English man of letters, fell under the Confederate spell. In early 1863, he scolded Charles Eliot Norton of Boston, the liberal art historian and tireless advocate for the Union, for mixing up a "fight for dominion" with a "fight for liberty."[21]

For many Confederate nationalists, the effort to win the support of men like Ruskin took on critical ideological importance. Recognition that their new republic stood for important liberal values, and not slavery alone, justified Confederate nationality, giving it moral authority and a tangible basis. Most white southerners held an unwavering faith in the reality of southern nationhood regardless of liberal support. During the winter of 1860–61, white southerners had written a constitution, elected a president, and chosen representatives to their new house and senate. By the time war broke out in April, most considered southern nationhood an accomplished fact. "We regard this war as one prevailing between two nations," an article in the *Richmond Enquirer* declared during the conflict. A Confederate citizen using the pseudonym "Planter" wrote the same paper about the importance of recognition from "across the Atlantic." The issue, the correspondent asserted, involved "nothing less than . . . national life and death." Some observers in Europe agreed. A prosouthern pamphlet that circulated in England and Ireland asserted that "a more united people never rose up in defence of their rights than those of the southern States." The French liberal intellectual Gustave de Beaumont, famous in America as the traveling companion of Alexis de Tocqueville, admitted to Boston businessman John Murray Forbes that "one cannot hide from one's self the fact that in the eye of public opinion the struggle has taken the character of a great war between two peoples."[22]

Beaumont's use of the word "peoples" highlighted one of the most important intellectual problems that confronted the promoters of southern nationhood. Europeans naturally conflated nationalism with ethnicity. Old World romanticism celebrated the cultural, linguistic, and ethnic differences that distinguished Europe's many "peoples" and "nations." By the middle of the nineteenth century, many intellectuals believed that possession of such distinguishing traits automatically gave a group of people a moral claim to form its own polity. White southerners could not claim any distinguishing traits that were readily apparent. Like many historians since, the Confederacy's advocates recognized the potentially tenuous nature of their claims to ethnic distinctiveness from their northern neighbors. Recognizing that northern and southern whites shared a common language and lacked religious or racial differences, one leader in Hotze's paper argued that "community of descent is not altogether a reliable criterion of nationality, for the descendents of the same stock often diverge very widely in national characteristics."[23]

The southern argument for separate nationhood faced another philosophical problem. Northerners and southerners had long enjoyed a shared British political heritage and, for the past eighty-five years, had shared the same government. Didn't their long-standing partnership prove the northern case that the United States constituted a legitimate nation? Hotze's secession-minded writers predictably answered that a nation did not necessarily consist of a "population living under the same government." They pointed out that "many distinct nationalities are brought under a common sway, without the least losing their distinguishing peculiarities."[24]

But northerners, after all, also claimed to fight to vindicate the existence of a sacred and inviolable nation. Many white southerners recognized the consequent need to distinguish between their attempt at independence and the North's effort at national unification. Some Confederate thinkers conceded that true nationalism could embrace either separation or unification. Their act of national self-determination involved seceding from a preexisting government; still, they could sympathize with national unification if it legitimately reflected the will of the people. "The heterogeneous populations of the Austrian Empire do not constitute a nation," the *Index's* formulation held, "and yet the subjects of all the kings and princes of Germany constitute only one."[25]

Still, as some recent historians have noted, since the defeat of revolution in 1848, most European nationalist movements of the mid-nineteenth century had focused on creating larger nations out of smaller polities. Confederate editors acknowledged that fact, but believed their nation represented the exception that proved the rule that "national movements were expected to be movements for national *unification* or expansion." The large geographical area occupied by the eleven Confederated states, and the profitable nature of the slave system they defended, they argued, "enlarged rather than restricted the scale on which human economies, societies and culture operated." Confederate advocates argued that, even though they sought separation from a larger political entity, their nationalist experiment protected a profitable slave economy, opened markets long closed by northern protectionism, and, most importantly, advanced the principle of the "self-determination of peoples" championed by all liberals.[26]

The definition of nationalism that Confederate diplomats and propagandists developed best matches the ideology surrounding what Eric Hobsbawm has termed the "heyday of the liberal bourgeoisie." From the period roughly between 1830 and 1880, Hobsbawm argues, nationalist thinkers viewed ethnicity as of only "secondary" importance. Cultural, economic, and military "viability" mattered most. The Confederacy's ability to meet the federal government in battle proved its viability as a nation. The military tests that the young nation faced only confirmed the strength and perfection of the Confederacy's institutions. The editors of the *Index* argued that the southern nation enjoyed "the obedience of a numerous and devoted population, in a degree which devotion to a cause or country has seldom reached in modern times." Its government, the editors argued, "waged war upon a scale unprecedented even in this century of Napoleonic Wars." They believed that fact gave white southerners an unmistakable claim to viable nationality: "If the South had not possessed the conditions of a vigorous nationality before, it would have derived it from the events of this war."[27]

Hotze's paper offered its own criteria for viable nationhood that superseded culture and ethnicity. An article in the *Index* argued that common economic priorities, a similar social organization, and shared reliance on an institution such as racial slavery might do the most to influence a population to set themselves apart. The editorial passionately proclaimed that "whenever and from whatever cause the consciousness of national identity pervades a population, a nation is born." This formulation eschewed legalism in favor of romantic sentiment and action. Men belong to nations, Hotze's paper argued, "not because of the operation of any political machinery, but because they have in common something which they cherish, whether that something be in the present or only in the past." That "something" could include a defense of slavery, or might also involve the unifying experience of war. The article concluded that the outbreak of violence between North and South destroyed any legitimate national bonds that might have remained between the two sections. "Whatever doubts might still have been entertained as to the radical and inherent differences of character between the peoples north and south of the Potomac," the paper asserted, "no doubt can be entertained that they are distinct nations now and henceforth. The currents of their history are forever diverted into different channels."[28]

Thinkers like Hotze and his writers gave Confederate supporters a complex philosophy to undergird their nation-building. To sustain the tremendous sacrifice required to achieve independence, however, white southerners would need proof that success would be possible. Historian Benedict Anderson has argued that in order for modern nationalist movements to develop, their supporters need both a sense of simultaneous action and prior examples from which to draw. The Confederacy's advocates believed they had both. The Confederate effort to influence European public opinion depended on linking the southern cause with that of nationalist revolutionaries throughout the Atlantic world. The events of nineteenth-century European history provided southern whites with powerful inspiration and justification for their arguments. They drew hope and encouragement from the patriots who had been successful, and took solace in knowing that others had fought bravely against long odds, no matter the result. They also believed that the great powers had established legal precedents in favor of recognition of new nations.

The example of the successful revolutionary movements in Belgium and Greece in the 1820s and 1830s encouraged Confederates to expect European aid. The *Index* reminded American and European readers that "the interference of the great powers wrested Belgium from Holland and Greece from Turkey." That line of argument picked up steam in late 1862 when G. W. Bentink, a member of Parliament for West Norfolk and a Confederate sympathizer, implored Parliament to recollect what Britain had done for Greece and Belgium. In his opinion, those precedents cemented the Confederacy's case in international law. The success of the Belgians and the Greeks, Confederate thinkers argued, also augured well for Confederate claims to national viability. An article in the *Richmond Daily Examiner* pointed out that the territories of Belgium and Greece did "not much exceed that of the single State of Virginia." If they had deserved independence, then surely so did the massive Confederacy. For any readers who worried about the strength of the Union war effort, the author reminded them that the British had justly "rallied to the side of feeble and expiring Greece" just when it teetered on the brink of complete annihilation.[29]

The revolutions of 1848 and 1849 did more to establish the Confederacy's place in world history. Those revolutions, although in most instances they met with failure, profoundly articulated what the *Index* referred to as "that idea of 'nationality' which by slow degrees is becoming a part of the political creed of the rising generation." Many Confederate journals hailed the similarities between their revolution and the struggles of the forty-eighters. They also argued that the policies of the United States and other powers in those years had established precedents in favor of the recognition of nations struggling for self-determination.[30]

Confederate nationalists argued that the United States had established a strong precedent in favor of nationalist rebellion with its French policy in 1848. One Richmond correspondent of the London *Times* reminded readers that the American minister in Paris quickly recognized the "establishment by the French people of a Republic" after the "expulsion of Louis Philippe from the French throne" in February 1848. The anonymous writer quoted extensively from Secretary of State James Buchanan's letter of approval to the foreign minister that had invoked the United States' "sacred regard for the independence of nations." In his letter, Buchanan had clearly articulated the guiding principles of American foreign policy. "In the intercourse with foreign nations," he wrote, "the Government of the United States has from its origin always recognized *de facto* governments. We recognize the right of all nations to create and reform their political institutions according to their own will and pleasure." In this regard, Buchanan, a staunch Democrat, charted a policy for the State Department that was indistinguishable from that of his Whig successors in the Taylor and Fillmore administrations. Daniel Webster and Edward Everett, who both served stints as secretaries of state under Fillmore, made similar statements.[31]

While the French revolution in February 1848 seemed to establish diplomatic precedents favorable to the Confederate cause, it worked less well as an ideological point of comparison. For that, the Confederacy's supporters turned to other movements of that year. Many southern nationalists felt that Ireland's struggle for home rule resembled the Confederate cause. Judah P. Benjamin, who took over as secretary of state in March 1862, believed that Ireland would prove such fertile ground for Confederate sympathy that he dispatched a special mission to the Emerald Isle. In late 1863, he and Jefferson Davis selected Father John Bannon, still popular with Irish Confederates from Missouri, to travel to Ireland to distribute pro-Confederate propaganda and stem the tide of Irish migration to the northern states. Bannon came increasingly to believe that the Confederacy fought for the same principles that Irish nationalists cherished. Upon arrival in the Old World he quickly cultivated the survivors of Young Ireland's revolt against British rule in 1848. He gravitated to prominent forty-eighters such as William Smith O'Brien and John Martin, men who favored the Confederacy because of its support for national self-determination and independence. Bannon quickly went to work publishing their thoughts on the conflict in widely circulated broadsides aimed at linking the Confederate cause with Irish nationalism and the revolutions of 1848. Bannon distributed one poster in which O'Brien attacked Thomas Francis Meagher for siding with the Union. "It is a spectacle painful and humiliating to all lovers of freedom," O'Brien lamented, "to find one of the representative men of the Irish race—himself an exile and a Catholic, vindicating a course of action similar to that which expelled the natives of Ireland from their possessions and their homes." Another one of Bannon's screeds publicized John Martin's contention that "the South has the right to self-government as clearly as the Belgians, Italians, Poles, or the Irish." The Irish American priest also found ammunition for his broadsides in John Mitchel's characterization of the federal war effort as "the foulest crusade of modern times."[32]

Confederate spokesmen, choosing from the many nationalist movements of 1848, most often drew parallels to Hungary's revolution in particular. To Confederate spokesmen, Austria's attempt to crush Hungarian independence in a war that lasted for more than a year closely resembled the North's effort to subjugate the South. "The cause of the Confederate States is very much that of Hungary," an editorial in the *Charleston Mercury* maintained. More than one article in the *Richmond Enquirer* seized on the memory of Louis Kossuth's visit to America and celebrated the principles for which he fought. One editorial reminded readers that Kossuth had praised America's "provision for *local self-government*" during his New

World tour. Southern whites, the article asserted, now fought to preserve self-government in the battle with what the paper called "the growth of *central power*." Another article offered the opinion that the South, like Kossuth, would risk death to prevent "dishonor," by resisting an attempt to "subjugate a free people." Even Union soldier Alfred Lewis Castleman acknowledged the relevance in comparing Hungary's struggle and the Confederate cause. He feared in 1861 that overconfident northerners had forgotten that "Hungary, with its population of only 3,000,000, and without revenue, withstood the whole power of Austria, till the hordes of Russia had to be called in to aid in their subjugation."[33]

The Hungarian struggle seemed to combine the best features of both the French and Irish uprisings. The Hungarians espoused the ideas behind Ireland's fight for freedom while reaffirming the practical precedents that had been established in France in 1848. One Confederate citizen in Richmond wrote a letter to the editor of the *Index* reminding the reader that in 1848 the Hungarians had successfully formed a provisional government and mounted a subsequent effort to dissolve their connection with the Austrian empire. The United States had reacted sympathetically, he pointed out. He recalled the fact that the State Department had sent A. Dudley Mann to Hungary to "watch the struggle" and to "be the first to welcome Hungary into the family of nations." The correspondent concluded that Hungary's bid for independence had failed in spite of American support. "The assistance given to Austria by Russia rendered nugatory the brave exertions of the revolutionary government," he maintained, "but its failure was not due to any want of encouragement from the great American Republic."[34]

To many white southerners, the northern half of the United States seemed to have lost its way over the course of the nineteenth century. The American republic had once stood for the rights of self-determination, self-government, and local rule. The war northerners now fought to destroy the aspiring southern nation only underscored their hypocrisy and justified the actions of the Confederate states. One article in the *Index* reminded readers of a speech delivered by a first-term representative named Abraham Lincoln in January 1848. In that speech, Lincoln defended the right of revolution, linked that right to the political progress and salvation of the world, and came close to predicting the events of the coming year. "Any people, anywhere, being inclined, and having the power, have a right to rise up and shake off the existing government," Lincoln had argued. "This is a most valuable, a most sacred right," he continued, "a right which we hope and believe is to liberate the world." Confederate vice president Alexander

Stephens defended secession by reminding Lincoln of his past treatment of forty-eighters in America. "You in your welcome to Louis Kossuth," Stephens wrote, "expressed high regard for any people struggling for liberty, yet the slaves of the south are in as good condition as were Hungarian serfs." Lincoln's sentiments became so notoriously well known that Democratic Party officials circulated a pamphlet in 1864 accusing him of hypocrisy. "What did Abraham Lincoln say in Congress in 1848?" the campaign sheet triumphantly asked. "ANY PORTION of such people that CAN, MAY revolutionize and make their OWN of so much Territory as they inhabit," it answered.[35]

For Confederates, that they had history on their side seemed clear. The trends of the recent past ran toward recognition of the rights of nationality. If northerners stubbornly refused to admit this point during the 1860s, then they were being less than honest with themselves. An article in the *Richmond Enquirer* concluded its discussion of the relevance of 1848 by laying out evidence of northern hypocrisy. The paper charged that northerners "were all agog at the notion of freedom for Ireland" and that "they exulted at the movement for Hungarian liberty." The article continued by pointing out that northerners had "rushed forward to flatter and fawn upon Kossuth when he landed on our shores," "raised a shout of gratulation at the overthrow of Austrian rule in Italy," and "hooted at the idea of union between Ireland and Great Britain, or between Austria and her dependencies." Yet, the author lamented, "they deny, in effect, the claim of thirteen sovereign States to be free."[36]

Events contemporaneous with the South's revolution of 1861 also provided the Confederacy with justification and inspiration. Though the revolutions of 1848 ended in universal failure, Confederates believed that the principle of nationalism remained alive and well in the modern world. Southern nationalists were hopeful because Italians, Poles, and others fought as southerners did to construct new nations. The failures of the revolutions of 1848 and 1849 had not resulted in a victory against the rights of self-determination; instead, they had merely intensified the struggle. "The cry of revolt," mused one correspondent, had "been raised . . . incessantly since 1848."[37]

Americans throughout the United States eagerly followed the drama of Italian unification that played out in the late 1850s and early 1860s. As Americans descended into civil war, Italian patriots led by Giuseppe Garibaldi and Count Camillo di Cavour of Piedmont successfully realized the dream of Italian nationhood. They completed the work begun in 1848 by throwing off Austrian rule and unifying the peninsula under one government. Although the principle of national unification would seem to prove more congruent with the federal cause, the Confederates championed the Italians as fellow freedom fighters invoking the sovereign rights of self-determination. The *Charleston Mercury* asserted that the military success of Italian patriots against the armies of Austria boded well for Confederate independence: "See what Southern men—Italians commanded by GARIBALDI, and fighting for their liberty—are doing to the Austrians, Northern men." The *Index*, probably hoping to counteract the many British supporters of Italian unification who favored the North, loudly hailed William Gladstone's speech in which he proclaimed himself a "warm advocate of the new Italian Kingdom, founded on the right of the States to choose the rulers and the nationality they prefer." Another editorial made the comparison between the Confederate and Italian causes more bluntly: "No one ever questioned the right of the eight millions, which form the population of the Two Sicilies, to give up their autonomy, and annex themselves to the kingdom of Victor Emmanuel—why, therefore, should the eight millions of Confederates be denied the rights of refusing to submit any longer to the government of Washington, and constitute themselves as an independent nation?"[38]

The success of the Risorgimento offered many Confederates grounds for hope as well as pride that their revolution evoked the spirit of the times. Italian nationalism had enjoyed widespread international sympathy. Garibaldi and Cavour had achieved worldwide fame and admiration. Some observers expected the Confederacy's leaders to rank among the greatest nationalist heroes of the modern age. Englishman and Confederate sympathizer A. J. B. Beresford-Hope gave voice to such sentiments when he enshrined President Jefferson Davis and General Thomas Jonathan Jackson among the era's greatest nationalists. "When this living age of ours—this second half of the nineteenth century—comes to tot up the head roll of its great men—those whose burning patriotism combined with calm statesmanship made them the fathers of a country struggling into new life," Beresford-Hope declared, "by the side of Cavour will blaze in history with equal glory the name of Jefferson Davis. Heroes will go with heroes—Davis with Cavour, and Stonewall Jackson with Garibaldi."[39]

In 1863, a revolt in Poland aroused the sympathies and captured the imaginations of the Confederate people. In January of that year, student protests against Russian rule prompted Polish and Lithuanian landholders and military officers to take up arms and join the cause of independence.

"Street Fighting in Naples." During the 1860s, the Italian Risorgimento inspired Confederates who were also fighting to establish a nation. (Author's collection)

Ironically, their aims included the protection of serfdom, which Czar Alexander II was in the process of destroying. More than one article made a specific comparison between southern slaveholders and Polish gentry whose estates were farmed by serfs. "Like the Confederates, the Poles are a nation of slave-holders," wrote one editorialist. The Confederate press believed white southerners and Poles also shared "courage, skill in arms, genius for command, a high development of individual character . . . and an unquenchable thirst for national independence." The Paris correspondent for the *Index* hailed the similarities between the Confederate cause and the Poles fighting "against tremendous odds in Eastern Europe." Scores of articles hoped that the "spirit of Polish nationality" would "fly strong and triumphant from the Baltic to the Carpathians," and condemned northerners for refusing to take a stand against the Czar.[40]

Confederate editorialists most frequently remarked upon the similarities between the Union war effort and Russia's contemporaneous war in Poland. The comparison worked on a number of levels. The Russians sought, as did the Federals, to fight the cause of national independence and proved willing to attack the foundations of the societies that sustained it. "Both are attempting to crush by brutal force an heroic people, superior to them in all attributes that constitute a title to national independence," proclaimed a writer for the *Index*. Another of the paper's correspondents asserted that, like the Russians, the federal government could only hope for a victory that would hold "by the bayonet certain subdued provinces as in the case of Poland or Hungary."[41]

The northern war effort also merited comparison with that of the Russians on the tactical level. As the first issues of the *Index* went to press, the Lincoln government was increasingly moving toward what historian Mark Grimsley has termed "hard war." Federal forces had not been able to destroy the Confederacy's armies on the battlefield, so Union soldiers took the war to the home front. Congress authorized confiscation of food, livestock, and slaves from some Confederate civilians in the First Confiscation Act of 1861 and expanded the law's reach in 1862. To Confederate thinkers, this violated the laws that governed war between nations. It instead resembled the despotic measures that European tyrants used to repress their own people. The *Charleston Mercury* asserted that Unionists employed the same harsh "restrictions" needed to subjugate "the Poles, or the Venetians, or the Irish." The *Richmond Enquirer* worried that the "revolting details" of the Czar's efforts to subdue the Poles foreshadowed what the Confederate people could expect if the "Yankee Muscovites" ever subjugated "our country." The policies of confiscation, conscription, and emancipation appeared to be similar to Russian policies that struck at serfdom and punished patriotic landholders. An article in the *Index* took both Russia and the United States to task for pillaging and burning "defenseless habitations" and for instigating "servants to rise against their masters." "If pillage on the largest scale be the right of Cossack officers," one observer asserted, "it is not less the privilege of the federals. Villages are burned on the Mississippi on not more provocation than on the Vistula."[42]

One federal general in particular embodied Union tyranny in countless Confederate newspaper articles. John Basil Turchin had been born Ivan Vasilevich Turchaninov "in the Province of Don, Russia." He attended military school at St. Petersburg and served on the staff of the Imperial Guards. Turchin listed among his military credentials his service in putting down the Hungarian revolution of 1848–49, and displayed equal zeal in prosecuting the Union war effort. One northern publisher asserted that "his method of treating rebel property, including slaves, at the commencement of his military career in this country was that of an experienced soldier, and was the people's key-note for a more vigorous prosecution of the war."[43]

While Unionists preferred to dub Turchin the "Russian Thunderbolt," Confederate propagandists placed him among "Lincoln's Cossacks." One Confederate editorialist expressed typical sentiments in finding "points in common between the tyranny of the Czar and that of President Lincoln." He compared generals such as Turchin to other "Russian butchers who . . . have towns plundered and sacked." Another editorialist declared General Benjamin F. Butler and General Robert H. Milroy, both of whom had taken early action in the field to free Confederate slaves, "worthy peers to Mouravieff," the Russian general who had served in Poland and had gained notoriety for his heavy-handed tactics during the Crimean War. The alleged rough treatment of civilians by General Ambrose E. Burnside and General William S. Rosecrans taught Confederates a lesson the "gallant Poles" had already learned: "There is no safety anywhere but in camp."[44]

An apparently real alliance between the United States and the Russian Empire served only to cement comparisons between the two governments. Russia consistently opposed British and French efforts to mediate the American conflict, and in the winter of 1863–64 the Russian fleet harbored in federal ports, ostensibly on a mission of goodwill. The *Index's* Paris correspondent reported that French public opinion expressed outrage at the "strange sympathy" that existed between "the degenerate republic of Washington, and the most despotic monarchy of the Old World." The apparent alliance called into question American values and standing abroad. Lincoln's behavior at home and friendship toward Russia tarnished his reputation as a progressive thinker and statesman. "Public opinion, which never forgives," the journalist claimed, "has now ceased to ask what may be expected from the Liberalism of a Government which unites its interests with those of Russia, and pretends to march with her to the deliverance of the world." Another observer proclaimed that "the only friend of Russia is the dictatorship of Mr. Lincoln." One editorialist sarcastically pointed out that the Union made "common cause with the Czar, as engaged, like themselves, in the suppression of an 'unjustifiable' rebellion." Supporters of the Confederacy could not escape the conclusion that they had been right all along in evaluating the intentions and character of the North. "Knowing what the United States is," one of Hotze's writers remarked, "we are not in the least surprised that it should gloat over the idea of an intimate alliance with a Government reputed the most despotic in Europe." One blunt headline in the *Richmond Enquirer* simply labeled Unionists "Yanko-Russians."[45]

The experiences of the Poles, the Italians, the Irish, the French, the Germans, and the Hungarians taught Confederates, and their Unionist counterparts, not only to hope, but to expect war. History taught that national movements on both sides of the Atlantic could expect to be met with force. Oppressive power continued to meet ascendant nationalism in armed conflict, Europe's recent history of revolutions notwithstanding. One of Hotze's correspondents wagered that the "immemorial practice of sovereigns and statesmen" would not be reversed by the bloodshed in 1848, the success of the Italian Risorgimento, or the threat of future revolt. Lincoln's choice to resort to arms appeared to many to bear this prediction out. An article in the *Richmond Enquirer* quoted the *New York World*'s assertion that the Civil War gave Americans firsthand experience with "the means by which old world governments are compelled to maintain their existence." "European dynasties," the author explained, "are always exposed to dangers of rebellion, or revolution, and all rulers . . . must resort to the most secret agencies and the sternest measures or yield the baton of power." According to the *Enquirer*, the war proved that the American republic found itself "no exception to transatlantic experience." The federal government, agreed the editors of the *Index*, "was bound to put down secession as a European government puts down rebellion—by force of Arms."[46]

According to Confederates, the North's resorting to war, like European tyrants' recourse to repressive force, threatened not only person and property. It also inevitably undermined the liberal political values that made the nineteenth century an enlightened and progressive age. The recent past taught that governments employing military power inevitably undermined the most basic liberties. "Coercion," one observer reflected, could never "be carried into effect without a systematic violation of every principle of constitutional law." In order to hold an oppressed people in check, authorities on both sides of the Atlantic suspended freedoms of the press, the right to trial by jury, and liberty of conscience. Articles compared Lincoln's decisions to impose martial law, tamper with legislatures, and imprison active dissenters to the actions of reactionary leaders like King William of Prussia, Napoleon III of France, and the secret police of Austria and Naples. Others condemned violations of a free press in the North and in Europe and asserted that "the echo of the armed heel rings forth as clearly now in America as in France or Austria." In a direct reference to the French government that replaced the revolutionary regime of 1848, the same article reflected that "it will soon be sixteen years that France has reflected and pondered over her lost liberty." The consequences for the French people included "despotism and ruin" that promised to lead "inevitably to the most terrible of all the revolutions that history has hitherto recorded." "Let us remember the teachings of history," the article urged.[47]

As southern armies hurled back repeated northern offensives, many white southerners grew increasingly convinced that their war would redeem the world as well as their own republic. The northern nation, one editorialist reflected, had lost its "moral and political greatness" in prosecuting the Civil War. An article in the *Richmond Enquirer* asserted that the Lincoln government threatened not only to "crush out all liberty in America" but hung "like a portentous thunder cloud over Europe." The author argued that the United States would join the governments of France and Rome in promoting the principles of "pure despotism," "centralization," and "imperial power." In 1863, the Confederacy sponsored a diplomatic mission designed to make similar arguments. Judah P. Benjamin dispatched Lucius Quintus Cincinnatus Lamar, a southern politician and military figure, as a goodwill ambassador to Great Britain. Upon his arrival in England, he declared himself a representative "of oppressed and downtrodden nations." He spoke at the annual dinner of the Chertsey Agricultural Society on the significance that the Confederate cause held for world history. He told his audience that "the South, abused, bleeding, her life blood draining away," fought "not for her own liberties," but "for the liberties of that people who were sending armed millions to subjugate and crush her." More than that, the South struggled for "freedom everywhere."

Lamar claimed that Confederate armies sought "to rid the world of one of the most intolerant, aggressive, overbearing powers that ever disturbed the repose of Europe, or menaced the peace of civilization."[48]

Even when Union victories tested Confederate resolve, Confederate leaders encouraged white southerners to find comfort in comparing themselves to the freedom fighters of the past. The lessons of history taught that no nation could be forged without undergoing a fiery trial of sacrifice and devotion. The *Richmond Enquirer* reminded its readers during the 1864 siege of Petersburg that Virginians had not yet "suffered as the Venetians did in 1849, when more than half of their grand old city was under the fire of bombs and red-hot balls." The *Charleston Mercury* struck a similar note when Union armies stood poised to capture Richmond in the spring of 1862. The paper pointed out that "in every other country of the world" citizens seeking liberty survived sieges "with infinite courage and fortitude." "Even luxurious Venice, of 1848," the paper recalled, "shut up by land and sea, with famine and pestilence in every house, with a population eating rats and making soup of old shoes, and the bombs crashing through every roof, stood it . . . for months. Is Richmond less brave?"[49]

Most Confederates refused to believe that their new republic would ever join the ranks of the oppressed nationalities of the age. If their bravery did not win them victory on the battlefield, past precedent had led them to expect that it might bring them recognition abroad. Heroic suffering, they hoped, would endow their cause with universal appeal, just as it had done for the Poles, the Irish, and the Italians. When the U.S. Navy threatened Charleston in 1864, one unidentified resident wrote his brother from Paris that the defense of the city won it sympathy in the Old World. "I glory in the pride, spunk & patriotism of our dear little city & chivalrous state of So. Ca.," he wrote. "She has won the admiration and respect of all Europe." He attributed French support to the nationalist ideologies the Confederacy and its leaders defended: "Genl Beauregard has an enviable position in the eyes of Europe for his manly & gallant defense against a foe . . . whose only aim is to crush out . . . a free and chivalrous people who are fighting for their Freedom & liberty." The blame for Europe's officially remaining on the sidelines, many southerners believed, should be laid entirely upon the imperfections of the monarchical system, not the Confederate cause. France's failure to intervene in the conflict, the Charleston resident held, was due to the unfortunate fact that in monarchies "the people do not think for the Government as we do."[50]

The Confederacy's advocates did not win recognition for the new nation.

In August 1864, another frustrated Confederate supporter in Paris wrote about the difficulties many of the Confederacy's advocates in Europe faced. He attributed their failure to win recognition to European liberals' grave misreading of the conflict. "By a strange phenomenon in moral optics," he lamented, "industry, commerce, national wealth, civilisation, enlightenment, justice, right, and liberty appear to many French Liberals to be exclusively on the side of the Federals." In the years afterward, some asserted, with the benefit of hindsight, that the white South's mission had been doomed from the start. Confederate diplomats, they argued, like the heroes of the "Lost Cause," fought an impossible battle against numbers and European public opinion. R. M. T. Hunter, who in 1861 had confidently lectured the British government on the rights of national self-determination, confessed in 1871 that the "new world" in which he lived "puzzled" him. He asked James Mason to "explain" to him the principles that had guided "the course of Foreign Nations towards" the Confederacy. The Confederate States, he believed, had done everything right. They had erected a powerful government, fought the United States for four long years, and inflicted tremendous casualties. Still, their government had disappeared from the face of the earth, while other nations survived even after failing the critical test of war in much more pathetic fashion. "I doubt if such a contest and for so long was ever kept up by any people with such terrible odds against them," he wrote. France's recent collapse in its war with Prussia only underscored the Confederacy's viability as a nation. The southern nation had not failed because it lacked the ingredients of a successful nation, Hunter concluded. It failed because European powers refused to recognize the heroism and merit in the white South's struggle: "Three or four to one actively and the whole world passively against us . . . Was success possible under the circumstances?"[51]

During the war, Hunter, Hotze, Mason, and the public they represented certainly believed it was. By the middle of 1862, the South had come close to convincing the world's great powers. In mid-September of that year, the British cabinet met to discuss intervention in the American conflict while U.S. and Confederate armies clashed on northern soil. The outcome of the battle, the English observers decided, would go a long way toward determining the British course of action. The results proved unfriendly to Confederate independence. The Union victory at Antietam convinced Britain's heads of state to postpone their decision. In the days that followed, President Lincoln issued his Preliminary Proclamation of Emancipation. The prospect of emancipation introduced new issues into America's clash of nations. Under the pressure of war, leaders in the United States and the Confederacy would seek to define the relationship between race, class, and the state. The world would now have to choose not only between two approaches to national legitimacy, but between two ways of structuring Western society.

5

The Last Best Hope of Earth

ON JANUARY 1, 1863, IN A MUCH-ANTICIPATED NEW YEAR'S DAY CERE-
mony, Abraham Lincoln signed his Emancipation Proclamation. The
order, in its final form, granted freedom to all slaves still held in bondage in
Confederate territory. The president's directive recast the U.S. military as
an army of liberation. It instructed members of the armed forces to act on
their new duty to "recognize and maintain" the freedom of the slaves they
encountered as Union armies marched deeper into the South. The new
federal policy also authorized African Americans to strike a blow for their
own emancipation. For the first time since the war began, black Americans
could officially enlist and serve in the Union army.[1]

Numerous observers remarked on the revolutionary nature of the act.
For some, it called to mind the most momentous events of the past half-
century. Frederick Douglass compared the promise of emancipation to the
promise that the revolutions of 1848 had held for "the death of kingcraft
in Europe and throughout the world." Lest the supporters of abolition pre-
maturely give up the struggle, he recalled with foreboding that in Europe
"the latent forces of despotism rallied." Thomas Wentworth Higginson, the
New England abolitionist and man of letters, also worried that the lessons
of the past spoke to the transience of progressive change. As he waited to
lead into battle one of the first African American regiments to take the
field, he confessed to fears that the president's promise might not be kept.
"After the experience of Hungary, one sees that revolutions may go backward," he remembered. In New York City, the Irishman and Democratic
politician James T. Brady spoke to a large gathering of citizens designed
to build support for the new policy. Brady, as did many of his countrymen,
admitted to having once bitterly opposed all abolitionists. He now considered emancipation necessary to save the U.S. government, a government
that he believed provided "a home and a refuge from the persecution and

oppression" of the Old Country. "I have within me," he wrote, "the hope of the poor serf in Russia, the enthusiasm of the young Hungarian, who, by the little flicking flame of freedom, even though it be in a dungeon, finds himself stimulated with . . . hope."[2]

As the reactions of Douglass, Higginson, and Brady attest, emancipation held more than domestic relevance. It also responded to recent history and held implications for the world. For contemporaries in Europe and America, Lincoln's decision to free Confederate slaves represented nothing less than an act of revolution. It gave the Union a common cause and a shared history with the thousands of revolutionaries in Europe who had taken up arms for liberty, equality, economic justice, and liberal nationalism in the years since 1789. But it did more than that. Emancipation forced northern intellectuals, politicians, and policymakers to rethink the meaning of American nationalism. They had heretofore avoided associating the Union cause with revolutionary values out of fear that such comparisons might hurt the United States' standing as a credible world power. They received little reward for their caution. The results of battle and growing sympathy abroad had helped solidify Confederate claims to separate nationhood. The deepening war demanded new approaches and new policies at home and abroad. As northern armies attacked slavery in America, Union officials in Europe discredited the Confederacy's nationalist experiment. In the process, they presented the world with a new model and a new message. When set in a global context, emancipation did not just destroy slavery in America. It made new statements about nation-building and the role of rank, class, labor, and citizenship in the emerging nineteenth-century state.

The arrival of emancipation marked a radical departure for the Lincoln administration. For more than a year, the president had resisted employing what he had termed "radical and extreme measures" in defeating the Confederacy. For the first year and a half of war, Union diplomats and policymakers had worked to convince the world that the United States represented a responsible and indivisible nation-state committed to law, order, legitimacy, and respect for private property. The First and Second Confiscation Acts had authorized the army to seize southern crops, farms, and slaves, but only as a just punishment for individuals who could be shown to be guilty of supporting the rebellion against the government. On the whole, Lincoln continued to insist that the Constitution protected property rights, including the right to own slaves, no matter how morally reprehensible those rights might be. He had rebuked and dismissed generals like

John C. Frémont for seeking to prosecute the war by freeing slaves. Lincoln believed Frémont's actions would undermine the rule of law and the protection of property, which justified national authority and gave purpose to national existence.[3]

By the summer of 1862, however, Lincoln had reached the conclusion that he could save the nation only by destroying slavery. Armed force alone had failed to vindicate American nationalism after a year and a half of war. The defeat at Bull Run, the bloodshed at Shiloh, and General George B. McClellan's repulse in seven days of fighting before Richmond convinced Lincoln that a more aggressive approach to the war would be needed to overcome the strength of the South. Lincoln defended emancipation as a military measure, first and foremost. Striking against slavery, he argued, would weaken the rebellion and thereby save the nation. Lincoln insisted that the purpose of the war had not changed. He had not abandoned his commitment to maintaining a stable American nation. Instead, he argued, emancipation would make a true American nationalism easier to achieve.

Still, it was evident to observers throughout the world that emancipation endowed the northern cause with an ideological and moral dimension that it had lacked. Lincoln himself deliberately chose to cast the conflict in universal terms. In late 1863, in commemorating the thousands of lives lost at the Battle of Gettysburg, he spoke of a "new birth of freedom," which he believed would rejuvenate the nation and the world. He held that emancipation would help preserve the American republic, a republic that, in turn, would promote liberty for all men across the globe. "We shall nobly save, or meanly lose, the last best hope of earth," he explained in his annual message to Congress on the eve of emancipation in late 1862. "Other means may succeed," he reasoned in defending his new policy, but "this could not fail."[4]

Numerous historians have commented on the relationship between emancipation and the evolving northern vision of American nationalism. As historian Howard Jones has shown, emancipation allowed Lincoln to forge a newer and "better Union," a Union held together without the need for compromise over human slavery. James McPherson and others have pointed out that the movement toward universal freedom in America excited people around the world with hopes that liberty and democracy might spread to all corners of the earth. Few scholars, however, have asked questions about how and why this new vision took shape. Why did Lincoln consider the United States the *last* hope of mankind? Why did emancipation augur the arrival of a new kind of nationalism not only in America but throughout the world? The answer lies in an understanding of recent world history. When set in an international context, the American experience appears in no way exceptional or unique. Emancipation responded to and in many ways followed the lead of nation-builders and revolutionaries of the last half-century.[5]

Especially in the years after 1863, the Civil War struggled to define the relationship between slavery and the nation-state, as did many of the conflicts of the late eighteenth century and the early nineteenth. Americans themselves had confronted the question during their war for independence when significant numbers of patriots, especially in New England, began to contest the institution's compatibility with republican values. The new United States could only resolve the issue through uneasy compromise. While some states abolished slavery and some individuals were voluntarily granted manumissions, the institution survived in the South. By the nineteenth century, slavery's existence there began to suggest possible tension between states' rights and national authority.[6]

The French Revolution of 1789 illustrated the conflict between slavery and the nation in much more dramatic fashion. The new French nation, unlike a medieval kingdom, was the embodiment of all its people or "citizens," not the property of a monarch. The state existed not to preserve privilege, but to protect the equality of all citizens before the law. In declaring the fundamental equality of all mankind, the French revolutionaries, most notable in their "Declaration of the Rights of Man and of the Citizen," leveled a withering attack on rank, hierarchy, inherited privilege, and subservience. The declaration set off fierce debates in Paris and in the colonies about whether or not slavery could exist in such a modern nation. Should slaves be considered men and citizens too? Amid the confusion, free blacks and slaves in Saint-Domingue took up arms to assert their rights. After a decade of bloodshed, Haiti emerged as the second independent republic in the New World, and the first nation to consist almost solely of former slaves.[7]

When in September 1862 Abraham Lincoln declared his intent to free blacks held in bondage, the precedents of the past remained alive in the minds of many observers. For some, Lincoln's Emancipation Proclamation conjured up bloody images of the Haitian Revolution. As historian Howard Jones has shown, the British governing class initially recoiled in horror at the news of emancipation and black military enlistment, fearing that Lincoln, unable to defeat the Confederacy in a conventional war, had resorted to inciting slave rebellion. White southerners certainly agreed, and the Confederate press teemed with references to Haiti and statements on a par with Jefferson Davis's denunciation of the act as "the most execrable measure recorded in the history of guilty man."[8]

Most white northerners, for their part, felt uncomfortable comparing their war to the French and Haitian Revolutions. By the mid-nineteenth century, most Americans, from North and South, had come to equate those events with anarchic violence and race war. As supporters of emancipation contemplated the end of slavery, however, they looked to other models to make comparisons and draw inspiration. In 1833, the British parliament passed a law peacefully abolishing slavery in its West Indian possessions in an act that provided some financial compensation for former owners. In the years that followed, measuring the effects of West Indian emancipation became a source of fierce debate for supporters and opponents of slavery in the United States. White southerners pointed to the crash of Jamaica's sugar economy as proof that abolition would lead to financial ruin, while abolitionists and free-soilers argued that the legacy of slavery itself had deprived the island of the work ethic and respect for labor that would have helped in making a successful transition to freedom. In 1861 and 1862, the example of the West Indies framed some northerners' discussions over the question of emancipation in the United States. An article in *Harper's Weekly* entitled "What to Do with the Negroes" cited the experience in the British Caribbean as one of two relevant "historical precedents." Abraham Lincoln himself held out the prospect of compensated emancipation as a solution to slavery in the Border States, though without success.[9]

By 1863, it had become clear to most observers that emancipation in the United States would not follow the path taken by Great Britain. The end of slavery in America would come as a revolutionary act in the midst of conflict, an act more comparable to the violent upheavals that had troubled the continent of Europe in the name of freedom and liberty. Some remembered that in 1848 the provisional government of France, upon seizing power, took immediate and direct action against slavery in the new republic's remaining colonies. *Harper's Weekly* reminded readers that "the revolutionary Government of France with a stroke of the pen freed all the slaves in the French West Indies." This method, the editorial argued, proved more relevant and successful than British efforts at compensated emancipation. The article noted with approval that "no compensation was granted to the owners, and the act took effect immediately." French intellectual Eugène Pelletan, in a pamphlet entitled *An Address to King Cotton*, also pointed out that Americans followed the French in striking against slavery in the midst of upheaval. He recalled that the revolutionaries of 1789 had been the first to "inaugurate negro emancipation and . . . grant the black the right of citizenship." The provisional government, he reminded his readers, finished the job in 1848.[10]

As liberals in Europe and America greeted Lincoln's Emancipation Proclamation, they joined the editors of *Harper's* in recalling the achievements of Europe's revolutionaries. The act seemed to promise at least partial realization of the hopes and dreams of 1848. As historians Thomas Bender, James McPherson, and David Potter have argued, Lincoln's vision for the reunited states linked nationalism and liberalism, the twin goals of Europe's midcentury revolutions. As 1863 arrived, progressives on both continents dared to hope that he might succeed in finally making nationalism synonymous with liberty. French liberal Édouard Laboulaye, in a pamphlet that circulated on the northern home front, compared the Civil War with the uprisings in Lombardy in 1848 and 1859 that had brought Italian unity. He favored the North because southerners, unlike the patriots of Italy, he claimed, had seceded in the "INTERESTS OF SLAVERY" and out of the "FEAR OF LIBERTY." Eugène Pelletan asserted that the Emancipation Proclamation revived the ideals of 1848. He conceded that the visionaries of 1848 failed to establish a lasting republic in France, but he and his fellow liberals now looked to America for fulfillment of their hopes and dreams. "There are at least others beyond the ocean," he declared, "to whom the last revolution has given the right to shout for Liberty!" Pelletan concluded with a stern admonition for the southern planters, a warning derived from the history of the first French revolution. Those who stood in the way of human progress, he contended, were doomed to destruction. "Tempt destiny no longer," he admonished the slaveholders. "Remember the example of the French nobility. They left the soil rather than submit to common law, and the soil passed from them into the hands of a class sprung from revolution and identified with liberty."[11]

The African American community in the North greeted news of the president's proclamation with similar hope and excitement. Many of its members displayed a keen awareness of emancipation's global origins and worldwide importance, as did Frederick Douglass. In Brooklyn, the congregation of Bridge Street African Methodist Church hosted a "grand jubilee" in early January that celebrated the act and commemorated similar milestones in the history of slavery and freedom. The celebrants decorated the pulpit with a banner whose inscriptions honored British abolitionists William Wilberforce and Thomas Clarkson while recalling "Emancipation in 1834" in the "British West Indies." In the pages of the *Christian Recorder*, the leading mouthpiece of the African Methodist Episcopal Church, Henry McNeil Turner mentioned the "serfs of Russia" as he reflected upon parallel acts of moral grandeur. Another correspondent hailed the proclamation as a "step in the progress of world history," and pointed out that a nation reunited without slavery would "excite the fears of despots." A letter from a young soldier in the Army of the Potomac, which the paper reprinted, rejoiced that the United States would join Germany, France, England, Holland, and Russia in lifting the darkness of bondage with "universal light and liberty." These interpretations remained fresh in 1865 when black advocates for a monument to Abraham Lincoln gathered in the nation's capital to celebrate the Fourth of July. William Howard Day opened the proceedings with a review of "the struggles for the principles of freedom in the Old World" and praise for the destruction of despotism in America.[12]

For some officers and men charged with applying Lincoln's emancipation policy, the lessons of the past offered guidance as well as inspiration and analogy. In late 1862, Benjamin Butler found himself in charge of Union-occupied areas of Louisiana. He quickly faced the problem of dealing with slaveholders seeking to evade emancipation. Some even claimed French citizenship and immunity from American military decrees. Butler looked to the past for precedents. He invoked a decree passed by the revolutionary government of France in 1848 and forwarded it to William Henry Seward. The statute forbade "any Frenchman" even "in foreign countries" from possessing, purchasing, or selling slaves. As a result, Butler believed he had the right to free the slaves of Americans and Frenchmen alike. Thomas W. Conway, superintendent of the Department of the Gulf's Bureau of Free Labor, headed a report on the confiscation of southern estates titled, "Withering Condition of the Old Land Aristocracy." Conway joined Pelletan in recalling with approval the example the French had set in the 1790s: "What was reaped from the French Revolution to the large land estates of France is being realized by Louisiana, as the most sweeping result of the war which she herself helped to inaugurate."[13]

Many of the Union's representatives abroad also thought of Europe as they contemplated Lincoln's change in policy. Emancipation allowed them to recast their diplomatic strategy and bring it in line with traditional republican predilections. Early in the war, Lincoln and his diplomats had tailored their message to the monarchs of Europe who had for the most part triumphed in the rebellions and revolutions of the past century. After 1863, however, the advocates of the Union increasingly spoke to the people, the progressives, and the revolutionaries of Europe. As historian R. J. M. Blackett and others have shown, significant portions of the European working class favored the Union cause. While early in the war the insistence of Lincoln and his administration that the northerners fought for reunion, not to end slavery, confused many Europeans, as Union supporters in Europe and America made progress toward linking reunion and emancipation, growing numbers of workers flocked to the Union side. They made use of speeches, rallies, pamphlets, and the press to argue that the North represented the cause of democracy and liberty throughout the world.[14]

In the wake of emancipation, administration officials were swamped with proof of the sympathy of European progressives. In March 1863, the British reformer Richard Cobden wrote to Charles Sumner, chairman of the Senate Foreign Relations Committee, assuring him that the Emancipation Proclamation had awakened "wide and deep" sympathy for "personal freedom" in the British people. On the eve of emancipation, an open letter from the working men of Manchester assured Lincoln that they would oppose any attempt of the British government to interfere in the conflict now that the United States was "undeniably and without exception, the home of the free." French liberals insisted that textile workers in Rouen, though they suffered terribly from the cotton famine, understood that the war involved a "superior cause." A group of Italian liberals led by Giuseppe Garibaldi praised Lincoln as the "pilot of liberty," and the Democratic Party of Barcelona hoped that the abolition of slavery in the United States would be "the signal for the abolition of all slavery among mankind." In England, Henry Adams attended what he called a "democratic and socialist meeting" aimed to prevent British interference on behalf of the Confederacy. He reported that "at this moment the American question is organizing a vast mass of the lower orders." These lower orders, Adams asserted, supported the Republican Party platform and celebrated the "rights of man." He concluded that "the old revolutionary leaven is working steadily in England."[15]

By 1863, reports like these encouraged administration officials to cultivate their new allies in the battle for world opinion. Late that year, Charles Sumner advised Abraham Lincoln to abandon his appeal to conservative European heads of state. He urged the president to proclaim to "*the people of Europe*" that the war for the Union was also a war for human liberty. "If our cause in Europe could be put openly on this ground," he wrote, "the Rebellion would receive a death-blow." He believed such a move would place America in the vanguard of world progress. He predicted that "slavery every where would tremble before the judgement of the civilized world."

When faced with war, Sumner, who was, in most cases, a pacifist, urged Lincoln to "get as much as possible for our own country and also for mankind out of all our bloodshed."[16]

Such a change in policy offered considerable risk. Stirring up European public opinion over slavery might anger the heads of state whose aid, favor, and recognition might prove critical to the nationalist hopes of either Unionists or Confederates. Still, two years of appeals to conservatism had not done much to convince the European governing classes of the right of the United States to remain undivided. Numerous observers noted that many of the same individuals who had opposed progress in Europe also supported the Confederacy. One article in *Harper's Weekly* suggested that Englishmen who sympathized with the Confederacy had been "conspicuous in history" as opponents of "freedom, democracy, and equal rights." A. J. Hamilton, a Texas Unionist who later served as wartime federal governor of that state, detected common institutions and interests between the Confederacy and the conservative powers of Europe. "The governing classes of some of the governments of the Old World," he wrote, sympathized with the "aristocratic principles of slavery," and had demonstrated a deep interest "in the preservation of the privileges of class." The only reason they had eschewed a more active role in the Civil War, Hamilton believed, was because the dangerous "masses of the people of those governments," who had rebelled before and could do so again, supported the Union and abolition.[17]

The well-known propensity of the European people to revolt gave the supporters of abolition courage in pressing forward with their plans to abandon appeals to conservatism and celebrate America's revolutionary destiny. Supporters of abolition became convinced that they had the mass of the European people on their side, and that any action by European governments on behalf of the Confederacy would be met with rebellion. Secretary of the Navy Gideon Welles believed that foreign involvement on behalf of the South in what he called America's "great conflict" would prompt "an uprising of the nations that will shatter existing governments and overthrow the aristocracies and dynasties not only of England but of Europe." John Bigelow predicted that, in the event of war between the United States and Great Britain, the common people of England would rise up against their government and rally to the Union cause, and Parke Godwin believed that the destruction of slavery in the New World would accompany the fall of monarchy in the Old. More than a few editorials in sheets ranging from *Harper's Weekly*, to the *Chicago Daily Tribune*, to a paper in rural Oskaloosa, Kansas, agreed. One sought to explain why England had not yet intervened in the American war. The answer lay in the apparently well-known sympathies of the country's tumultuous lower classes. The article asserted that the "great masses of the British people, who are not represented in Parliament, in the Press, or in the Clubs, are on our side." These sympathies could be explained by the ideological connections members of the British lower class saw between the struggle in America and their cause in Europe. "They believe," the article maintained, "that ours is the cause of freedom against slavery, of democracy against privilege, of labor against hereditary capital and property." Although they held little legal power, these people represented, in the author's opinion, "Great Britain's dangerous class" because "they can make revolutions, and, if goaded too far, the presumption is that they would do so." In such an event, monarchy would be left in the dust. "The throne and aristocracy of England," the paper predicted, "would crumble in an afternoon."[18]

The northern press and political leadership naturally focused much of their attention on Great Britain. By 1863, however, the likelihood of France's meddling in the Civil War may have been even greater than that of England. Napoleon III, who had taken the French throne after the upheavals of 1848, had what one paper in Marysville, Kansas, termed a "penchant for intervention." The editor pointed to Napoleon III's destruction of the Roman Republic in 1849, his complicity in the Crimean War, and his betrayal of the "cause of Italian independence." After the outbreak of the Civil War, Napoleon III intently sought to capitalize on the crisis in the United States by reestablishing a French empire in the Americas. As in the case of England, many Unionists believed that the revolutionary nature of the war, especially in the years after 1863, prevented the French from risking any involvement. An article in *Harper's Weekly* asserted that France, in addition to England, knew "perfectly well" that "in case of universal war . . . a vast popular revolution would immediately develop itself throughout Europe." Henry Raymond, editor of the *New York Times*, wrote to fire-eater William Lowndes Yancey during the secession crisis to make the same point. Raymond explained that Napoleon III might go to war on behalf of "enslaved Italians," but any "interference on behalf of Slavery" would shake "the Imperial throne." Henry Adams agreed: "So sure as Napoleon proves so false to France as to take up the cudgels for monarchy against democracy, just so sure he will lose his throne."[19]

The supporters of emancipation made connections with the European past not only because it provided them a convenient point of comparison, but also because it reshaped a discussion about American nationalism that northern thinkers had begun in 1861. The European past endowed their cause with universal significance, ideological importance, and intellectual depth. Politicians, editors, and intellectuals used the knowledge that many European conservatives favored the Confederacy to develop new ideas about progressive nationalism in the modern world. Like their forty-eighter supporters, they compared southern planters to European aristocrats and argued that the privileged classes on both continents had prevented the full realization of the nationalist impulse. They produced a new definition of nationalism that cast aristocratic owners of serfs, slaves, and vast tracts of land as enemies of the people and of the state. True nationalism, they argued, valued free labor, equality before the law, and the protection of civil rights. Rank, hierarchy, and legal class distinctions were incompatible with the modern state, and illegitimate "aristocrats" in Europe and America stood in the way, as the bloody history of the nineteenth century had shown.

Since the late eighteenth century, Americans had often compared their political enemies to aristocrats. As historian R. R. Palmer has pointed out, the "Age of Revolution" in Europe and America revolved around the struggle between "democrats" and "aristocrats." The American Revolution of 1776 had encouraged Americans to value egalitarianism and denounce all the trappings of monarchy, hierarchy, and legal rank. To be labeled an "aristocrat" implied that one was not a "citizen" and that one stood in the way of social progress by clinging to outmoded beliefs that encouraged those with wealth and land to cultivate a false sense of authority and superiority. The French Revolution of 1789 cemented these ideas in the minds of many Americans. The most radical supporters of the French Revolution believed that the struggle promised to remake the world in America's image. They took to wearing tricolored badges and donning the simple republican garb of the *sans-culottes*. When domestic political conflict flared during the turbulent decade of the 1790s, they naturally compared their opponents to the "aristocrats," the enemies of the people in both Europe and America. Jeffersonian Republicans especially employed the language of class and rank in their battles with the Federalists.[20]

There can be no doubt that by the nineteenth century the labels "aristocrat" and "democrat" had become firmly ingrained in the American rhetorical tradition. It must be acknowledged, however, that these ideas had always held a tangible reality. During the first French revolution, the abbé Sieyès had argued that aristocrats were the enemies of the people and therefore incompatible with the emerging modern nation in which labor was valued and the people could never legally be divided by rank. Americans of the 1790s understood that their fragile republic represented an experiment in representative government, an experiment that might easily fail if confronted with an invasion by the British king or subverted by an ambitious tyrant at home. If the history of the 1800s had not unfolded as it did, these fears may have dissipated and accompanying modes of political discourse might have faded in meaning and use, as they would in the twentieth century. During the 1800s, the discourse regarding aristocrats and democrats did not become anachronistic, however. Indeed, that discourse remained a vital part of the unfolding discussion about the nature of the nation-state that would emerge during the nineteenth century. Events in the mid-nineteenth-century Atlantic world provided many observers with abundant proof that a powerful, landed ruling class could pose a real threat to nationalist aspirations. Americans watched in the years after the French Revolution as European aristocrats thwarted popular movements for representative governments that would extend the rights of suffrage to landless workers. In 1861, many northerners feared that southern oligarchs would similarly destroy the American republic.[21]

By the time war broke out in America in 1861, many northerners were prepared to join the Unionist forty-eighters in interpreting the conflict as a historic battle between the forces of aristocracy and the supporters of liberal nationalism. In early 1861, as southern delegates established the Confederate government in Montgomery, Alabama, the moderate New York Republican George Templeton Strong confided to his diary his fears for their motives. "It becomes plainer every day," he wrote, "that secession is the act of an oligarchy, and ignores or contradicts and overrides the 'self-evident truths' of all the Democratic platforms of the last half century." He raged at "Lord" and "Prince" Jefferson Davis and his "chivalric pals" who, Strong feared, meant to rule the southern people with no intention of submitting their authority to a popular vote. He predicted that the new Confederate government would amount to nothing more than a "strong, unscrupulous aristocracy," and would trample upon "Democratic theories of universal suffrage and the Rights of the People." When General P. G. T. Beauregard's gunners fired on Fort Sumter in mid-April, Strong declared, "This is a continuation of the war that Lexington opened—a war of democracy against oligarchy."[22]

Strong's views on the conflict owed much to the indictment of southern society that the Republican Party and radical European immigrants had developed in the years before the war. As historian Michael Holt and others have shown, the Kansas-Nebraska Act, the *Dred Scott* decision, and the struggle over the Lecompton Constitution led many northerners in the 1850s to develop the fear that a small group of wealthy slaveholders had conspired to seize control of the U.S. government and subvert it to its own ends. Belief in this "Slave Power Conspiracy" helped Republicans rally voters across the North. As the war approached, thinkers, editors, and politicians sketched out the Slave Power thesis in growing complexity and detail. In 1863, it was employed to win support for emancipation. Such an argument could not have developed the way it did without the actual existence of a titled and privileged European ruling class that had weathered the rebellions and revolutions of the past half century. The nobility of the Old World provided northerners with a point of constant comparison to the slave owners of the New. Both based their political power on the illegitimate monopolization of land, subjects, and slaves, and both threatened the values of free labor and egalitarianism that promised to redeem the world.[23]

The war's most complete articulation of the Slave Power thesis was initially developed for a European, not an American, audience. John Elliott Cairnes, an Irish university professor and supporter of liberal causes, published his book *The Slave Power, Its Character, Career and Probable Designs* in 1862 to influence public opinion in the United Kingdom. It proved such a powerful statement of the Union cause that an American edition appeared immediately afterward. Cairnes argued that blame for the war lay squarely on the shoulders of a small cabal of powerful, wealthy planters. Their vast holdings in land and slaves, he believed, gave them economic and political power disproportionate to their numbers. Cairnes asserted that the infamous "three-fifths clause" in the constitution that counted slave property toward political representation had given slaveholders an artificially large role in American government. When the American people elected a president opposed to this powerful class, Cairnes argued, the southern aristocrats chose to destroy the nation rather than submit to the natural workings of the democratic process.[24]

Though Cairnes's work was initially intended to make the Civil War intelligible to Europeans, his ideas about the Slave Power and the three-fifths clause held tremendous relevance to the unfolding domestic discussion about the nature of American nationalism. Leading Republicans widely circulated similar ideas. Like the abbé Sieyès, and the forty-eighters after him, Republicans held that a dangerous aristocracy had developed that threatened national unity and existence. Early in the war, the liberal intellectual Richard Henry Dana wrote to John Bigelow, U.S. consul in Paris, to express his opinion that the American republic could not survive unless the Slave Power, which he compared to an "oligarchy," were destroyed. Bigelow evidently agreed. A Free-Soil Democrat before the war who had written for William Cullen Bryant's *New York Evening Post*, Bigelow became one of the leading northern expositors of the Slave Power thesis. Bigelow believed, as did Dana and Cairnes, that the Constitution had given slaveholders undue influence in the U.S. government. While the northern states remained committed to upholding the "right of suffrage" and "political equality before the law," the three-fifths clause had tied the exercise of political power in the South to the possession of human and material wealth. In his analysis of the origins of the Civil War, Bigelow charged that the founding fathers had "created in the Southern States a privileged class, an aristocracy, on the basis of property in slaves." In Bigelow's opinion, if the Constitution had not included the three-fifths clause, then sectional conflict over the expansion of slavery would never have occurred because northerners would never have had a political motive to exclude slavery from the West. John Lothrop Motely agreed, though he believed that the South would have developed an aristocratic class regardless, because "slavery itself" permitted the "concentration of much power and property in few hands."[25]

The ideas of Cairnes, Dana, Bigelow, and Motely circulated widely in the pages of the prowar press. Newspapers that appealed to Republicans and War Democrats constantly compared southern planters to dangerous aristocrats. Horace Greeley's *New York Tribune* regularly ran a series of columns written by Karl Marx in which he blamed a "Southern slavocracy" or "oligarchy" for instigating the war. The rural Pennsylvania *Waynesboro Village Record* urged the defeat of the "Slave Power" lest a monarchy be established in America that would destroy all liberty. "The real issue," a *Record* editorial declared, "is not so much between freedom and African slavery, as between an aristocratic and free form of government." One article in *Harper's Weekly* contended, "Southern society is composed of the aristocracy who own the laborers." Another article drew a clear parallel between social organization in the Old World and the New. The "350,000 slaveowners of the South," the author reasoned, considered themselves "an aristocracy to be classed with the lords of England, the boyars of Russia, and the barons of France." Southerners, the editor suggested, subscribed to the fiction that mankind could be divided into two classes, the aristocracy, which included monarchs, noblemen, and southern gentlemen, and the "working people," which included "the merchants and operatives of Europe, the whole people of the North, and the white trash at the South." The Democratic-leaning *New York Herald* took a similar view of the situation. The newspaper hailed a speech by British member of Parliament John Bright in which he quoted Kossuth, Garibaldi, and Victor Hugo in lauding the United States as "the free home of the working classes, with free vote and free career for the humblest."[26]

John Murray Forbes, the Boston abolitionist, businessman, and promoter of the Union war effort, was one of the first Republicans to seize on the idea that the comparison of slave owners to aristocrats could mobilize for the war effort broad constituencies beyond the tightly knit forty-eighter communities. He understood that he could bring together northerners with a variety of views on the slave question by avoiding discussion of the morality of slavery and instead focusing attention on the effects it had on the American political system. More than anyone, he worked tirelessly to spread these views in organized fashion. In July 1862, he forwarded to Republican politician William Curtis Noyes a bundle of statements "from the rebels." The package contained clippings from speeches by Confederate politicians proclaiming themselves "aristocrats and masters bound to rule us." Forbes instructed Noyes to print and distribute those statements in an effort to "enlighten the working classes." Such articles, Forbes believed, would "be of great value in raising recruits." He hoped they would open "the eyes of the people to the real nature of the contest," which, Forbes believed, pitted "aristocracy *vs.* popular government, and slave labor *vs.* free labor."[27]

One year later, Forbes pressed his arguments upon President Lincoln. He approached Secretary of the Navy Gideon Welles to urge Lincoln to "make the issue before the country distinctly perceptible to all as democratic and aristocratic." Forbes told Welles that "the whole object and purpose of the leaders in the Rebellion is the establishment of an aristocracy." Forbes also wrote Lincoln himself. "My suggestion," he told the president, "is that you should seize an early opportunity and any subsequent chance, to teach your great audience of plain people that the war is not the North against the South, but the people against the aristocrats." He also hoped Lincoln would direct his generals to issue bulletins or general orders that would instruct Union soldiers and any "rebels" that could be reached. The people of Europe, Forbes explained, already grasped the true nature of the conflict. He asserted that John Bright and other English republicans saw that Unionists were "fighting for democracy: or (to get rid of the technical name) for liberal institutions." Consequently, he believed, "the democrats and the liberals of the Old World" supported the Union. Forbes asserted that even the enemies of the United States shared his view of the question: "The aristocrats and the despots of the Old World see that our quarrel is that of the people against an aristocracy." This "truth" would only have to be expressed in America. "Let the people North and South see this line clearly defined between the people and the aristocrats," he declared, "and the war will be over!"[28]

The fruit of Forbes's labor is especially evident in the pamphlets issued by the Union's Loyal Publication Society. Society members recruited prominent forty-eighters and European liberal intellectuals to write pamphlets that took a transatlantic view of American affairs. The society distributed its message widely among soldiers and on the northern home front. After the society's inception in February 1863, it published at least ninety different titles and issued close to one million copies, mostly in the critical years of 1863 and 1864. The pamphlets reached hundreds of Union Leagues, ladies' associations, and newspaper editors across the North. Tens of thousands of private individuals subscribed. The society's officials sent at least as many pamphlets to the army for direct circulation in the field. John Murray Forbes's New England branch of the society specifically targeted editors by sending broadsides and clippings of particularly relevant articles to 867 northern newspapers. One Indiana editor told Forbes that his efforts were especially helpful in reaching rural audiences, since small-town publishers often relied on the forwarded material in crafting their editorials.[29]

These efforts ensured that an international perspective on the Civil War reached wide audiences. Francis Lieber, the German liberal who had participated in an abortive revolution in his home country in 1830, and who later sympathized with the movements of 1848, served as the first chairman of the society's publications committee. In that post, Lieber took responsibility for selecting material for publication. He authored ten pamphlets himself, and later became president of the society. More than 20 percent of the society's pamphlets contained international themes or comparisons of conditions in Europe and America. That number is all the more impressive considering the fact that many of the pamphlets had very specific purposes that included responding to political controversies, addressing the sacrifices of women on the home front, and promoting the reelection of Abraham Lincoln. If the pool is reduced to only those pamphlets that dealt with the meaning of the war, then an international perspective becomes even more prominent.[30]

Under the leadership of men like Forbes and Lieber, the society developed the most complete, thorough, and sophisticated explanation of why the Slave Power, slavery, and slaveholders threatened the rights of white men in Europe and America alike. The society's thinkers argued that an economy based on slavery encouraged the growth of large landed estates in the same way feudal economies had. That growth had similar consequences in Europe and America. As more land fell into fewer hands, the ranks of the yeomanry dwindled, poverty increased, and freedom withered. Thomas Francis Meagher, in a series of letters to the Irish people reprinted by the society for circulation in America, explained that while southern slaveholders lacked the titles and inherited privileges of their European counterparts, their peculiar institution gave them a functional equivalent. Slavery, Meagher believed, "constituted the basis" of the aristocracy's "wealth," "social consequence," and "political power." Francis Lieber, in an exegesis entitled *Slavery, Plantations, and the Yeomanry*, provided examples from European history, noting that the ancient Romans had first coined a word for the "overgrown possessions of the land-owners," calling them latifundia. In England, he asserted, the growth of the latifundia had led to the "extinction of the class of small farmers and comfortable peasants." These developments left the common people in an "abject state." Lieber compared their plight to that of the peasantry of Central Europe, where the "feudal tenure of land" had been finally abolished in 1848. For Lieber, the plantations of the South differed little from Europe's infamous latifundia. Both made it almost impossible for modest men to earn an honest living. Lieber conceded that "no feudal law" promoted the "land devouring tendency" in America. He declared, however, that "THE INSTITUTION OF SLAVERY TAKES ITS PLACE."[31]

Meagher's and Lieber's indictment of the Slave Power rested implicitly, as did the indictments of most northern thinkers, on the free-labor ideology that Republicans had used before the war to critique southern society. As historian Eric Foner has shown, northern politicians during the 1850s and 1860s celebrated the common man's ability to rise to prosperity through hard work and fair competition. For Republicans, slavery proved antithetical to those values. Slave labor hurt productivity by removing the worker's ability and incentive to climb the social ladder. It also drove down the wages of free laborers by preventing fair market competition. As a result, Republicans in the 1850s and 1860s insisted that the southern social system had led to economic stagnation. One Loyal Publication Society pamphlet examined the material well-being of the "mechanics of the South" and concluded with the familiar charge that Confederate leaders had "reduced their misguided, deluded and betrayed people" to a "miserable condition." The author attributed the supposed penury of the region's poor whites, as did many advocates of free labor, to the growth of the landed planter class. The "abject posture" of labor in the South, the author argued, should have served as a warning to the mechanics of the North who could "plainly see what their fate would be should the rebel hopes of success be fulfilled."[32]

While Foner situated the discussion over free labor in a domestic context, the issues he identified had always formed part of a larger conversation about the future of labor throughout the world. The celebration of America's promise depended upon a comparison with and an indictment of the conditions workers faced in Europe. One unidentified pamphleteer argued that the United States was "the very paradise of labor." He argued, "Here is no place for idlers, be they rich or be they poor! Labor here makes all men equal; here the European noble and peasant work side by side!" The author contended that the social system in the New World surpassed even the progress that the Old World had made in recent years in "facilitating intercourse amongst the different peoples, in the abolition of river dues, guilds, the progress of free labor, and the emancipation of the serfs." Still, the state of labor in the mid-nineteenth century included a confusing array of wage work, slavery, and servitude. In industrializing regions of Europe and the United States, increasing numbers of journeyman artisans and mechanics found themselves forced to resort to permanent paid labor in the mills and shops owned by the small number of wealthy men who had access to the capital needed for large-scale production. At the same time, in the rural hinterlands of the growing cities, chattel slaves and peasants lacking civil rights still toiled on great estates, the former in the American South and the latter on the European continent.[33]

Though progressives in both Europe and America hoped the future lay with unfettered free labor, that outcome was far from assured during the early 1860s. Liberals and abolitionists still called for an end to slavery, and socialists began to question the growing power of capital to enslave workers. Attempts to resolve this "labor question" had driven a great deal of the violence that rocked Europe during the nineteenth century. The revolutions of 1848 had succeeded in abolishing serfdom in parts of Eastern Europe and liberating the slaves in the French West Indies, but had failed to establish for both the urban and the rural proletariat the right to vote, serve in office, or obtain meaningful and sufficient work. One article in *Harper's Weekly* recited the depressing litany of recent failures that had called the future of free labor into question: "The Chartist follies, the potato rebellion in Ireland, and the disastrous end of the Continental movements of 1848, gave Privilege an extension of its lease, and threw Democracy in England back for nearly a generation."[34]

The Confederate rebellion now threatened to inflict the same results on America. One pamphleteer wrote that the Confederacy's attempt to found a nation whose cornerstone rested on slavery was "a crime against this Nineteenth Century, . . . an attempt against all recognized human rights." For this observer of recent history, the disintegration of the American Union seemed so out of step with modern progress as to appear absurd. "As well might we assume that England would reenact its former system of protective duties, its corn laws, and navigation act," he incredulously asserted, and "that Germany would revive the old guilds, soccage service, and religious persecutions, that Russia would restore the just abolished serfdom." He continued, "We might as well assume that civilization would retrograde, and that the great civilized nations of Europe would go back to the feudal system of the middle ages!" Thomas Francis Meagher worried that a Confederate victory would encourage the "imperial *parvenu*" of Austria and England's "old Tory monarchy" to perpetuate "hereditary burthens, the stingy franchises, the domination of privileged classes, the monopolized land, the surfeited Church Establishment, and all the other gilt and bloated follies" of old Europe. Édouard Laboulaye similarly warned that the separation of the United States into two nations would re-create the difficulties of the Old World. "Custom-house and frontier difficulties, rivalries, jealousies—all the scourges of old Europe," he wrote, "would at once overwhelm America.[35]

The advocates of northern free labor argued that the semifeudal economies of Europe and the aristocratic Slave Power in America represented two sides of the same coin. The editors of *Harper's Weekly* asserted that the "labor question" that the world confronted took "the name of the slavery question" in the American South. Another editorial, while conflating feudalism with an emergent capitalism, asserted that the Confederacy fought to protect the great "principle" of the "aristocratic class" that held that "capital ought to own labor." The popular minister Henry Ward Beecher, who late in the war toured England to promote the Union cause, told his followers that capitalist exploitation of the working class and the slaveholders' exploitation of their chattel stemmed from the very same ideological roots. "The same thing that leads to the oppression of the operative," he explained, "leads to oppression on the plantation." Beecher denounced the "grinding of the poor," the "advantages which capital takes of labor," and the "oppression of the shop." In Beecher's opinion, capitalist violations of the rights and dignity of the worker shared "the same central nature" and stood "as guilty before God" as "the more systematic and overt oppression of the plantation."[36]

Northern thinkers did not confine their analysis to economic questions. They also explained why aristocracy threatened good government. Advocates for the Union argued that an aristocratic society, whether it was found in the Old World or the New, inevitably trampled on civil and political rights, rights without which the American republic would have no meaning or purpose. Union officer J. W. Phelps argued that slavery had to be destroyed because of its negative effects on representative political institutions. "It is vain to deny," he wrote, "that the slave system of labor is giving shape to the government of the society where it exists, and that that government is not republican either in form or spirit." Colonel Charles Anderson, a Texas resident and Kentucky native who opposed secession, agreed. He had traveled extensively in Austria, whose imperial government had put down revolt in 1848, and served as a U.S. diplomat in Turkey, the country that had fought the nationalist aspirations of the Greeks early in the century. He claimed to have "seen considerable of the working of absolute government" and concluded that the Confederacy compared with the worst authoritarian oligarchies. "Does every man not know that the most fearful tyrannies of the world are aristocracies?" he rhetorically asked his readers. A. J. Hamilton stood convinced that Confederate slaveholders wished to establish "an order of nobility at the South" that would threaten "civil liberty and free government." Robert Dale Owen, abolitionist, politician, and son of the famous Scottish social reformer, offered proof of designs for that noble order by pointing out that the southern government, like the "despotic monarchies" that defended "the right divine of Kings" upon pain of death, suppressed "all opinions teaching the sinfulness . . . of slavery."[37]

Comparisons between the problems of slavery and the problems of the proletariat served more than a rhetorical purpose. They endowed America's Civil War with worldwide importance. The celebration of the North's free-labor society had always rested on the long-cherished assumption that the United States was an exceptional place. Its republican political

"Rev. H. W. Beecher Defending the American Union in Exeter Hall, London."
In 1863, Beecher toured England and gave a series of speeches designed to win
support for the Union war effort. He especially developed themes that linked
slavery with the oppression of the white working class. (Author's collection)

and social structure eliminated hierarchy, dignified labor, and had much to teach Europe and the world. One rural Pennsylvania newspaper reprinted an article from the *London Daily News* that described the contest in America as a "great conflict between free and servile labor" in which "the working men throughout the world have a supreme interest." Indeed, the editor joined a rural Kansas newspaper in suggesting that the Confederacy actively campaigned for slavery as a solution to the world's labor problem "irrespective of race or complexion." Missouri senator A. L. Gilstrap advanced a similar interpretation of the war in a letter to General William S. Rosecrans. James McKaye of the Loyal League of New York asserted that the Civil War held "the deepest interest" for "the people of France." "All men," he declared, would benefit if the "slave power" were "utterly overthrown and extinguished." An article in *Harper's Weekly* made the link with European struggles explicit: "We are fighting the battle of Democracy against Aristocracy—labor against capital—manhood against privilege—which has been fought out in most of the countries of Europe."[38]

By 1863, many northern politicians, pamphlet writers, and policymakers had developed an intellectual justification for emancipation that drew on the events of the past century. The southern aristocracy had to be destroyed because it fostered a system that thwarted national development. Northern soldiers and politicians increasingly understood that in order to achieve victory they would have to strike against the wealth that supported the power of the planter class. That meant seizing land as well as freeing slaves, as the French revolutionaries had done to break the power of the nobility. And as fighting intensified, the U.S. military, which had once been reluctant to take the war to southern civilians, began to view a war on the southern home front in a new way. In late March 1863, Henry W. Halleck wrote General Ulysses S. Grant to explain the administration's evolving policy on slavery and the treatment of southern civilians. The Union general-in-chief ordered his subordinate to assume a more active role in taking fugitive slaves into the lines and putting them to work for the government. "The character of the war has very much changed within the last year," Halleck explained to Grant. Halleck believed that destroying slavery held both military and ideological importance. "The North must conquer the slave oligarchy or become slaves themselves," he asserted. Confederate victory, according to the general-in-chief, would turn northern "manufacturers" into "mere 'hewers of wood and drawers of water'" who would serve what he called "Southern aristocrats." Striking at slavery would undermine that aristocracy's power by depriving it of its most important source of private wealth. "This is the phase which the rebellion has now assumed," Halleck declared.[39]

Grant would do as much as any Union officer to commit the United States to a policy of "hard war." By 1865, Union armies increasingly struck at the Confederacy's will and ability to resist the government by freeing slaves, seizing farms, and burning crops. Though these policies always remained controversial on the northern home front, especially among Democrats, soldiers in the field increasingly viewed them as necessary. While many native-born soldiers rejected emancipation for moral reasons alone, as did their forty-eighter counterparts, the destruction of the power of wealthy, aristocratic planters also won approval and praise. Now that emancipation had arrived, the comparison of wealthy white southerners to aristocrats won support for the policies that targeted property in people and land for confiscation and destruction. Samuel B. Shepard, a soldier in the Sixth Connecticut Regiment, opposed equality for African Americans but fought because he believed that the government founded by the "Revolutionary forefathers" had degenerated into a "pro-slavery aristocracy." General Hiram Berry conceded, as had many forty-eighters before him, that contact with the regressive southern social system caused him to qualify his allegiance to the Democratic Party. "I am a Democrat still. I am not, however, a Southern Democrat," he wrote, "for I find Democracy here nothing less than aristocracy, to make the rich richer and the poor poorer." Ebenezer Gilpin, a Union cavalryman, and Hallock Armstrong, a chaplain with a Pennsylvania regiment, also came away from their experiences in the South convinced that the southern social system represented an "aristocracy." They were joined by Chauncey Herbert Cooke, a Union common soldier, in arguing that emancipation would liberate poor whites as well as blacks from the rule of "rich" aristocrats. Hallock Armstrong applauded policies that brought destruction to the planter class. "Our generals," he wrote, "have done well in allowing the soldiers to take what they wanted from the rich planters. They deserved their fate. How are the mighty fallen!" David Day, a soldier in the 25th Massachusetts Infantry, gloried in delivering the harsh blows of war as he marched through the South with his regiment. He reported that his unit "made a desolation of the country through which we passed." He reflected with satisfaction on what war and emancipation had done to the wealthy planters. "That proud aristocracy," he wrote, "can now look over their desolate fields, and in vain call the roll of their slaves." He concluded that the harsh tactics would prevent the rich from ever again testing the power of the people. "I reckon the landed nobility up the country through which we traveled will never care to see another excursion of the same kind," he wrote.[40]

In late 1864, the policy of "hard war" reached its apogee. In November, Union General William Tecumseh Sherman cut loose from his supply lines in Atlanta and began his destructive "March to the Sea" through Georgia and the Carolinas. His soldiers subsisted on the crops and stores they found in their path. They burned what they could not use. A column of former slaves, freed forever from bondage, trailed the army. George S. Bradley, an army chaplain who served during the march, remarked that it seemed "sad to burn such beautiful residences," but explained that "our boys" reasoned "correctly." They justly blamed the planters for starting the war and just as understandably made them pay for it. "The wealthy people of the South," Bradley wrote, "were the very ones to plunge the country into secession—*now let them suffer—let South Carolina aristocracy have its fill of secession*." Charles Fessenden Morse, another soldier on Sherman's March, reported from the army that wherever the men marched, "in nine cases out of ten, before night all that [was] left to show where the rich, aristocratic, chivalrous, slave-holding South Carolinian lived, [was] a heap of smoldering ashes." Morse believed such treatment of secessionists was justified. "They have rebelled against a Government they never once felt; they lived down here like so many lords and princes," he explained. Morse asserted that "each planter was at the head of a little aristocracy in which hardly a law touched him." Morse seethed with class resentment when he reflected that the privileged had brought war upon the majority. They had everything, thought Morse, but still wanted more. "This didn't content these people," he argued, "they wanted 'their rights,' and now they are getting them."[41]

While not all these soldiers would have been astute students of recent world history, more than one developed his beliefs from contemplating the wider world. Just as it had been in the minds of the forty-eighters who joined the northern armies in 1861, the fate of Europe seemed intertwined with the future of the Union to many northern soldiers. John C. Myers, a soldier in the 192nd Pennsylvania, believed that slavery's defeat "shook to their centre two continents." He believed that the destruction of the "great privileged class at the South," which he compared to an "order of nobility," "an aristocracy without hereditary title," justified the losses of war: "What are barren fields, depopulated plantations and other consequential damages compared with results which will be beneficially realized for ages to come?" General and former Democrat Robert H. Milroy denounced the members of his old party who opposed the war effort he considered "a struggle which involves not only the fate of free government in our own country, but for all the world." Another native-born Union private believed that the failure to preserve the nation would retard "the onward march of Liberty in the Old World" for "at least a century." He feared, most certainly with the results of 1848 in mind, that "Monarchs, Kings and Aristocrats will be more powerful against their subjects than ever."[42]

Union supporters increasingly believed that the defeat of the Slave Power held universal importance. The institution of slavery threatened republican government by creating a powerful class of wealthy landholders whose political values proved antagonistic to democracy and equality for white men. Americans had only to look to Europe to confirm their beliefs. Reactionary aristocrats in the Old World had consistently opposed workers' rights and the expansion of the franchise. In 1848 they had violently repressed the downtrodden masses that yearned for liberty. That example served as a warning to Americans of the fate that awaited them should Confederate leaders succeed in defeating the federal government and dividing the American nation. The destruction of the wealth and property in people and land that formed the basis of the southern aristocracy's material power would best ensure the preservation of an American nationality that embodied "the last best hope of earth."

The emancipation of the slaves made it much easier for some sections of the European public to believe in the providential role in world history that the United States had claimed for itself. That did not mean that alternative visions were not proposed. The supporters of southern independence refused to give up their cause easily. Even as the slave system eroded wherever armies marched, Confederate nationalists made a final effort to convince the world that their "peculiar institution" provided the firmest foundation for the future of Western civilization.

6

———•———

The White Republic

THE CONFEDERACY'S TASK OF CONVINCING THE WORLD THAT THEIR
new nation represented the principles of liberal revolution grew more difficult in the spring of 1863. The European public's supposed sympathy for the
rights of self-determination had not enticed any Old World nation to risk
war and intervene on behalf of the South. The Emancipation Proclamation
proved most problematic. The Lincoln administration's policy increasingly
appealed to the antislavery sentiment of the European masses. Many of
the Union's supporters argued that their cause championed human rights
the world over. Confederate agents reported that their European contacts
would recognize the Confederate nation only if it abandoned slavery.[1]

Emancipation posed a real problem for the would-be revolutionaries of
the Confederacy. The northern government's policies and the rhetoric of
the government's supporters increasingly reminded Confederates that, in
1848, Europeans had linked the principles of self-determination to human
freedom, social equality, free labor, and the right to work. These radical
goals openly challenged the southern defense of racial slavery. Confederates, however, did not abandon their peculiar institution. Nor did they
retreat from the rhetoric of modern nationalism. In fact, they remained
fiercely committed to both. Emancipation forced Confederates to reflect
upon slavery and its role in their new nation. In the process, the Confederate press, pamphlet writers, and politicians further developed their
complex vision of the Confederacy's role in world history. They continued to insist that their cause helped advance the principle of national self-
determination. At the same time, they began to argue that their social
system would enhance national stability across the globe. Though they remained inspired by the struggles of Hungarians, Italians, Irish, and Poles,
the arrival of emancipation caused them to evaluate the prospects their
own revolution held for success. As they did so, they reflected upon the

reasons why so many of the recent movements they admired had failed. Radical excesses, they concluded, had too often marred good causes by dooming the attempts of Europeans to achieve stable nationhood. They came away determined to avoid those mistakes. Confederate spokesmen claimed that the enslavement of the black laboring class would give their nation the strength to survive where others failed. Some referred to the concept as "white republicanism" and argued that it would achieve a successful nationalist revolution by opposing both the "black republicanism" of the abolitionists and the "red republicanism" of the most radical European revolutionaries.

Confederate supporters again turned to Henry Hotze and the *Index* for help in winning European aid. The editors of the *Richmond Enquirer* noted that his advocacy for self-determination and the right of revolution had made his paper "a really influential exponent of the Confederate cause." They now hoped Hotze could set Europe right on the question of emancipation. The editors asked him to explain to the world that slavery was not open to compromise. "Let the 'Index' tell our 'friends' who desire to open negotiations with us about Slavery," they advised, "that this is precisely the subject on which we can never negotiate with them at all." In fact, the *Index* argued defiantly, Confederates proposed to give slavery "a fuller development and firmer basis, if possible." Even as the institution crumbled in many parts of the South, the architects of Confederate nationality held to it tightly as a source of unity and strength. Moreover, the enlightened opinion of Europe, the editors of the *Enquirer* implied, had much to learn from the Confederate experiment. "Instead of being disposed to take any English dictation in the matter of our social and industrial system," they wrote, "we feel ourselves enabled and entitled to teach that country many important principles."[2]

The editors argued that racial subordination gave Confederate nationality a stable basis that many European nations lacked. The editors of the *Enquirer* believed that Union arms had been "kept at bay for more than two years" because slavery imparted peculiar strength to the southern social system. Slavery, the editorial claimed, gave "only five millions" of white southerners "such a power of resistance to aggression and invasion as no European empire has ever yet exhibited." The secret to the South's success lay in its peculiar solution to the problems of class and labor in an increasingly industrial world. The North, like the monarchies of Europe, they argued, had a "vicious and unjust industrial system" that produced "a vast mass of discontented and disfranchised white labor." Such unruly workers often provided the brute force for revolutions against constituted governments. White southerners, by contrast, claimed to enjoy an unusual degree of unity and commitment to the cause of national independence. The paper claimed that Confederates, by enslaving the black working class, prevented the white radicalism and class conflict that had marred the revolutions of 1848, weakened the North, and doomed any European nationalist endeavor. "The beneficent institution of slavery," the editors argued, "relieves these Confederate States of that terribly urgent social question which is always keeping European empires uneasy at the feeling that they are standing upon ground pregnant with the elements of volcano and earthquake." In short, the southern social system, *Enquirer* editors believed, would provide the stability that had so often eluded new nations in the past.[3]

The argument that slavery promoted a stable social order in the South had long played a role in the defense of the peculiar institution. George Fitzhugh famously argued in the 1850s that slavery proved superior to free-labor capitalism. Enslavement of the working class, he argued, solved the problems of industrial poverty by replacing class conflict with employer paternalism. Less well-known white southerners advanced similar arguments. Albert Taylor Bledsoe, a University of Virginia professor who would later travel on a mission to England to promote the Confederate cause, developed one of the clearest articulations of this point of view. In 1856, he published *An Essay on Liberty and Slavery*, which attacked the popular doctrine of absolute human equality. In his book, Bledsoe argued that no man held "inalienable rights." Instead, political communities regulated individual liberty to achieve a greater good. Bledsoe posited that an undue emphasis on man's natural, unfettered rights led to society's disintegration into violence, disorder, and anarchy. In Bledsoe's estimation, the purpose of society lay in restricting the rights of the individual to ensure the liberty of the many. Slavery, he claimed, ensured public order in the southern states. Bledsoe believed that the South's social order, by depriving African Americans of their individual rights, promoted the liberty of the white majority. Abolition, Bledsoe argued, would produce anarchy. "The very . . . institution which is supposed by fanatical declaimers to shut out liberty from the Negro race among us," he maintained, "really shuts out the most frightful *license* and disorder from society."[4]

Southern nationalists increasingly believed that slavery and the social stability it afforded would aid the region's quest to become a great power amid the world's "family of nations." The institution, they argued, facilitated the trade in cotton and textiles upon which the prosperity of Western civilization depended. They also believed that slavery enhanced national unity by excluding darker-skinned peoples from civic life, and promoted national stability by refuting notions of the universal equality of mankind. As Nicholas Onuf and Peter Onuf have argued, white southerners did not believe that their defense of slavery tied them to the values of the distant past; instead, they asserted that their peculiar institution would help them lead the world to a progressive future. They developed their ideas from their study of recent history and current events. The Reverend William A. Hall, a member of New Orleans' Washington Artillery, gave a series of addresses in Richmond and Petersburg during the spring of 1864 under the title of *The Historic Significance of the Southern Revolution*, even as the progress of emancipation and the advance of Union armies threatened the viability of the South's nationalist experiment. He began his exegesis by asking, "What does this great revolution mean when considered as a movement in history?" He answered by arguing that the Confederacy would lead the world into its final stage of development.[5]

According to Hall, the world in 1860 stood at the tail end of a great era of "individual freedom." Inspired by Hegel, he divided human history into periods, which he believed engaged each other in dialectical fashion. Hall explained that the inexorable progress of history would usher in the millennium by building on the accomplishments of the ages. During the nineteenth century, he explained, the masses had seized power for themselves from the consolidated despotisms of the past. While that important development had many positive consequences for human liberty, the disintegration of the American republic, which he attributed to the influence in the North of "foreign and radical ideas," proved to Hall that the world also faced the negative effects of extreme equality. Slavery and the Confederate Revolution, he believed, would lead the world into a stable and harmonious "period of conservatism."[6]

Such a position raised awkward questions about the Confederate war's relationship to past progressive struggles. As historians Eugene Genovese and Elizabeth Fox-Genovese have shown, the wars and revolutions of the late eighteenth century and the early nineteenth put white southern thinkers in a difficult intellectual predicament. While they approved of the destruction of monarchy and aristocracy in favor of republican governments, they worried about the attacks on slavery that increasingly accompanied progressive change. Still, Confederates did not abandon their support for the most basic goals of the revolutionaries of the past century; instead, they offered ideas for how they might be perfected. The lessons of the past seemed to suggest that too much liberty had led to destructive license. An emphasis on universal equality had led to class conflict, which, in turn, caused the failure of every major European nationalist revolution since 1789. By the time war broke out in America in 1861, Confederates had convinced themselves that racial slavery alone could provide a solid basis for successful nationalism.[7]

Southern nationalists never abandoned their celebration of the principles of self-determination. They frequently drew on European examples as well as America's revolutionary heritage. They most often celebrated the ordered liberty of the early American republic, which afforded political rights to all white male property-holders, and embraced the right of revolution for those they deemed worthy to exercise it. William Hall argued that the South's bid for independence sought only to conserve "the perfection of republican government" embodied in the original values of the American Revolution, and adopted by the most responsible European revolutionaries, like the Polish and Hungarian gentry. One Confederate pamphleteer spoke for many when he praised the founding fathers for combining "the saving element of English conservatism" with "a liberal infusion of the Democracy of France." The resulting constitution proved "conservative, yet elastic." It "restrains, without oppressing; and protects, without infringing the equal rights and liberties of an equal people," he concluded.[8]

As the Federals announced their new policy of emancipation, however, they could not help but be reminded that revolutions had not always adhered to such conservative principles. The French Revolution of 1789, first and foremost, had introduced to the world new principles in the struggle for progress. Most white southerners initially celebrated the French Revolution for its promise to spread the principles of republicanism. Though white southerners continued to approve of self-determination, the slave revolt in Haiti and the excesses of the terror quickly cooled their ardor for all other French doctrines. Two articles in *DeBow's Review* denounced the French for their attempt "to reorganize society upon the principle of strict political and social equality," and blamed the failure of the French to create a lasting republic on the workings of the "democratic spirit" left "unchecked by conservative restraints." Frank H. Alfriend, writing in the *Southern Literary Messenger*, learned from the lessons of the French Revolution that "pure democracy is indeed a form of despotism . . . utterly repugnant to the true spirit of liberty." Albert Taylor Bledsoe explained that the damaging doctrines of absolute equality and the "inalienable rights of men" were "born in France" and "cradled" in that country's revolution.[9]

Even more disturbing were the principles of abolitionism, first promoted by some members of the French general assembly. The fruits of their heresy could be seen in what Bledsoe considered the "diabolical massacres of St. Domingo." According to Bledsoe, "les Amis des Noirs" of the first French Revolution had formed a "prototype" for the "friends of the Blacks at Boston." Together, they spread dangerously radical notions of racial equality throughout the world. By the time of the Civil War, Confederates believed that what they called "black republicans," best exemplified by northern abolitionists and the revolutionaries of Haiti, threatened national unity and stability on both sides of the Atlantic. In the estimation of white southerners, these black republicans had perverted the true meaning of republican government by insisting upon racial equality.[10]

Many Confederates argued that these dangerous doctrines of universal equality did not die with the French and Haitian revolutions. For many southern observers, the revolutions of 1848 provided a particularly complicated case in point. While they applauded and indeed seized upon their advocacy of self-determination, Confederates believed that Europeans had failed in 1848 to create lasting nations because of the attachment of some of the revolutionaries to radical social and economic change. Americus Featherman, a contributor to *DeBow's Review*, blamed the failure of the revolutions of 1848, and the failure of the French Revolution of 1789, on the attempt to provide "strict political and social equality" to all men. A correspondent of the *Richmond Enquirer*, identified only as "E. Y.," used the case of the "discontented" people of Austria as an example. The efforts of the country's most moderate revolutionaries, claimed "E. Y.," had been repeatedly hijacked by the "more radical" who demanded "the same latitudinarian liberty which more than once deluged Europe with blood." The Reverend William Hall agreed. He praised the American Revolution's "noble *protest of individual freedom*," but believed that those principles had been carried too far in the subsequent revolutions it inspired. German "transcendentalism" and French "materialism" had, according to Hall, placed too much emphasis on the rights of the individual. "Individual liberty," he lamented, now took imperial precedence over "every interest of society." That development, he believed, explained the failure of recent nationalist movements in Europe. "Chiefly for this reason poor Poland had bled and struggled in vain," he cried, "and sweet Erin lies shorn of her strength and beauty." Would the United States share their fate?[11]

The revolutions of 1848 provided an instructive lesson not only because they failed to vindicate the principles of nationalist self-determination, but also because they built upon the legacy of the French Revolution by introducing to the Western world new definitions of liberty. By the mid-nineteenth century, many European radicals had advanced beyond the first French revolutionaries in thinking about equality in economic as well as political terms. Socialists and communists argued that workers had the right to the full value of the products that their hard work produced. It seemed unjust that wealthy owners of shops and factories prospered off of the labor of others while wage workers and the unemployed starved. In 1848, the French were the first to experiment with socialism by establishing national workshops that would provide a subsistence wage to all workers who lacked one. Slaveholding southern planters considered these new doctrines of economic equality nothing less than an attack on the rights of property, whether those rights involved land, cash, or people.

Though no historian has yet uncovered evidence that any southerners read Karl Marx's *Communist Manifesto*, "they did not have to," as historians Elizabeth Fox-Genovese and Eugene Genovese have pointed out. White southerners saw the ideas of communism and socialism catching fire around them, and they denounced their effects on social stability and national life. In 1862, George Fitzhugh explained to the Confederate readers of *DeBow's Review* that "socialists" threatened modern civilization by seeking to dismantle all forms of exploitation and restraint, which he considered necessary for the survival of all societies. One editorial in the *Richmond Daily Examiner* contrasted the success of the South with the failure of the French to achieve a lasting republic in 1848. The author, as had Louisa McCord before him, blamed Alphonse de Lamartine, the president of the provisional French republic, for giving in to the demands of the masses for the "right to work." The article reminded readers that "Lamartine announced that the State must furnish labour for its citizens," which, the *Examiner*'s editors contended, subverted "the true function of government." The editors argued that Lamartine's attempt to "eke out any man's income by class legislation" had sealed the fate of the French republic. "On this theory his Government broke down," they declared, "and the common sense of the age dismissed him as a dreamer and visionary theorist."[12]

White southern thinkers blamed the failure of nationalism in Europe on the radical ideologies of socialism, communism, and extreme equality, which they most often conflated and called "red republicanism." Red republicans, white southerners feared, would betray the cause of self-determination and introduce anarchy into global politics by attacking property rights and economic privilege in the name of universal equality. In the summer of 1865, for instance, the southern diarist Catherine Devereux Edmondston denounced the freed slaves' desire for land as red republicanism. The *New York Herald* exhibited a similar understanding of the term by pointing out the southern fear that "proletarianism" would soon become the modern substitute for abolitionism. "The rights of property," Confederates warned, would be "discussed as a religious question, involving sin in the capitalist and dire oppression, to be resisted to the blood by those whom accumulated wealth employs."[13]

The term "red republicanism," along with "black republicanism," filled the writings of Confederate citizens, statesmen, and journalists throughout the war. They were much more than simple rhetorical epithets. They referred to a comprehensive worldview that identified dangers to representative government across the globe. While Confederate supporters continued to celebrate America's conservative revolution, and conceded that they shared with northerners and European radicals a commitment to republican government, they feared and derided the innovations introduced by some of the most extreme progressives of the nineteenth century. As the war deepened, Confederate spokesmen stood convinced that the world was awash in utopian schemes like abolitionism, socialism, and communism. They called these maladies "isms," and believed they undermined not just Europe, but the United States and Western civilization itself. Albert Taylor Bledsoe pointed out to his readers that "the French are not the only people who care but little for liberty, while they are crazy for equality." He feared that the "same blind passion" that had disturbed the Old World was possible "even in this enlightened portion of the globe."[14]

By 1863, many southerners had become convinced that European "isms" of all kinds had infected northern society, as a characteristic article in the *Richmond Daily Examiner* pointed out. Edward Pollard blamed the popularity of isms in the North on New England public schools and their propensity to teach "a vain passion for reform, infidelity, and the agitations of revolution." A contributor to the *Southern Literary Messenger*, identified only as "An Alabamian," praised the South for its freedom from isms and denounced the "free-soilism, Mormonism, free-loveism, and abolitionism" that disgraced the North. He declared that political ferment in the North, as it had in France, produced not only a healthy regard for the right to self-government, but also "infidelity and socialism." The Reverend William Hall agreed that America's democratic beginning had made her people especially susceptible to the radical ideologies that troubled and thwarted Europe. Northern society in particular, he argued, had proved particularly susceptible to the "French atheism" of Thomas Paine and the "Transcendental Philosophy of Germany" that had influenced abolitionism and had "given birth to almost every other *ism* that afflicts that people." The *Index* triumphantly printed a letter from an English traveler in America praising the South for distinguishing between "democracy and red republicanism."[15]

One of the most frightening of these isms was the specter of "agrarianism," which many southerners linked to communism, socialism, and red republicanism. Southern thinkers derived the concept of "agrarianism" from the ancient world. Tiberius and Gaius Gracchus of Rome, in an effort to revive the fortunes of the declining middle and lower classes, divided the estates of the wealthy and distributed them to the people. Though their efforts ultimately failed in the face of conservative reaction, Confederate thinkers feared their tactics had been revived in a misguided attempt to solve the problems of the modern world. Americus Featherman believed that all free-labor societies, given their commitment to social equality and the blurring of distinctions between the "labor class" and the "supervisory and intellectual class," inevitably adopted policies of agrarianism. Frank Alfriend argued that too much democracy led to a "spirit of leveling agrarianism" that "sought to equalize all," and he denounced the "Fourierites" and "Socialists" of the North whom he accused of "Roman agrarianism." The *Charleston Mercury* declared that northern "Republicanism" consisted of nothing more than "Radical Mobocracy—the will of the majority—Agrarianism, Red Republicanism."[16]

Confederate partisans argued that the North had weakened the antebellum republic by increasingly accepting the more radical doctrines that had doomed Europe's nationalities in 1848 and 1849. The American Revolution of 1776, they believed, had established a well-ordered republic that offered self-government to all white citizens. Some Europeans had attempted to follow its example in 1848. Confederates feared, however, that nineteenth-century progressives' increasing emphasis on racial and economic equality subverted the original intention of the republic and threatened its very existence. The *Richmond Enquirer* blamed sectional strife on the deterioration of northern democracy, a democracy that had been "changed and degraded into the Radicalism which deluged Europe with blood at the end of the last century, and which shook its thrones again in the convulsions of 1848." Northern politicians, the editors charged, had adopted "all the radicalism, the discontent, the poverty and the crime of Europe," thereby threatening "Republican freedom." The editors of the *Index* similarly denounced the "New World apotheosis of vulgarity and democracy," which, they believed, had too often been "preached to the nations of the earth as the approach of a political and social millennium." The white South, the paper believed, now fought the "world's battles" against this "insidious social disease" that had made "alarming progress" and had to be "fought" in "all countries."[17]

The architects of Confederate nationalism noted that the modern world, unlike the world of 1776, offered several competing theories of republican government. They hoped that their revolution would help the world sort through some of those competing philosophies, as had most of the violent uprisings of the past century. Confederates hoped to conserve what they took to be the original goals of the American Revolution and the best goals of 1848 by discrediting republicanism of the new black and red varieties. One Confederate supporter coined the term "white republicanism" to describe the South's nationalist project. In a book intended for circulation at home and abroad, he took the pen name "White Republican." He began by declaring that, as an American, he was "by birth and education a *Republican*." In his effort to promote the Confederate cause he explained that he adopted "the word '*white*' in order not to be confounded with either the '*Black* Republicans' or the '*Red* Republicans.'" The "white republican" banner called attention to the South's attachment to representative government while making clear that Confederates disagreed with those who would include African Americans in civic life. At the same time, the moniker reemphasized Confederate commitment to the rights of self-determination while rejecting the radical anarchic socialism that Confederates believed had doomed the revolutions of 1848.[18]

Confederate thinkers acknowledged that southerners had once found much to admire in the revolutionaries of Europe. Indeed, they argued that the South acted in the tradition of the European nationalists of 1848 who had fought for the rights of self-determination. They hoped that the Confederacy would succeed where others had failed by eliminating radical social goals from the revolutionary agenda. In the process, an independent South would provide an example for the entire world to follow. The editors of the *Index* triumphantly reprinted an article that asserted that the Confederacy never indulged in "such crimes and excesses as have often marred the brilliancy of struggles for national freedom." A. Dudley Mann assured the Belgian foreign minister that Confederates rejected all "Utopian theories." The *Charleston Mercury* likewise praised the Confederate revolution for its lack of "vain social theorists." The paper took comfort from the fact that "no Kossuth, no Mazzini, no Louis Blanc" could be found among southern statesmen. The editors held that if Confederates had tainted self-determination with radical ideology as Europeans had done in 1848, the Confederacy would have crumbled just as quickly as France, Germany, and Hungary. "Riot and confusion would have ensued," the editors wrote, "and Anarchy, with torch, stake and scaffold-blood, barricade and guillotine, would have driven her blood stained chariot wheels over the ruins of the Confederacy."[19]

As emancipation progressed, the supporters of the Confederacy increasingly insisted that the southern nation introduced a new kind of progressive force to the world—a republicanism that eschewed radicalism and unrest. Dr. Cartwright, writing in *DeBow's Review*, believed that the Confederate experiment would "demonstrate the strength, stability and permanency of a government founded on natural instead of artificial distinctions in society." An unnamed Texan explained that, like the imagined government of White Republican, his ideal government combined "liberty" with "order and law." He declared himself "heart and soul a democrat" but only "*as we* in the Confederacy *understand democracy*." Henry Hotze coined the term "liberal conservatism" in explaining the Confederate project. His concept stressed the willingness of Confederates to embrace modernity tempered by caution. Hotze declared that the South's new doctrine meant "progress without subversion, liberty with order, fraternity without equality, love & good-will to all men without professional philanthropy." By avoiding extreme doctrines, it would oppose "Yankeeism of whichever hemisphere and whatever tongue or nationality."[20]

Confederate nationalists took no pains to hide the fact that slavery would occupy an important place in their new republic. Indeed, they regarded it as the key to their nationalist experiment. Only subordination of the working class could prevent the spread of anarchic socialism in Europe and America. Like many of their northern adversaries, Confederates believed that race in America played the role of class in Europe. While a growing number of northerners argued that true nationalism could be achieved only by removing illegitimate wealth and power based on distinctions of race and class, Confederates argued that the republican experiment could succeed only by maintaining those distinctions. Maintaining slavery, they held, prevented the class divisions among whites that manifested themselves in the radical doctrines of socialism and communism. Racial slavery especially, Confederates believed, provided the social stability necessary for any viable nationality. The South, like Europe's most successful nations, one article maintained, "eschewed" the "doctrine of political equality" because it contained "a real and marked social distinction of classes." To make the African American "the free citizen of a free country, equal with the white man," the editorial argued, "would be to carry out logically that principle of equality which European democrats deduce from American precedents." The *Richmond Enquirer* considered slavery the South's "guaranty against mob-law, our bulwark against anarchy and socialism." The *Enquirer* contended, "It [slavery] makes our democracy safe and substantial and is the life and strength of our social organization." Robert R. Howison, writing in the *Southern Literary Messenger*, took a similar stance in asserting that slavery allowed for harmony between "the highest, the middle, and the lowest classes." Another editorialist agreed: "Those institutions supply us with that just and humane balance between capital and labor which society in Europe so deeply needs" and too often sought "in their various theories of communism."[21]

Slavery, Confederates argued, provided the stability that nations needed in modern times. Recent history had taught Confederates that, without slavery, class conflict would lead to the disintegration of all civil society. Such an observation did not augur well for the future of the North. As a result, Confederates argued that through secession they sought not to destroy the Union, but only to abandon the sinking ship. The *New York Herald* reported that throughout the war "sundry Southern journals" daily predicted "riots, conflagrations and hangings" in the northern states. Americus Featherman predicted that northern laborers "urged on by poverty, hunger, and destitution" would inevitably raise "the war cry of social equality." The *Richmond Enquirer* detected the "elements of a terrible revolution" in the future of the North. Opposition to the rights of slaveholders, the *Enquirer* editors maintained, signaled not humanitarianism, but seething resentment for the capitalist social order. The article warned that abolitionism was only a manifestation of the desire of the poor to strip property from the wealthy. The paper asserted that "beneath the thin crust of Black Republican hostility to the South, there rage the awful fires of civil anarchy and social chaos." The editors charged that northern conservatives and "Northern capital" trembled for "safety" from the "laboring classes" and "hordes of hungry and reckless men." They believed that Lincoln and his advisors constituted "revolutionary committees" that hoped to use the war, the slave question, and the promise of confiscation to distract the "fearful mob" and "precipitate upon the South all the dangerous element of free society." The defeat of northern armies, they believed, would precipitate a crisis in the remaining states of the Union. The paper predicted that greedy soldiers would "sack New York" instead of southern plantations, and universal "anarchy and crime" would then "reign over the free States of the late Union."[22]

Events in the North seemed to confirm these apocalyptic predictions. The New York City draft riots of 1863 offered proof to many Confederates of northern society's downward spiral. In July of that year, New York exploded in violence as working-class whites, including large contingents of Irish immigrants, sacked government offices and lynched free blacks in protest of emancipation and the draft. Although the Lincoln administration succeeded in quelling the rioters, the incident showed Confederates that the radicalism inherent in the northern government's policies would undermine the North's effort at nation-building. Europe's nationalist revolutions in 1848 and 1849 had failed for the same reasons, Confederate editors believed. The *Index* argued that the riots marked "the sad beginning of a revolution produced by the oppression of the working classes." The *Richmond Enquirer* jokingly observed in July 1863 that working-class New Yorkers had been initiated into the "mysteries of the barricades" by the "accomplished professors in the celebrated Parisian university of revolution." An observer in New York mistakenly believed the mob favored emancipation, but made a similar comparison in a letter to the Paris correspondent of the *Index* in which he blamed the draft riots on radical ideology. "These black Republicans," he wrote, "are also Red Republicans; their heroes are the heroes of the Red Republic in Europe, whose portraits decorate the walls of the lager beer-cellars where they congregate." He compared the spectacle to an uprising in Paris or Lyon and marveled that "even a few barricades at last appeared." The supposed radicalism of the rioters served as a warning to the South of the political consequences of defeat. One article asserted that if the South were "subjugated" then "its lands" would be "parceled out among those who commit such crimes."[23]

Many Confederate observers, though they welcomed moderate European revolutionaries to their ranks, argued that the presence of large numbers of immigrants in the North abetted the trend toward radical democracy. The results could be observed in the declension of northern society. A. Jeffery, writing in the *Southern Literary Messenger*, linked the rise of abolitionism and "European Red Republicanism" in New England to immigration from the Old Country. A writer known as "Fowler" warned against the establishment of manufacturing industries lest it attract "European infidelity and socialism." White Republican attributed the radicalism of the Republican Party in part to the presence of "trade unions, German turners,

"Sacking Brooks's Clothing Store." Confederates believed that the draft riots in New York City offered proof of northern society's descent into radicalism and class conflict. (Courtesy of Prints and Photographs Division, Library of Congress, Washington, D.C., LC-USZ62-16601)

Irish associations, &c." in the "Wide-Awake" militia clubs. A contributor to *DeBow's Review* pointed to the antislavery sentiment of the foreign-born population in St. Louis and the border South as proof of the radicalism of European immigrants. A writer known as "Signa" explained to readers of the *Southern Literary Messenger* that the Confederacy fought against the "mad agrarianism" of the "scum" of Europe and the "reddest of all German red republicans" who had settled in the American West. More than one article in the *Index* asserted that the influx of the foreign born rendered the North "more radical, more fond of change, more ultra-Democratic," while the South still clung to "the political traditions and institutions of the fathers of the Republic."[24]

In the wake of emancipation, many Confederates feared that the most extreme foreign revolutionaries also influenced the U.S. military. They denounced the presence in the Union armies of what many southerners considered some of the most radical of the immigrants and forty-eighters. White Republican wildly and erroneously estimated that the "Northern army . . . is composed of forty-one per cent of Irish and Germans, to say nothing of other alien nationalities." A. Dudley Mann told the Belgian foreign minister that the Union army was filled with "German, Irish, and other European mercenaries," and one Confederate attacked General Franz Sigel, whose revolutionary fame had won him admirers across the North. The traveler Fitzgerald Ross ridiculed the many German immigrants who had settled in the North after 1848. He sarcastically labeled them "*Freiheits helden* [*sic*]," or heroes of freedom, who, he believed, had "left their country for their country's good," only to become as much of a "nuisance" in the New World as they had been in the Old. University of Virginia professor Basil Lanneau Gildersleeve, though he had sympathized with the struggle for self-determination in 1848, saw little reason to believe that those who had embraced radicalism in Europe, thereby dooming their nations, would enjoy any more success in America. He encouraged Confederates to eschew the aid of radicals and leave them to their fate in the North. "The Southerner, especially," Gildersleeve cautioned, "has good reason to turn with aversion from all the 'democratic' movements of Germany; for he recognizes in the Yankee crusade a strong infusion of the German spirit, and among the crusaders themselves a considerable sprinkling of the actors, some ridiculous, some brutal, who have been hustled off the German stage."[25]

In the first two years of the war, the policies of the federal government offered Confederates confirmation of their fears that northern society was deteriorating under the influence of the worst kind of European radicalism. Confederates denounced the suspension of civil liberties in states like Maryland and recoiled at the adoption of "hard war" policies that brought destruction to the southern home front. Confederate representatives found Lincoln's decision to sanction the confiscation of Confederate property and land even more disturbing. By 1863, the Treasury Department took possession of abandoned plantations and seized stores of cotton. Confederates maintained that such acts arose from a premeditated policy that threatened Western civilization as a whole. They pointed to recent history to make their case. The most radical revolutionaries in Europe had often attacked the rights of property, and white southerners believed that the North now followed their example. One editorial in the *Index* cited the influence of "five hundred thousand Yankees and Irishmen and Germans" on policies that resulted in "tens of thousands of estates confiscated; tens of thousands of families driven into exile; a nation denationalized by the destruction of all that gives to a people national life and unity of spirit." Another expressed similar sentiments by reprinting the remarks of Robert J. Walker, delivered before Pittsburgh's Democratic committee in 1856. The Republican Party, he charged, advocated "doctrines agrarian and revolutionary, subjecting all property to division or confiscation." "The truth is," he told his audience, "the Black Republican platform is revolutionary and agrarian; it involves principles which must strike down the tenure of all property in every state as well as in every territory of the Union." White Republican agreed. The Lincoln administration, he claimed, had sanctioned an "incalculable amount of private robbery and official theft . . . unequaled in the annals of the rottenest of Republics." He asserted that the "white men" who opposed such measures languished "enslaved and imprisoned" in direct violation of constitutional law. Such abuses, derived from the red republican style, demonstrated for the Confederate supporter the nature of "black Republican liberty."[26]

The seizure and liberation of slaves received the most criticism. Confederates argued among themselves and to the world that emancipation did not involve the issues of slavery and human freedom. Instead, emancipation engaged the principles of property rights and anarchic socialism that had increasingly concerned the modern world. A citizen of New Orleans wrote a letter to the editors of the *Index* declaring that Unionists fought only to posses the "property of the South." An editorial in the same paper claimed that "northern soldiers" and "New England abolitionists" took their inspiration from French theorist Pierre Proudhon, the "extremist of communists and Red Republicans" who declared that "all property is robbery." Another asserted that "abolitionism," "infidelity," and "French and German socialism" were linked "political theories." The *Richmond Daily Examiner* believed the war had "attracted the attention of Europe" for that very reason. "Behind the proximate causes of the war," the paper declared, "lies the spoliation of slave property and vested rights." The editors held that an attack upon these principles "strikes at the titles of all property and throws all goods of life into one general scramble for the bold or adroit robber." A caucus of Confederate clergy met to reinforce these opinions on the home front. The group issued a joint "appeal" that linked emancipation with European socialism. The religious leaders told southerners that "the same class of persons" who supported abolitionism also espoused "heresies of a kind unparalleled," heresies that included "communism," "women's rights," and "Free Love."[27]

As the war progressed, Confederates grew increasingly confident that their struggle would prove vital to the peace of the world. They believed they fought to halt the spread of the threatening ideologies of communism and abolitionism that had infected not just the United States but the world. Confederates frequently pointed out that the ties of sympathy between radicals on both sides of the Atlantic would prove particularly dangerous for the stability of European nations, as well as the United States. Victory for the Union would bolster the cause of radical reform in the Old Country, Confederates warned. George Fitzhugh attributed the Czar's decision to free the serfs to the "Jeffersonian-French fever" that he believed would produce nothing but "red republican hymns, riots, barricades, and bloody revolutions." White Republican stressed the hostility that all manner of "theoretical democrats, whether of the Black Republican or of the Red Republican stripe," held against kings and their realms. An editorial in the *Index* claimed, "The masses of the North—composed, as they are, of fragments of every nation on earth—absolutely hate the social institutions of England." Several observers noted that prominent Irishmen in the North planned to renew the struggle for Irish independence, including a citizen in Halifax who asserted that the Civil War was being used as "neutral soil" to drill Irish soldiers for future use in England. One editorial in the *Index* summed up the far-reaching importance for Britain these developments held: "The Radical journals, it is true, are incessantly urging that the success of Northern arms is proof of the triumph of democracy, and throwing out warnings of their coming fate on what they are pleased to call the aristocracy of England."[28]

Confederate agents cemented their point by arguing that the most dangerously radical classes in Europe favored the North. The *Richmond Enquirer* printed a letter from a supportive Frenchman who argued that the majority of his fellow nationals sympathized with the South. The only exceptions could be found, he argued, among "the demagogues, the Red Republicans, the Communists," and those "who decreed the abolition of slavery in the colonies" in 1848. Another observer agreed. The leading pronorthern paper in France, this observer warned, displayed "radical and communist principles" and "diligently sought to keep alive and stimulate that senseless prejudice in the French mind on the subject of slavery." The *Index* spoke of the "unrelenting" opposition of "the Red Republicans of Germany" toward the southern cause. More than a few articles in the Confederate press attacked the Europeans who supported the North, Europeans including "socialists" like Louis Blanc and Alphonse de Lamartine, and British reformer John Bright, who was accused of wishing to seize "the lands of the rich" so that they might be "divided among the poor." One editorial asserted that radical politicians in England naturally coupled support for the Union with "bitter denunciations of the possessors of hereditary wealth and influence," "attacks on the holders of property in land,"

and suggestions that parliament enable poor men to become landholders by ordering "a general confiscation and gratuitous distribution of landed property."[29]

Even as slavery and the nation it had sustained collapsed under the weight of northern arms in 1864 and 1865, Confederates held firm faith in the worldwide importance of their mission. They continued to hope for recognition abroad, even as their case grew more difficult by the day. Until the bitter end, they expected action from Europe. History told them that the principles of the Confederate revolution demanded the support of the world. "E. Y." pointed out that Great Britain had fought the revolutionary legions of France and quelled Chartist demonstrations in England. Surely Great Britain would aid the South by opposing red republicanism in America, too. England, he pointed out, had already proved "willing to spend untold sums of money to kill" radicalism, which he compared to a "hydra . . . threatening the civilization and wholesome progress" of the European continent. The people of the South, he asserted, were "now found battling against the imported spawn of this dire enemy to mankind." England must have felt "equally bound to at least throw her moral weight in the scale" on behalf of the Confederate states. White Republican also believed that the inevitable success of the Confederate cause would uphold the self-interest of all those who valued stable government and a well-regulated social order. He held out hope that Europeans would eventually succumb to reason and help defend those principles in America, thereby winning the admiration of all thoughtful statesmen throughout the world. "The conservative and wealthy class of citizens on both sides," he argued, "would hail such an act of friendly interposition with delight."[30]

No interposition was forthcoming. In mid-1863, the Confederate department of state had recalled James Mason, minister to Great Britain, in protest for that country's lack of attention to Confederate agents. Mason joined A. Dudley Mann, John Slidell, and others in a quixotic quest to talk Napoleon III, Pope Pius IX, and King Leopold I of Belgium into recognizing the Confederacy and intervening in the Civil War. At home, the new southern nation began its slow but bloody collapse. The Union policies of emancipation, confiscation, and hard war devastated the southern economy and the peculiar institution on which it depended. At the same time, U.S. armies methodically battered southern defenders into submission. When Robert E. Lee surrendered his Army of Northern Virginia to Ulysses S. Grant at Appomattox Court House in April 1865, most southerners abandoned the hope of establishing an independent Confederacy.

Still, even among the wreckage of the southern nation, some of the Confederacy's supporters clung to the belief that their expiring nationalist experiment was the world's most effective model of republican government. Confederate supporters had always believed that their revolution represented the solution to the problems of nationalism that troubled the mid-nineteenth-century Atlantic world. Their revolution would eschew the class conflict and radical social goals that had ultimately doomed so many of Europe's aspiring nations. Now that Confederates' so carefully constructed alternative had been cast aside, no observer could foresee the consequences. Henry Hotze, for one, refused to abandon the fear that the defeat of the Confederacy foretold a dire fate for the North and the world. He failed to grasp that emancipation would produce a stronger nation. He wrote to a correspondent in New York in late April 1865 that although "the armed resistance of the South [was] about to cease," the United States stood "on the eve of a civil revolution more momentous than the war itself."[31]

As had many of his southern countrymen, Hotze believed that the North had made a disastrous error in accepting the radical doctrines of emancipation and confiscation. Hotze asserted that even in defeat the South's racial hierarchy offered a more stable basis for lasting nationality than the North's apparently successful effort at reunification. He felt certain that most northern whites would refuse to accept what he called "the Africanization of the Union" as an "equivalent of its 'restoration.'" Hotze believed that citizenship rights for African Americans could only be maintained with the use of armed force, which would inevitably turn the U.S. government into a "centralized despotism."[32]

Hotze believed that only if northerners rejected the radical theories that had led to emancipation, then a viable nation could be salvaged from the wreckage of war. Indeed, in such circumstances, Hotze was willing to stay on hand to reconstruct a white republic. "If there is manhood and common sense enough left in the victorious section," he wrote, "to construct a white man's government out of the smoldering ruins that negrophilism & all the other accursed isms of your section have left, I should like to have my part in the work." If northerners did not reject their radical theories, Hotze would stay away from his adopted country. The American nation, he argued, would join the other failed experiments of the age in presenting "the miserable spectacle of the South and Central American Republics."[33]

Conclusion

American Nationalism and the
Nineteenth-Century World

AS THE CONFEDERATE NATION COLLAPSED IN 1865 UNDER THE
weight of unrelenting military pressure, Ernest Duvergier de Hauranne remained on hand to witness its death throes. The French thinker marveled
at the grandeur of a struggle that had been carried on for so long by the
people of two republics without ever succumbing to dictatorship or dema-
goguery. The history of the French Revolution, the revolutions of 1848, and
so many other conflicts of the recent past had demonstrated how often
violence had led the way to political tyranny. That had not happened in
America. "Enormous armies sprang into being in a few weeks," Duvergier
de Hauranne declared in awe, "and after five years they were discharged
in several months without trouble, without disorder, without causing the
slightest peril to the freedom of the country." Duvergier de Hauranne believed Americans had succeeded in fighting a "people's" war, whereas Europeans had failed, because of the strength of their representative institutions. "Great revolutions reveal the true character of a people and the real
value of the institutions that govern it," he asserted.[1]

He lavished most of his praise on the supporters of the Union. Duvergier
de Hauranne interpreted Union victory as a vindication of the principle
of nationality, as would many observers after him. He hailed the defeat
of the Confederacy as a reaffirmation of the importance of national unity,
integrity, and strength. He assumed with the benefit of hindsight that the
United States had been destined to prevail in the American struggle. The
law of nations had foreordained it. The United States had been a strong
and viable nation before the war, he reasoned, and would remain one regardless of any disorder, discord, and strife that might trouble it. Indeed,
the North's great victory reminded Duvergier de Hauranne of his own
country's experience during the late 1780s and 1790s. "France emerged
from the Revolution to find itself once again a nation, as united as in the

past," he wrote. The French intellectual had no reason to assume that the national future of the United States would prove any different. "Civil wars may bathe a nation in blood and may even dismember it," he declared, "but they never completely destroy it."[2]

Indeed, Duvergier de Hauranne held that the United States would surpass the nations of Europe in presenting the world with a stable model of nation-building. He even foreshadowed Bismarck's conception of conservative nationalism as he condemned the Confederacy to the ash heap of failed revolutionary movements. The South, he pointed out, had fought to break up a government, not to consolidate national authority and power. "I become indignant each time I hear talk of the 'great conservative cause of the South,'" he raged. "The South," he scoffed, "is conservative of nothing except slavery." The North, by contrast, had defended the principles of consolidation and centralization, so crucial to nineteenth-century projects of nation-building. The North, he pointed out, had "taken up arms only in order to defend national unity and the rule of law." Duvergier de Hauranne argued that the Union cause was too often "labeled revolutionary," emancipation notwithstanding. "Make no mistake," he advised his European readers, "the men of the North are the true conservatives."[3]

Still, Duvergier de Hauranne found himself forced to admit that the Confederacy had looked very much like a nation during its brief life. He conceded that the white South's attempt at self-determination perfectly conformed to the spirit of the nineteenth century. "I am aware," he wrote, "that today nations are in fashion and that this sonorous word is considered the answer to everything." As a result, he admitted, many Europeans had embraced the Confederate cause regardless of its faults. They overlooked the barbarism of slavery, he confessed, because white southerners had presented slavery as "a national cause." Even Duvergier de Hauranne had found something to admire in the white South's struggle. "There is," he mused, "something heroic, in this perseverance on the part of a small population which, though cut off, invaded and decimated for two years, still finds resources to stand up against the immense strength of the Union." He wondered if he should grant them the benefit of Edmund Burke's belief that a true nation, once established, could never be "obliterated." The Confederacy, he finally concluded after careful consideration, might have founded an independent polity, but it had not existed long enough to establish a permanent pedigree. "I am perfectly willing to admit," Duvergier de Hauranne conceded, "that a nation should be inviolable when its roots are profoundly planted in history. But it needs at least some time to take shape; it can't be improvised in four years."[4]

Duvergier de Hauranne had difficulty concealing his ambivalence. While he morally objected to the white South's embrace of slavery, he could not easily convince himself that the Confederacy had not been a nation. The dilemma troubled the doctrinaire liberal. Shouldn't the South have been granted the right of self-determination after all? The Irish, the Italians, the Germans, and the Hungarians had been applauded in 1848 for very similar revolutionary endeavors. The Latin Americans, the Belgians, and the Poles had, at other times and on other occasions, received the blessing of the century's most modern thinkers. Some of the nationalist heroes of those recent movements had also once held serfs or slaves. The Confederacy's cause did not appear radically different from the more ideologically palatable revolutionary projects of the recent past.

Duvergier de Hauranne's confusion is understandable. Two American nations fought for existence between 1861 and 1865. Armed force would ultimately settle the question on the battlefield. In the meantime, however, advocates fought in the realm of diplomacy and public opinion. Nineteenth-century thinkers and politicians believed wholeheartedly in the existence of a "family of nations." In order for a polity to cement its independence, it had to be welcomed into the circle of nations through recognition by its fellow members. The United States and the Confederacy worked hard to convince the world's powers that they were entitled to recognition as inviolable nations. Both sides described themselves to the world in their newspapers, diplomatic dispatches, and official pronouncements. In the process, they developed one of the clearest and most thorough definitions of nationalism the nineteenth century ever produced.

The two sides shared a remarkable number of assumptions. The similarities of their descriptions teach us not only about the North and the South, but also about the developing ideology of nationalism in the nineteenth century. Both Unionists and Confederates held a millennialist faith in the development of the world's growing "family of nations." They both believed that the establishment of nation-states would bring harmony, unending peace, and unbroken prosperity to the globe. To observers living in the middle of the nineteenth century, the recent past seemed to confirm that the path of world progress lay in violent nationalist upheaval. The wars and revolutions of the preceding decades had demonstrated that nations could only be forged through violence. Oppressed peoples in Europe and

North and South America had been struggling for more than fifty years to replace kingdoms with nation-states and monarchies with republics. Some had succeeded and some had failed, and the fate of society on both sides of the Atlantic still hung in the balance in 1860.

For that reason, both northerners and southerners in America believed that the outcome of their civil war held urgent importance for the future of the world. The shape and content of the nation-state had not yet taken final form. The war in America would give northerners and southerners the chance to influence the development of the nation-state as their predecessors had in 1776. The revolutions Americans had witnessed in Europe in 1848 dramatically revealed the principles at stake. New and dangerous ideologies threatened to undermine the stable society of nations that had been developing since the first American Revolution. Northerners looked with alarm at the apparently growing tendency of legitimate nations to fracture as leaders on both sides of the Atlantic repeatedly used force to thwart the will of the people. Many northerners became convinced that a cabal of aristocrats whose power rested on land, slaves, and inherited privilege stood behind these developments. Only the utter defeat and destruction of those classes on both sides of the Atlantic would ensure a stable future for the world's nations and peoples. Confederates, on the other hand, believed that society was disintegrating in Europe and America under the influence of radical doctrines such as socialism, communism, and human equality. They believed that only their "white republic," based on slavery, could successfully balance representative government with national stability.

Americans in the North and in the South believed that the outcome of the Civil War would go a long way toward resolving these troubling problems. They recognized, however, that events contemporaneous with their revolution engaged some of the very same issues. Nineteenth-century people throughout the world, Americans believed, were struggling to define the relationship between race, class, and nation.

One episode in particular seemed to illustrate that point. In 1864, Emperor Napoleon III moved to install a puppet ruler, Archduke Ferdinand Maximilian of Austria, upon the Mexican throne. Napoleon hoped to capitalize on the United States' distraction with the Civil War by reestablishing a European empire in Latin America. Many northerners and southerners responded to events in Mexico according to the nationalist ideologies they had developed during the war. The French incursion into Mexico dramatically revealed to them the principles at stake in their own conflict. The hopes, fears, predictions, and warnings of Union and Confederate thinkers and statesmen seemed to be coming true at home and abroad.[5]

Confederates hailed the French incursion as the first foreign application of their doctrine of white republicanism. The Mexican nation's infamous instability, an editor of the *Index* asserted, had brought "a scandal and disgrace to modern civilization." He believed that Mexico had failed to progress because it lacked anything that could properly be termed "the nucleus of a nation." The Confederate author attributed Mexico's failure to establish a stable national republic to its mixed-race population. "Of the eight millions that are loosely termed Mexicans," he scoffed, "scarcely one and a half million are white, that is of pure European descent. The rest are Indians, Negroes, and the infinite mongrel breeds produced by the mixture of the races." In such a case, the author believed, European tutelage would bring welcome order to what he considered a hopeless population.[6]

Northern observers viewed the question very differently. For Union politicians and opinion-makers, Napoleon's interference in Mexico, like secession itself, represented nothing less than an aristocratic plot aimed at subverting popular government. William Henry Seward believed that Napoleon acted in Mexico out of the conviction that "a new European monarchical system can and ought to be permanently established on the American continent, and in territory bordering on this republic." The editors of *Harper's Weekly* feared that Maximilian's Mexican adventure, to which they attributed ideological motives, foreshadowed European interference in the Civil War. "The assent of the Governments of Europe to French participation in our affairs will be based upon their natural and earnest wish that a popular Government may conspicuously fail," the editors wrote, "for our success would be an inspiration to the people of Europe too threatening to be calmly contemplated by the aristocratic class." Wendell Phillips suggested that the United States retaliate by calling upon the revolutionary masses of 1848 to rise once again. "If France plants the germ of aristocracy and thrones on the soil of the American continent," he wrote, "my answer to her is that reconstructed Union holding out its right hand with $50,000,000 for Garibaldi, saying, 'Take possession of Rome,' and $100,000,000 for the republicans of Paris, saying, 'Make Napoleon sit uneasy,' and $100,000,000 for Germany, saying, 'Make kings tremble.'"[7]

The reconstructed Union did not carry its ideological fight to Europe. After the collapse of the Confederacy, the administration of President Andrew Johnson rushed U.S. troops to the Mexican border in a show of force.

Napoleon backed down. Maximilian's regime collapsed as France withdrew its support. The resolution of the crisis seemed to offer confirmation of the complete triumph of the northern conception of the future of nationalism around the world.

By 1865, northern nationalists believed that a restored United States would uphold legitimate, viable, representative governments throughout the world. The defeat of the Confederacy and the end of the French experiment in Mexico would mark the turning point in the fight against the illegitimate aristocrats and monarchs who had apparently triumphed in 1848 and 1849. Charles Francis Adams looked forward to the moment when America's "troubles" passed and her people settled "down again into a nation." He believed that the disintegration of the American republic had "revived" the "hopes" of "all the privileged classes in Europe." The defeat of the Confederacy and the French withdrawal from Mexico demonstrated to Adams, however, that the Union's principles held the key to the future of the world. Maximilian's miserable fate confirmed that the age of aristocracy had passed. "An Austrian prince aided by French soldiers," Adams concluded, "has not a very brilliant prospect in the nineteenth century of founding a dynasty." The defeat of the Confederacy and the overthrow of Maximilian would ensure, Adams believed, that "the existence of the United States as a prosperous republic" would continue to serve as the most compelling model for emerging nations to emulate in the modern world.[8]

Ironically, as the nineteenth century progressed, the boundaries between northern and southern ideas about nationalism began to blur. Americans, regardless of region, increasingly agreed that the United States would become a great nation. They believed, however, that America would define its greatness not only through its republican example, but also by expanding its borders and ruling over non-European peoples. America's ideology of republican government, they insisted, would have to be taught to less "civilized" nations. White republicanism reappeared in the form of the white man's burden as the United States extended its rule over Hawaii, Puerto Rico, Cuba, and the Philippines. The definition of American nationalism developed by Unionists and Confederates gradually merged into the ideology of American imperialism.[9]

Between 1861 and 1865, the merging of ideologies did not seem so clear. The two sides were locked in a deadly struggle for the future of the world. Unionists and Confederates alike would have considered themselves progressives who subscribed to the radical notion that national self-determination and representative government would protect the fate of liberty and civilization throughout the world. Still, they acknowledged that their struggle was not new. The patriots of the first American Revolution, they believed, had introduced those concepts to the world. The European revolutionaries of 1848 had, most recently, exposed problems and proposed principles that had not been contemplated in 1776. The American Civil War responded to both, confirming the view of Ernest Duvergier de Hauranne that "Radicalism in America looks to Europe while European Radicalism looks to America."[10]

Notes

Abbreviations

AM   American Memory, http://memory.loc.gov/ammem/index.html

CA   Chronicling America, http://chroniclingamerica.loc.gov/

CW   The Civil War: A Newspaper Perspective

CWLD   The American Civil War: Letters and Diaries

HW   HarpWeek, http://www.harpweek.com/

MOAC   The Making of America, http://moa.cit.cornell.edu/moa/

MOAM   The Making of America, http://quod.lib.umich.edu/m/moagrp/

OR   *The War of the Rebellion: A Compilation of the Official Records
          of the Union and Confederate Armies*

ORN   *Official Records of the Union and Confederate Navies*

VS   The Valley of the Shadow: Two Communities in the American
          Civil War, http://valley.vcdh.virginia.edu/

Introduction

1. Bowen, *A Frenchman in Lincoln's America*, 1:xlvii–xlviii.

2. Ibid., 1:10, 13–14, 105.

3. Ibid.

4. Hobsbawm, *The Age of Revolution*; Palmer, *The Age of the Democratic Revolution*; Anderson, *Imagined Communities*, 67, 159. Don Doyle and Marco Pamplona point out that in the early nineteenth century, nationalism was almost always tied to liberal ideals. They also discuss the importance of New World nationalism in this regard. See Doyle and Pamplona, *Nationalism in the New World*, 1–3.

5. The work of Timothy Roberts has revealed the importance of the revolutions of 1848 in American culture, society, and government. See Roberts, *Distant Revolu-*

tions; Timothy Roberts, "The United States and the European Revolutions of 1848," in Thomson, *The European Revolutions of 1848 and the Americas*, 76–99; Timothy Roberts and Daniel W. Howe, "The United States and the Revolutions of 1848," in Evans and Pogge von Strandmann, *The Revolutions in Europe*, 157–79. See also Tuchinsky, "'The Bourgeoisie Will Fall and Fall Forever.'"

The most recent scholarship on the revolutions of 1848 argues that the conflagration can best be viewed as a "European event" in which the revolutions had similar goals, even if each movement developed unique aspects that eventually formed the basis of nationalist myth-making. The contention that the revolutions of 1848 can be seen as a Europe-wide event certainly proved true for nineteenth-century Americans who hailed the movement for European freedom but later distinguished between its more particular goals as they applied 1848's legacy to sectional conflict and civil war. For the most important recent discussions, see Dowe, Haupt, Langewiesche, and Sperber, *Europe in 1848*; Evans and Pogge von Strandmann, *The Revolutions in Europe*; Körner, *1848*; Price, *The Revolutions of 1848*; Sperber, *The European Revolutions*; Stearns, *1848*; Tacke, *1848*.

6. For a discussion of 1848's influence on the development of socialism and communism, see Browne and Moggach, *The Social Question and the Democratic Revolution*.

7. Beard and Beard, *The Rise of American Civilization*, 2:6. For variations on the Beard thesis, see Moore, *Social Origins of Dictatorship and Democracy*; Ashworth, *Slavery, Capitalism, and Politics in the Antebellum Republic*; McPherson, *Abraham Lincoln and the Second American Revolution*; Egnal, "The Beards Were Right." For a recent work that challenges the basic premise of these works, see Ayers, *In the Presence of Mine Enemies*.

8. Marx and Engels, *The Civil War in the United States*, 23–24, 81.

9. White quoted in McPherson, *Battle Cry of Freedom*, 233; Jonathan Worth to H. B. Elliot, May 30, 1861, in Worth, *The Correspondence of Jonathan Worth*, 153, CWLD. The American Civil War: Letters and Diaries is a digital database of hundreds of books originally published during the nineteenth century. They are reprinted in their entirety. This collection was accessed at Alderman Library, University of Virginia, Charlottesville. Claytor, *Diary of William Claytor*, 1:248, CWLD; Larcom, *Lucy Larcom*, 87, CWLD; Jones, *A Rebel War Clerk's Diary*, 1:29, CWLD; Nevins and Thomas, *The Diary of George Templeton Strong*, 3:85, 95.

10. On the importance of the legacy of the American Revolution to the Civil War and the era of political divisions that preceded it, see McPherson, *What They Fought For*, 9–12, 27–31; Faust, *The Creation of Confederate Nationalism*, 14–15; Thomas, *The Confederacy as a Revolutionary Experience*, 1–2; Gallagher, *The Confederate War*, 64–67, 146–48; Rubin, *A Shattered Nation*, 14–25.

11. "President Lincoln and His Policy," *New York Herald*, August 5, 1861, CW. CW is a database of full-text newspaper articles. This collection was accessed at Alderman Library, University of Virginia, Charlottesville. Ingersoll, *A Letter to a Friend in a Slave State*, 1, 23, CWLD.

12. For accounts that stress the imperfect nature of the nation created in 1776, see

John M. Murrin, "1776: The Countercyclical Revolution," in Morrison and Zook, *Revolutionary Currents*, 65–90; Onuf and Onuf, *Federal Union, Modern World*.

13. See Bayly, *The Birth of the Modern World*, 86–120, 199–212; Onuf and Onuf, *Nations, Markets, and War*, 142–72; Marx and Engels, *The Communist Manifesto*. My characterization of the first French revolution relies on William H. Sewall Jr., "The French Revolution and the Emergence of the Nation Form," in Morrison and Zook, *Revolutionary Currents*, 91–125.

14. For a discussion of the effects of Italian unification on American identity, see Gemme, *Domesticating Foreign Struggles*.

15. David Potter, "The Civil War in the History of the Modern World: A Comparative View," in Potter, *The South and the Sectional Conflict*, 287. For a scholarly work that examines the unique "Americaness" of the Civil War, see Royster, *The Destructive War*. For some exciting recent works that take a global perspective on the Civil War, see Bender, *A Nation among Nations*, 116–81; Clavin, *Toussaint Louverture and the American Civil War*; Doyle, *Secession as an International Phenomenon*; Guterl, *American Mediterranean*; Roberts, *Distant Revolutions*; Rugemer, *The Problem of Emancipation*; Schoen, *The Fragile Fabric of Union*. For works that consider the effect Union victory had on the spread of democratic government across the globe, see Rawley, "The American Civil War and the Atlantic Community"; James M. McPherson, "'The Whole Family of Man': Lincoln and the Last Best Hope Abroad," in May, *The Union, the Confederacy, and the Atlantic Rim*, 132–48.

Chapter 1

1. Onuf and Onuf, *Nations, Markets, and War*, 222–46.

2. Weed quoted in Van Deusen, *Thurlow Weed*, 22.

3. Tochman, *Poland, Russia, and the Policy of the Latter towards the United States*, 20, 21–22.

4. Ibid., 25, 28.

5. For a discussion of the uncertainty with which the revolutions of 1848 were received, see Roberts, *Distant Revolutions*, 21–41.

6. My account of 1848 relies on Dowe, Haupt, Langewiesche, and Sperber, *Europe in 1848*; Evans and Pogge von Strandmann, *The Revolutions in Europe*; Körner, *1848*; Price, *The Revolutions of 1848*; Sperber, *The European Revolutions*; Stearns, *1848*; Tacke, *1848*; Jones, *The 1848 Revolutions*.

7. Nevins and Thomas, *The Diary of George Templeton Strong*, 1:334. Timothy Roberts, "The United States and the European Revolutions of 1848," in Thomson, *The European Revolutions of 1848 and the Americas*, 76–80; Timothy Roberts and Daniel W. Howe, "The United States and the Revolutions of 1848," in Evans and Pogge von Strandmann, *The Revolutions in Europe*, 165, 166, 167; Roberts, *Distant Revolutions*, 42–62. For an intriguing discussion of the impact of the revolutions on the literature of Emerson, Hawthorne, Melville, Whitman, and others, see Reynolds, *European Revolutions and the American Literary Renaissance*.

8. Roberts, "The United States and the European Revolutions of 1848," 76–80; Roberts and Howe, "The United States and the Revolutions of 1848," 165, 166, 167.

9. Nevins and Thomas, *The Diary of George Templeton Strong*, 1:316, 317, 332.

10. Roberts, "The United States and the European Revolutions," 77; Morrison, "American Reaction to European Revolutions," 114.

11. Foner, *Frederick Douglass*, 97, 106; Charles Sumner to Joshua Giddings, April 21, 1848; Charles Sumner to John Pringle Nichol, September 17, 1849; Charles Sumner to William Bates and James W. Stone, August 12, 1850, in Palmer, *The Selected Letters of Charles Sumner*, 1:223, 270, 308. For a complete discussion of the effect of the revolutions of 1848 on American abolitionism and reform, see Roberts, *Distant Revolutions*, 81–104.

12. Lounsbury, *Louisa S. McCord*, 58–59, 65, 66, 73. For more on Calhoun, slavery, and the Dorr Rebellion, see Roberts, "The United States and the European Revolutions," 85–86, 89; Roberts and Howe, "The United States and the Revolutions of 1848," 162, 170; Morrison, "American Reaction to European Revolutions," 118–19.

13. Holt, *The Rise and Fall of the American Whig Party*, 600, 601. For more on the Hülsemann affair, see Roberts, "The United States and the European Revolutions," 91–92; Roberts and Howe, "The United States and the Revolutions of 1848," 170–71. For discussion of 1848 and Young America, see Spencer, *Louis Kossuth and Young America*.

14. *The Life of Governor Louis Kossuth with His Public Speeches in the United States*, 41–42, 43.

15. Ibid., 68, 74, 133.

16. Ibid., 44. On the political ramifications of Kossuth's visit, see Holt, *The Rise and Fall of the American Whig Party*, 692–97; Roberts, *Distant Revolutions*, 146–67; Spencer, *Louis Kossuth and Young America*, 116–17, 137–45, 177–78; Morrison, "American Reaction to European Revolutions," 111–14, 122–32. See also Roberts, "The United States and the European Revolutions," 93–96; Roberts and Howe, "The United States and the Revolutions of 1848," 174–75.

17. Wittke, *Refugees of Revolution*, 36–37.

18. Mitchel, *Jail Journal*, 357, 358, 369. For biographical sketches of Mitchel, see Williams, "John Mitchel, the Irish Patriot," 44–56; Claudine Rhett, "Sketch of John C. Mitchel, of Ireland, Killed whilst in Command of Fort Sumter," in *Southern Historical Society Papers* 10: 268–72; McGovern, *John Mitchel*.

19. Schurz, *The Reminiscences of Carl Schurz*, 1:400, 401. For a recent biography of Schurz, see Trefousse, *Carl Schurz*.

20. Kapp, *Vom radikalen Frühsozialisten des Vormärz*, 66; "Free Homes for Free Men," *Citizen*, March 25, 1854; Lohmann, *Radical Passion*, 10. Hartz argued that America was "born liberal" in the absence of feudal institutions (Hartz, *The Liberal Tradition in America*). For a biography of Assing and an account of her relationship with Douglass, see Diedrich, *Love across Color Lines*.

21. Levine, *The Spirit of 1848*, 15; Wittke, *Refugees of Revolution*, 43; Lohmann, *Radical Passion*, 4.

22. Notable papers with forty-eighter editors included August Becker's *Baltimore Wecker*, Carl Bernays's and Heinrich Boernstein's St. Louis–based *Anzei-*

ger des Westens, Gustav Bloede's *New York Demokrat*, Lorenz Brentano's *Illinois Staatszeitung*, Theodore Canisius's *Freie Presse* in Alton, Illinois, and his *Staats-Anzeiger*, in Springfield, Illinois, Carl Daenzer's *St. Louis Westliche Post*, Johann Georg Guenther's *Milwaukee Herold*, Theodor Hielscher's *Indianapolis Freie Presse*, Friedrich Hassaurek's *Cincinnati Hochwaechter*, and Oswald Ottendorfer's *New York Staatszeitung*. Zucker, The *Forty-Eighters*, vii–xi; Levine, *The Spirit of 1848*, 4–5, 15–19; Wittke, *Refugees of Revolution*, 3–5; Wittke, *The Irish in America*, 75.

23. "Anniversary of the French Revolution," *Citizen*, March 4, 1854.

24. Ibid.

25. "St. Patrick's Day Celebrations," *Citizen*, March 25, 1854; "St. Patrick's Day in Cincinnati," *Citizen*, April 1, 1854, April 8, 1854.

26. "Patriotism in Fall River," *Citizen*, April 8, 1854; "The Meagher Republican Grenadiers," *Citizen*, November 4, 1854.

27. "Mr. Meagher to Mr. Houghton," *Citizen*, April 8, 1854; "Mr. T. F. Meagher's Visit to California," *Citizen*, April 8, 1854; "Meagher's Lecture in Boston—Great Success," *Citizen*, November 25, 1854.

28. "The Citizen in England," *Citizen*, March 4, 1854. For an account of Mitchel's role in fostering an anti-British Irish nationalism in America, see McGovern, *John Mitchel*, 95–96.

29. "Land Tenure in Austria," *Citizen*, March 4, 1854; "The Irish Pacha," *Citizen*, March 4, 1854; "The Pope—Essay the Second," *Citizen*, March 11, 1854; "Postscript to the Right Rev. John Hughes, Catholic Archbishop of New York," *Citizen*, September 9, 1854; "Free Homes for Free Men," *Citizen*, March 25, 1854; "Rights and Wrongs of Labor," *Citizen*, April 8, 1854.

30. Levine, *The Spirit of 1848*, 84–86; Eitel W. Dobert, "The Radicals," in Zucker, *The Forty-Eighters*, 161–62; Wittke, *Refugees of Revolution*, 10–17.

31. For a discussion of the importance of the German generation of 1848 in forming a politicized American working class, see Levine, *The Spirit of 1848*, 111–43. For discussion of many more such endeavors, see Hildegard Binder Johnson, "Adjustment to the United States," in Zucker, *The Forty-Eighters*, 55, 58–59.

32. For a detailed discussion of the Turner movement, see Augustus J. Prahl, "The Turner," in Zucker, *The Forty-Eighters*, 79–106; Wittke, *Refugees of Revolution*, 147–61. Turner mission statement, quoted in Prahl, "The Turner," 93.

33. *Sozialistischer Turnerbund*, quoted in Prahl, "The Turner," 98–99.

34. Levine, *The Spirit of 1848*, 102–6.

35. Potter, *The Impending Crisis*, 158, 159–76.

36. Anbinder, *Five Points*, 38–41, 50–51, 306, 312; Ignatiev, *How the Irish Became White*, 40–44; Roediger, *The Wages of Whiteness*, 133–34, 139.

37. Anbinder, *Five Points*, 154–55, 303–4; Ignatiev, *How the Irish Became White*, 6–19, 68–70; Roediger, *The Wages of Whiteness*, 134–35, 140, 143.

38. Foner, *Frederick Douglass*, 106; "The Citizen in England," *Citizen*, March 4, 1854. For a full discussion of Mitchel's views, see McGovern, *John Mitchel*, 119–54.

39. "The Citizen in Ireland," *Citizen*, March 4, 1854; "Anti-Slavery," *Citizen*, March 4, 1854; "Nebraska," *Citizen*, March 4, 1854.

40. "The Citizen in America," *Citizen*, March 4, 1854; "Mr. Mitchel's Address, Delivered before the Literary Societies of the University of Virginia, on the 28th June, 1854," *Citizen*, July 15, 1854.

41. "The Legislature of Louisiana and Mr. Mitchel," *Citizen*, April 15, 1854.

42. "German Meeting Against the Nebraska Bill," *Citizen*, March 11, 1854; Carl Schurz to wife, March 23, 1854, Carl Schurz to Gottfried Kinkel, January 23, 1855, in Bancroft, *Speeches, Correspondence, and Political Papers of Carl Schurz*, 1:13–14, 17; Schurz, *The Reminiscences of Carl Schurz*, 2:56.

For a detailed discussion of the German reaction to the Kansas-Nebraska Act and the act's importance in spurring defection from the Democrats and later support for the Republicans, see Levine, *The Spirit of 1848*, 149–208.

43. Prahl, "The Turner," 100.

44. Kapp quoted in Lawrence S. Thompson and Frank X. Braun, "The Forty-Eighters in Politics," in Zucker, *The Forty-Eighters*, 121. Carl Schurz to Gottfried Kinkel, January 23, 1855, in Bancroft, *Speeches, Correspondence, and Political Papers of Carl Schurz*, 1:16–17.

45. "Saving the Union," *Citizen*, May 27, 1854.

46. Robinson, *Kansas*, 79, 166, 249–50, CWLD. For further testimony on the Kansas crisis, see Roberts, *Distant Revolutions*, 174–84.

47. Kapp, *Vom radikalen Frühsozialisten des Vormärz*, 68; Carl Schurz to Gottfried Kinkel, December 1, 1856, in Bancroft, *Speeches, Correspondence, and Political Papers of Carl Schurz*, 1:23–24, 25; Heinzen quoted in Wittke, *Refugees of Revolution*, 195–96.

48. Carl Schurz to Henry Meyer, November 20, 1856, in Schafer, *Intimate Letters of Carl Schurz*, 174; Schurz, *The Reminiscences of Carl Schurz*, 2:72.

49. Bancroft, *Speeches, Correspondence, and Political Papers of Carl Schurz*, 1:149, 150; Schurz, *The Reminiscences of Carl Schurz*, 2:89, 119.

50. Student of Schurz and *Wächter am Erie* quoted in Wittke, *Refugees of Revolution*, 214, 216; Lohmann, *Radical Passion*, 130; Charles Sumner to Salmon P. Chase, September 18, 1857, in Palmer, *The Selected Letters of Charles Sumner*, 1:481.

51. Whitney quoted in Levine, *The Spirit of 1848*, 5; *Cleveland Plain Dealer* quoted in Wittke, *Refugees of Revolution*, 207.

52. "The Citizen in America," *Citizen*, March 4, 1854; Williams, "John Mitchel, the Irish Patriot," 44–56; McGovern, *John Mitchel*, 157–62; Roediger, *The Wages of Whiteness*, 140–43.

53. Carton, *Patriotic Treason*, 237–39; Victor Hugo to London *News*, December 2, 1859; Victor Hugo to Paul Chenay, January 21, 1861, in Sideman and Friedman, *Europe Looks at the Civil War*, 5, 9. Timothy Roberts also discusses the degree to which Brown may have been influenced by the revolutions of 1848 in Roberts, *Distant Revolutions*, 187–89.

Chapter 2

1. Russell, *My Diary, North and South*, 92, 98–99, 368, 369, 370, CWLD.

2. For discussion of the Germans in St. Louis, see Rowen, *Memoirs of a Nobody*;

Gerteis, *Civil War St. Louis*, 43–45; Arenson, *The Great Heart of the Republic*, 19–20; and Öfele, *German-Speaking Officers in the U.S. Colored Troops*, 10. This study does not seek to claim that all Germans in America agreed with the outspoken forty-eighters. Öfele rightly warns of giving too much credence to the "Myth of 1860," which celebrated German contributions to the nation by arguing that Germans unanimously supported the Union and single-handedly saved the country through their actions in St. Louis. Significant evidence suggests, however, that large numbers of Germans of all sorts concurred with the overwhelmingly Unionist forty-eighters' comparison of the war to the events of 1848. Even some conservative Germans who continued to support slavery spoke of the war in terms that invoked European revolution. On the importance of workers, ethnic groups, and southern cities in shaping the ideological terms of the debate on secession, see Towers, *The Urban South and the Coming of the Civil War*, 1–7. For a discussion of one of the rare German forty-eighters who remained loyal to the Democratic Party and defended slavery throughout the 1850s, see Stanley Nadel, "The Forty-Eighters and the Politics of Class in New York City," in Brancaforte, *The German Forty-Eighters in the United States*, 51–66. For a community study that illuminates the diverse political views of German immigrants, see Nadel, *Little Germany*.

3. Anneke, *Der Zweite Freiheitskampf.*

4. Rowan, *Germans for a Free Missouri*, 51.

5. "Working Men, This Day to Our Country," *Daily Missouri Democrat*, February 18, 1861; Rowan, *Germans for a Free Missouri*, 124, 134.

6. Arenson, *The Great Heart of the Republic*, 33, 65–81, 93; Rowan, *Germans for a Free Missouri*, 91.

7. "From Jefferson City," *Daily Missouri Democrat*, January 7, 1861; letter to the editor, *Daily Missouri Democrat*, December 31, 1860; "Monarchism of the South," *Daily Missouri Democrat*, February 16, 1861; "The Cotton States after Secession," *Daily Missouri Democrat*, December 7, 1860; "Progress of the Disunion Movement," *Daily Missouri Democrat*, December 19, 1860. St. Louis's Republican paper was known as the *Democrat*, and the Democratic paper was called the *Republican*. For more on Brown and his paper, see Gerteis, *Civil War St. Louis*, 58.

8. "Monarchical Tendencies of South Carolina," *Daily Missouri Democrat*, December 13, 1860; "To the Working Men of St. Louis," *Daily Missouri Democrat*, January 15, 1861; "Monarchism of the South," *Daily Missouri Democrat*, February 16, 1861.

9. Rowan, *Germans for a Free Missouri*, 136, 139–41; Arenson, *The Great Heart of the Republic*, 108–11. Historians have exposed as myth the claim that German support tipped the balance for Abraham Lincoln during the campaign of 1860. In fact, significant numbers of Germans remained conservative members of the Democratic Party. The forty-eighters who led the German press in St. Louis appealed to their countrymen by invoking the legacy of 1848. On the complicated German involvement in the presidential campaign of 1860, see Schafer, "Who Elected Lincoln?"; William E. Gienapp, "Who Voted for Lincoln?" in Thomas, *Abraham Lincoln and the American Political Tradition*, 50–88; James M. Bergquist, "People and Politics in Transition: The Illinois Germans, 1850–1860," in Luebke, *Ethnic Voters*

and the Election of Lincoln, 196–226; Thompson and Braun, "The Forty-Eighters in Politics," 115–40; James M. Bergquist, "The Forty-Eighters and the Republican Convention of 1860," in Brancaforte, *The German Forty-Eighters*, 157–74; and Wittke, *Refugees of Revolution*, 207–17.

10. Rowan, *Germans for a Free Missouri*, 152, 154; Gerteis, *Civil War St. Louis*, 92; Arenson, *The Great Heart of the Republic*, 111–14; "Progress of the Disunion Plot in Missouri: A Military Despotism Projected," *Daily Missouri Democrat*, February 2, 1861; "Arming the State at the Expense of St. Louis," *Daily Missouri Democrat*, April 30, 1861.

11. "The Open Secret of the Disunion Movement," *Daily Missouri Democrat*, February 8, 1861; Rowan, *Germans for a Free Missouri*, 272, 316–17.

12. Rowan, *Germans for a Free Missouri*, 203, 241; "The Union Resolutions," *Daily Missouri Democrat*, January 15, 1861.

13. "The Defenders of the Flag," *Daily Missouri Democrat*, May 24, 1861; Rowan, *Germans for a Free Missouri*, 187. See also Gerteis, *Civil War St. Louis*, 80–81; Arenson, *The Great Heart of the Republic*, 112–15.

14. Sigel quoted in Engle, *Yankee Dutchman*, 57. See also, Rowan, *Germans for a Free Missouri*, 195–97.

15. "The Story About the Arsenal," *Daily Missouri Democrat*, December 31, 1860; "From Jefferson City," *Daily Missouri Democrat*, January 7, 1861; Rowan, *Germans for a Free Missouri*, 151, 240.

16. See "The Result," *Daily Missouri Democrat*, April 2, 1861; "About the Police Commissioners," "Will Trade Revive," *Daily Missouri Democrat*, April 6, 1861; Tucker, *The Confederacy's Fighting Chaplain*, 13–14; Faherty, *Exile in Erin*, 29; Gerteis, *Civil War St. Louis*, 90.

17. Soldier quoted in Tucker, *The Confederacy's Fighting Chaplain*, 64. Bevier, *History of the First and Second Missouri Confederate Brigades*, 14.

18. Rowan, *Germans for a Free Missouri*, 207; Arenson, *The Great Heart of the Republic*, 116.

19. Gerteis, *Civil War St. Louis*, 108, 122; Arenson, *The Great Heart of the Republic*, 116–17; Tucker, *The Confederacy's Fighting Chaplain*, 18.

20. Gerteis, *Civil War St. Louis*, 122; Arenson, *The Great Heart of the Republic*, 118; Rowan, *Germans for a Free Missouri*, 238, 239; "Constantine Blandowsky," *Daily Missouri Democrat*, May 29, 1861.

21. Rowan, *Germans for a Free Missouri*, 226–27, 240; Tucker, *The Confederacy's Fighting Chaplain*, 18; Bevier, *History of the First and Second Missouri Confederate Brigades*, 25. For a record of Bannon's military service with the Confederacy, see John Bannon Diary, John Bannon Papers, South Caroliniana Library, University of South Carolina.

22. "A Word to Irishmen," *Daily Missouri Democrat*, May 10, 1861; "A Word to Irishmen in St. Louis," *Daily Missouri Democrat*, May 14, 1861; "St. Patrick's Day in New York," *Daily Missouri Democrat*, March 22, 1861; "Irish Brigade," *Daily Missouri Democrat*, May 22, 1861; "The Irish Brigade," *Daily Missouri Democrat*, May 25, 1861; "The Defenders of the Flag," *Daily Missouri Democrat*, May 24, 1861; "The Irish and Secession," *Daily Missouri Democrat*, February 18, 1861; Lonn, *For-*

eigners in the Union Army and Navy, 673; Lonn, *Foreigners in the Confederacy*, 122–23, 499. The unit nicknamed the "Irish Brigade" actually consisted of several companies.

23. "The Garibaldi Guard," *Harper's Weekly*, June 8, 1861, HW. HarpWeek is a full-text digital database of articles from *Harper's Weekly*. The collection was accessed at Alderman Library, University of Virginia, Charlottesville.

24. *New York Times*, May 3, 1861; Wittke, *Refugees of Revolution*, 221, 224; Prahl, "The Turner," in Zucker, *The Forty-Eighters*, 101, 108.

25. Carl Schurz to wife, December 24, 1860, in Schafer, *Intimate Letters of Carl Schurz*, 236, 240.

26. Ibid., 236–37, 240.

27. Schurz, *The Reminiscences of Carl Schurz*, 2:224, 228, 233.

28. Cavanagh, *Memoirs of Gen. Thomas Francis Meagher*, 368, 369; Conyngham, *The Irish Brigade and Its Campaigns*, 5; "Corcoran and His Countrymen," *Harper's Weekly*, September 6, 1862, HW. For a thorough discussion of the reasons that induced the Irish to join the Union army, see Randall M. Miller, "Catholic Religion, Irish Ethnicity, and the Civil War," in Miller, Stout, and Wilson, *Religion and the American Civil War*, 261–96.

29. Josef Dünnebacke to Ernst, May 3, 1862; Eheleute Pack to Schwager und Schwägerin, October 12, 1863, in Helbich and Kamphöfner, *Deutsche im Amerikanischen Bürgerkrieg*, 180, 280. A translated edition of *Deutsche im Amerikanischen Bürgerkrieg* was published in 2006 with the title *Germans in the Civil War*.

30. Albert Krause to Eltern und Geschwister, September 11, 1862; Albert Krause to Mutter und Geschwister, August 19, 1863; Carl Hermanns to Schwager und Schwester, April 12, 1862; Adolph Frick to Mutter und Geschwister, December 20, 1862; Dietrich Gerstein to Bruder, October 1, 1862; August Horstmann letter fragment, June 16, 1862; August Horstmann to Eltern, September 18, 1863, in ibid., 176, 184, 186, 257, 271, 334, 401; Peter Welsh to wife, February 3, 1863, in Kohl and Richard, *Irish Green and Union Blue*, 65–66.

31. Gould and Kennedy, *Memoirs of a Dutch Mudsill*, 72, 294; Byrne and Soman, *Your True Marcus*, 62, 140, 269, 321; Magnus Brucker to "frau," September 18, 1864, in Helbich and Kamphöfner, *Deutsche im Amerikanischen Bürgerkrieg*, 323.

32. *Case of General Tochman*; "To the Refugees in America from Foreign Lands," *Richmond Enquirer*, June 4, 1861.

33. "To the Refugees in America from Foreign Lands," *Richmond Enquirer*, June 4, 1861.

34. Ibid.; "Gen. Tochman, the Polish Veteran," *Richmond Enquirer*, August 2, 1861.

35. "Gen. Tochman, the Polish Veteran," *Richmond Enquirer*, August 2, 1861; *Case of General Tochman*; *Gen. Tochman's Case*.

36. *Case of General Tochman*.

37. *Richmond Enquirer*, January 13, 1863. For an account of Mitchel's career as a Confederate journalist and a discussion of his son who died during the war, see McGovern, *John Mitchel*, 176–84; Claudine Rhett, "Sketch of John C. Mitchel, of Ireland, Killed whilst in Command of Fort Sumter," in *Southern Historical Society*

Papers 10: 268–72. For an examination of the opinions of nationalists in Ireland on the American Civil War, see Hernon, *Celts, Catholics, and Copperheads*, 3–4, 18, 53–60, 90–101; Hernon, "The Irish Nationalists and Southern Secession," 43–53.

38. *Richmond Enquirer*, January 13, 1863; "The Irish Yankees," *Richmond Enquirer*, November 24, 1863; "The American War: Answer of William Smith O'Brien to General Meagher," *Richmond Enquirer*, January 8, 1864.

39. Raines, *Six Decades in Texas*, 454, CWLD; Carl Coreth to Rudolph, May 6, 1861; Rudolph Coreth to Carl, March 5, 1862; Rudolph Coreth to family, March 16, 1862, in Goyne, *Lone Star and Double Eagle*, 1–16, 17, 46, 48. For a discussion of the many German forty-eighters in Texas who remained loyal to the Union for many of the same reasons as their countrymen in Missouri, see Marten, *Texas Divided*, 117–18. On the many Germans who fought in Texas regiments, including the members of the Houston Turnverein, see Lonn, *Foreigners in the Confederacy*, 124–26.

40. Wittke, *Refugees of Revolution*, 222; Zucker, *The Forty-Eighters*, 351; Voigt quoted in Helbich and Kamphöfner, *Deutsche im Amerikanischen Bürgerkrieg*, 449; Anderson, *Brokenburn*, 26–27; see also Lonn, *Foreigners in the Confederacy*, 124–25.

Chapter 3

1. Bowen, *A Frenchman in Lincoln's America*, 1:114; Gerteis, *Civil War St. Louis*, 146–47; Arenson, *The Great Heart of the Republic*, 119–20.

2. Bowen, *A Frenchman in Lincoln's America*, 1:114, 306; Gerteis, *Civil War St. Louis*, 149–50; Arenson, *The Great Heart of the Republic*, 120–21.

3. Gerteis, *Civil War St. Louis*, 150–51, 158; Arenson, *The Great Heart of the Republic*, 121–22; Rowan, *Germans for a Free Missouri*, 296; *OR*, ser. 1, vol. 22, 565 (emphasis added).

4. Abraham Lincoln, First Annual Message to Congress, December 3, 1863; Abraham Lincoln to O. H. Browning, September 22, 1861, in Basler, *Abraham Lincoln*, 613–14, 630. This chapter's emphasis on Lincoln's conservatism complicates the interpretations presented in accounts that stress his determination to spread liberal values across the globe. The seminal works on this theme are Randall, *Lincoln the Liberal Statesman*, and Lillibridge, *Beacon of Freedom*. See also Crook, *The North, the South, and the Powers*, vi; James McPherson, "'The Whole Family of Man,'" in May, *The Union, the Confederacy, and the Atlantic Rim*, 132–48; Rawley, "The American Civil War and the Atlantic Community," 185–94; Jones, *Abraham Lincoln and a New Birth of Freedom*, 1–18.

5. Thompson and Braun, "The Forty-Eighters in Politics," in Zucker, *The Forty-Eighters*, 141, 142.

6. Ibid.; *Vanity Fair* 3 (1861): 142, MOAM. The Making of America is an online database of digital reproductions of hundreds of books and journals from library collections at Cornell University and the University of Michigan. The Burlingame episode is described in Tyrner-Tyrnauer, *Lincoln and the Emperors*, 31–32.

7. Giuseppe Garibaldi to George P. Marsh, October 7, 1862, in Sideman and Friedman, *Europe Looks at the Civil War*, 68–69, 73. For a representative arti-

cle that celebrates Garibaldi, see "Garibaldi and the Liberation of Italy," *Big Blue Union*, September 2, 1862, CA. Chronicling America is an online Library of Congress archive of American newspapers.

8. *New York Herald*, September 9, September 23, 1861; March 1, 1862; October 4, October 5, 1862, CW.

9. William L. Dayton to William H. Seward, September 23, 1862, in U.S. State Department, *Papers Relating to Foreign Affairs*, 392.

10. Seward, *The Works of William H. Seward*, 1:172–85, 186–95, 196–221, 4:348–49. See also Bender, *A Nation among Nations*, 123–24, 167–68.

11. William H. Seward to George G. Fogg, May 15, 1861, in U.S. State Department, *Diplomatic Correspondence of the United States*, 329.

12. London *Times*, May 20, 1861; John Lothrop Motely, "The Causes of the American Civil War: A Paper Contributed to the London Times," in Freidel, *Union Pamphlets of the Civil War*, 1:31–32; "State Rights," *Continental Monthly* 1, no. 5 (May 1862): 535, 539, MOAC. For a discussion of the importance of the concept of a united nation in northern thought, see Onuf and Onuf, *Nations, Markets, and War*, 278–307.

13. Motely, "The Causes of the American Civil War," 1:33; London *Times*, May 20, 1861; Adams, *The Education of Henry Adams*, 113. For a discussion of how the cause of law and order shaped northern ideological arguments, see Hess, *Liberty, Virtue, and Progress*, 1–3, 9.

14. "The True Interest of Nations," *Continental Monthly* 1, no. 4 (April 1862): 430, MOAC.

15. Ibid.; "American Nationality," *Princeton Review* 33, no. 4 (October 1861): 613, MOAM.

16. Joseph P. Thompson, "The Test-Hour of Popular Liberty and Republican Government," *New Englander and Yale Review* 21, no. 79 (April 1862): 241–44, MOAC; Motely, "The Causes of the American Civil War," 1:36–37; "Peace at Any Price," *Chicago Daily Tribune*, January 21, 1862; "Our War and Our Want," *Continental Monthly* 1, no. 2 (February 1862): 113, MOAC.

17. William H. Seward to William L. Dayton, April 22, 1861, in U.S. State Department, *Diplomatic Correspondence of the United States*, 199; "The Great Crime of History," *Big Blue Union*, September 6, 1862, CA.

18. "The United States and Europe," *Atlantic Monthly* 8, no. 45 (July 1861): 95, MOAC; "American Nationality," *Princeton Review*, 613, MOAM.

19. "Our War and Our Want," *Continental Monthly* 1, no. 2 (February 1862): 113, MOAC.

20. Robert McClelland to H. K. Sanger, January 2, 1861, *Letter on the Crisis*, 11, CWLD; Gertrude de Vingut, "Our Unity as a Nation," *New Englander and Yale Review* 21, no. 78 (January 1862): 98, MOAC.

21. Father to Theodore Heard, February 22, 1861; Mother to Theodore Heard, February 22, 1861; Mother to Theodore Heard, March 5, 1861; Mother to Theodore Heard, April 2, 1861, J. Theodore Heard Letters, 1855–1862, Harrison-Small Special Collections Library, University of Virginia, Charlottesville.

22. "What Will Monarchy Do," *Independent*, April 12, 1862, CA; William H.

Seward to Norman B. Judd, March 22, 1861; William H. Seward to Henry S. Sanford, March 26, 1861; William H. Seward to Charles Francis Adams, April 10, 1861, June 19, 1861, in U.S. State Department, *Diplomatic Correspondence of the United States*, 38, 54, 72, 107.

23. Henry C. Murphy to William H. Seward, May 27, 1861, in U.S. State Department, *Diplomatic Correspondence of the United States*, 349.

24. August Belmont to Baron Lionel de Rothschild, May 28, 1861, in Belmont, *The Letters, Speeches, and Addresses of August Belmont*, 51–52, CWLD; William Henry Seward to Rufus King, April 29, 1861, in U.S. State Department, *Diplomatic Correspondence of the United States*, 291.

25. William H. Seward to Charles Francis Adams, April 10, 1861, in U.S. State Department, *Diplomatic Correspondence of the United States*, 79; London *Times*, 20 May 1861; Motely, "The Causes of the American Civil War," 1:42, 43; "British Friendship," *Harper's Weekly*, September 13, 1862, HW; "Why Has the North Felt Aggrieved with England?" *Atlantic Monthly* 8, no. 49 (November 1861): 620, 621, 623, MOAC. For just a few examples of similar commentary regarding British interests in Ireland and their relevance to the Civil War, see "Gladstone Upon the War," *Harper's Weekly*, May 24, 1862, HW; "An Epistle to the London Times," *Vanity Fair* 4, no. 87 (August 24, 1861): 94, MOAM; "Diplomatic: Vanity Fair Remonstrates With the British Lion," *Vanity Fair* 3, no. 79 (June 29, 1861): 276, MOAM; "Our Danger and Its Causes," *Continental Monthly* 1, no. 2 (February 1862): 221, MOAC; "England and America," *Princeton Review* 34, no. 1 (January 1862): 174, MOAM; "Where Will the Rebellion Leave Us," *Atlantic Monthly*, 8, no. 46 (August 1861): 238, MOAC.

26. William H. Seward to Charles Francis Adams, April 10, 1861, May 21, 1861, in U.S. State Department, *Diplomatic Correspondence of the United States*, 79, 90; William H. Seward to William L. Dayton, March 26, 1862, in U.S. State Department, *Papers Relating to Foreign Affairs*, 325–26; William H. Seward to John Bigelow, April 5, 1862; John Bigelow to William H. Seward, July 17, 1862, in Bigelow, *Retrospections of an Active Life*, 1:477, 512.

27. Joseph A. Wright to William H. Seward, May 8, 1861; J. Glancey Jones to William H. Seward, April 15, 1861; John P. Stockton to William H. Seward, September 14, 1861; George P. Marsh to William H. Seward, July 6, 1861; Theodore S. Fay to William H. Seward, June 7, 1861, in U. S. State Department, *Diplomatic Correspondence of the United States*, 38–39, 188, 292, 323, 333.

28. "Patriotism," *Harper's Weekly*, March 2, 1861, HW.

29. Ibid.

30. Basler, *Abraham Lincoln*, 585; "State Rights," *Continental Monthly* 1, no. 5 (May 1862): 535, MOAC; John Pendleton Kennedy, "The Great Drama: An Appeal to Maryland," in Freidel, *Union Pamphlets of the Civil War*, 1:91; "American Nationality," *Princeton Review*, 645, MOAM; "Loyalty," *North American Review* 94, no. 194 (January 1862): 156, 158, MOAC; "The Right of Secession," *North American Review* 93, no. 192 (July 1861): 220, MOAC; Henry S. Sanford to William H. Seward, May 26, 1861, in U.S. State Department, *Diplomatic Correspondence of the United States*,

55–56; Agénor de Gasparin quoted in "England and America," *Princeton Review*, 172, MOAM.

31. John Stuart Mill, "The Contest in America," in Freidel, *Union Pamphlets of the Civil War*, 1:337–38.

32. Orestes Brownson, "Brownson on the Rebellion," in Freidel, *Union Pamphlets of the Civil War*, 1:140.

33. "Self Preservation," *Chicago Daily Tribune*, February 7, 1862; "The Question of Rebellion," *Harper's Weekly*, June 22, 1861, HW; Rev. Joseph P. Thompson, "The Test-Hour of Popular Liberty and Republican Government," *New Englander and Yale Review* 21, no. 79 (April 1862): 225, MOAC; "The Right of Secession," *North American Review*, 219, MOAC; Edward Ingersoll, "Personal Liberty and Martial Law: A Review of Some Pamphlets of the Day," in Freidel, *Union Pamphlets of the Civil War*, 1:256.

34. Basler, *Abraham Lincoln*, 598, 608; "A Strong Government," *Chicago Daily Tribune*, May 30, 1862.

35. Russell, *My Diary, North and South*, 471, 473–74, CWLD.

36. Rev. J. M. Sturtevant, "The Lessons of Our National Conflict," *New Englander and Yale Review* 19, no. 76 (October 1861): 895, MOAC; "The History and Theory of Revolutions," *Princeton Review* 34, no. 2 (April 1862): 248–50, MOAM; Rev. Joseph P. Thompson, "The Test-Hour of Popular Liberty and Republican Government," 244–45, MOAC.

Chapter 4

1. For information on the Yancey-Rost-Mann mission, I have relied on Hubbard, *The Burden of Confederate Diplomacy*, 29–32; Owsley, *King Cotton Diplomacy*, 51–86.

2. Robert Toombs to Yancey, Rost, and Mann, March 16, 1861, *ORN*, ser. 2, 3:193; Thomas, *The Confederate Nation*, 81.

3. My argument diverges from traditional accounts that depict an inept, bumbling, and ill-informed Confederate diplomatic effort. This interpretation was first offered in Owsley, *King Cotton Diplomacy*. It has found more recent support in Hubbard, *The Burden of Confederate Diplomacy*. For a discussion of the importance recognition held for the Confederacy's nationalist hopes, see Rubin, *A Shattered Nation*, 44–49.

4. On the geopolitics of Civil War diplomacy, see Crook, *The North, the South, and the Powers*; for a recent discussion of the problems slavery posed for the Confederate diplomatic effort, see Hubbard, *The Burden of Confederate Diplomacy*; the main introductory work on European public opinion remains Jordan and Pratt, *Europe and the American Civil War*. For more recent specialized studies, see Blackett, *Divided Hearts*; Blackburn, *French Newspaper Opinion on the American Civil War*; West, *Contemporary French Opinion on the American Civil War*.

5. Owsley, *King Cotton Diplomacy*, 51–86.

6. Chesnut quoted in Eaton, *A History of the Southern Confederacy*, 71; James

Mason to Nathaniel Tyler, editor of the *Richmond Enquirer*, November 23, 1860, in Mason, *The Public Life and Diplomatic Correspondence of James M. Mason*, 157.

7. R. M. T. Hunter to James Mason, September 23, 1861, *OR*, ser. 2, vol. 2, 1212.

8. Historians of Confederate foreign relations have argued for some time that an almost exclusive reliance on the power of "King Cotton" doomed diplomatic overtures from the start. See Owsley, *King Cotton Diplomacy*, 1–53; Hubbard, *The Burden of Confederate Diplomacy*, xi–xvi.

9. Paul Ambrose to William Winston Seaton, October 1863 and January 1864, in Kennedy, *Mr. Ambrose's Letters on the Rebellion*, 69, 112, CWLD.

10. Hotze quoted in Burnett, *Henry Hotze, Confederate Propagandist*, 109. My account of Hotze's life relies on Burnett's excellent introduction. See Burnett, *Henry Hotze, Confederate Propagandist*, 1–33. For other accounts of Hotze, his ideas, and his career, see Cullop, *Confederate Propaganda in Europe*, 18–19, 28–64; Oates, "Henry Hotze"; and Bonner, "Slavery, Confederate Diplomacy, and the Racialist Mission of Henry Hotze."

11. Burnett, *Henry Hotze, Confederate Propagandist*, 11, 13–14, 101.

12. Ibid., 15–16, 72; R. M. T. Hunter to Henry Hotze, November 14, 1861, Henry Hotze to R. M. T. Hunter, February 28, 1862, *ORN*, ser. 2, 3:293–94, 353.

13. Blackett, *Divided Hearts*, 7–14, 72, 102–3, 110–20; Cullop, *Confederate Propaganda in Europe*, 57–61.

14. Henry Hotze to Dr. Nichols, May 28, 1864; Henry Hotze to Sr. F. Manetta, June 1864; Henry Hotze to Edward Lucas, September 3, 1864, Henry Hotze Papers, Library of Congress, Washington, D.C. For an account of Thompson's activities in England and the articles he wrote for the *Index*, see "Journal of John R. Thompson," John Reuben Thompson Papers, Harrison-Small Special Collections Library, University of Virginia, Charlottesville; letter of introduction from Cornelia Grinnan to the Duke of Argyll, September 12, 1863, Letters of Albert Taylor Bledsoe, Harrison-Small Special Collections Library, University of Virginia.

15. "A Long War," *Index*, May 14, 1863; "What Constitutes a Nation?" *Index*, February 26, 1863.

16. "What Constitutes a Nation?" *Index*, February 26, 1863.

17. Ibid.

18. Ibid.

19. Ibid.

20. "The Anomaly of the Age," *Index*, March 19, 1863; *Richmond Enquirer*, June 4, 1861.

21. "The Anomaly of the Age," *Index*, March 19, 1863; *Richmond Enquirer*, June 4, 1861, March 20, 1862; "European Political Heresies," *Index*, May 29, 1862. See also "Errors of the Past," *Index*, June 12, 1862; John Ruskin to Charles Eliot Norton, February 10, 1863, in Sideman and Friedman, *Europe Looks at the Civil War*, 218.

22. *Richmond Enquirer*, January 16, 1864, November 6, 1863; "The People of the United Kingdom of Great Britain and Ireland to the People of the United States of America," in Sideman and Friedman, *Europe Looks at the Civil War*, 255; Gustave de Beaumont to John Murray Forbes, August 15, 1865, in Hughes, *Letters and Recollections of John Murray Forbes*, 2:148, CWLD.

23. "What Constitutes a Nation?" *Index*, February 26, 1863. For a discussion of the white South's attempt to portray itself as ethnically different from the white North, see McPherson, *Is Blood Thicker than Water?* 40, 43. McPherson asserts that Confederates advocated the principles of "ethnic nationalism," while their northern counterparts valued a "civic nationalism" that stressed the common subordination of all citizens to a sovereign government embodied in institutions such as Congress. McPherson argues that a "growing impression that Northern and Southern whites were two peoples with increasingly hostile interests" prompted southerners to found their nationalism on the claim that "Northern and Southern *whites* belonged to distinctive ethnic groups—or races, as ethnic groups were usually described in the nineteenth century." While some of the evidence backs up McPherson's claim, separate ethnicity was never the white South's most important justification for independence.

24. "What Constitutes a Nation?" *Index*, February 26, 1863.

25. Ibid.

26. Ibid. Hobsbawm, *Nations and Nationalism*, 33, 41. Dal Lago echoed Hotze in his comparison of the unifying nationalism of southern Italian landlords and the nationalist separatism of white southerners. See Dal Lago, *Agrarian Elites*, 238. For an account that stresses the similarity between the relationships of the Italian and American souths to their respective nations, see Doyle, *Nations Divided*, 5, 66–89, 73–74. On the tendency of historians to distinguish between "liberal unification" and "reactionary separation," see Thomas, *The Confederate Nation*, 167.

27. Hobsbawm, *Nations and Nationalism since 1780*, 20, 32, 33, 41; "The Anomaly of the Age," *Index*, March 19, 1863; "What Constitutes a Nation?" *Index*, February 26, 1863.

28. "What Constitutes a Nation?" *Index*, February 26, 1863.

29. "Mediation: A Northern Notion," *Index*, September 18, 1862; "The Want of a Policy," *Index*, October 23, 1862; "England," *Index*, November 6, 1862; *Richmond Daily Examiner*, February 5, 1862. For Anderson's thoughts on the importance of prior examples of nationalism, see Anderson, *Imagined Communities*, 159.

30. "The Letter of Invitation," *Index*, November 19, 1863.

31. "The United States and the Doctrine of National Independence," *Index*, January 12, 1865.

32. Martin, Mitchell, and O'Brien quoted in Stock, "Catholic Participation in the Diplomacy of the Southern Confederacy," 3–4. For information on Bannon's mission and beliefs, see Tucker, *The Confederacy's Fighting Chaplain*, 170–75; Faherty, *Exile in Erin*, 134–35.

33. *Charleston Mercury*, August 2, 1862, CW; *Richmond Enquirer*, July 4, 1861, September 28, 1861; Castleman, *The Army of the Potomac*, 6, CWLD.

34. "The United States and the Doctrine of National Independence," *Index*, January 12, 1865.

35. "The Pamphlet of Hon. W. B. Reed," *Index*, January 22, 1863. Alexander Hamilton Stephens to Abraham Lincoln, January 25, 1860, in *Some Lincoln Correspondence*, 14, CWLD; "The Lincoln Catechism, Wherein the Eccentricities and beauties of Despotism Are Fully Set Forth," in Freidel, *Union Pamphlets of the Civil War*, 2:1003.

36. *Richmond Enquirer*, October 3, 1861.

37. "The Magazines For June," *Index*, June 4, 1863.

38. *Charleston Mercury*, February 4, 1861, CW; "Mr. Gladstone on America," *Index*, October 16, 1862; "Foreign Correspondence—Paris," *Index*, October 23, 1862. For a discussion of opinion on the war and on Italian unification, see Blackett, *Divided Hearts*, 206.

39. "Social and Political Aspect of the American Question," *Index*, January 29, 1863.

40. "A Parallel and a Contrast," *Index*, August 6, 1863; "Foreign Correspondence—Paris," *Index*, February 26, 1863; "The Confederate Cause in France," *Index*, September 1, 1864; *Richmond Enquirer*, April 3, 1863, May 1, 1863, September 12, 1863.

41. "A Parallel and a Contrast," *Index*, August 6, 1863; "A Voice from Philadelphia," *Index*, August 28, 1862.

42. *Charleston Mercury*, January 12, 1864, CW. For a discussion of the Union's shift toward "hard war," see Grimsley, *The Hard Hand of War*, 67–119. "A Parallel and a Contrast," *Index*, August 6, 1863; "Paris Topics," *Index*, December 31, 1863; *Richmond Enquirer*, September 18, 1863.

43. Turchin, *Chickamauga*, 5. Turchin's given name has been rendered a variety of other ways, including Vasilevitch Turchininoff, Vasilyevich Turchaninov, Vasilovitch Turchinoff, and Vasilovitch Turchinov.

44. "Mrs. Greenhow's Imprisonment," *Index*, December 3, 1863; "Foreign Correspondence—Paris," *Index*, February 26, 1863; *Richmond Enquirer*, September 18, 1863.

45. "The Confederate Cause in France," *Index*, September 8, 1864; "Mrs. Greenhow's Imprisonment," *Index*, December 3, 1863; "A Parallel and a Contrast," *Index*, August 6, 1863; "Foreign Topics," *Index*, August 21, 1862; *Richmond Enquirer*, November 20, 1863. For more on the visit of the Russian fleet, see James McPherson, "'The Whole Family of Man,'" in May, *The Union, the Confederacy, and the Atlantic Rim*, 138–39.

46. "The Letter of Invitation," *Index*, November 19, 1863; "A Northern Revolution," *Index*, August 27, 1863; *Richmond Enquirer*, September 3, 1861.

47. "A Northern Revolution," *Index*, August 27, 1863; *Richmond Enquirer*, September 3, 1861; "Mr. Lincoln's Honesty and Capacity," *Index*, April 14, 1864. For an excellent discussion of how northern infringements on civil liberties in Maryland helped Confederates define their cause, see William A. Blair, "'Maryland, Our Maryland': Or How Lincoln and His Army Helped to Define the Confederacy," in Gallagher, *The Antietam Campaign*, 74–100.

48. "The Confederate Cause in France," *Index*, September 1, 1864; "Speech of Colonel L. Q. C. Lamar," *Index*, October 22, 1863; *Richmond Enquirer*, February 11, 1863.

49. *Charleston Mercury*, May 16, 1862, January 16, 1864, CW; *Richmond Enquirer*, September 27, 1864.

50. Unknown to "Bro," January 20, 1864, Papers of the Kendrick, Smith, Currier, and Owen Families, University of Virginia, Charlottesville.

51. "The Confederate Cause in France," *Index*, August 25, 1864. See also, Gavronsky, *The French Liberal Opposition and the American Civil War*, 95–96; R. M. T.

Hunter to J. M. Mason, February 14, 1871, Carter-Blackford Papers, Harrison-Small Special Collections Library, University of Virginia, Charlottesville.

Chapter 5

1. Basler, *Abraham Lincoln*, 689–91.
2. Foner, *Frederick Douglass*, 555; Higginson, *Army Life in a Black Regiment*, 47, CWLD; *The Great Mass Meeting of Loyal Citizens at Cooper Institute*, 3, 4.
3. Basler, *Abraham Lincoln*, 630.
4. Ibid., 688, 734.
5. Jones, *Abraham Lincoln and a New Birth of Freedom*, 1, 5, 12; Rawley, "The American Civil War and the Atlantic Community," 185; James McPherson, "'The Whole Family of Man,'" in May, *The Union, the Confederacy, and the Atlantic Rim*, 132–48; Crook, *The North, the South, and the Powers*, vi. The seminal works on this theme are Randall, *Lincoln the Liberal Statesman*, and Lillibridge, *Beacon of Freedom*.
6. For a discussion of the problem of slavery during the age of the American Revolution, see Wood, *Empire of Liberty*, 508–42; Davis, *The Problem of Slavery in the Age of Revolution*; Nash, *Race and Revolution*.
7. Sewall, "The French Revolution and the Emergence of the Modern Nation Form," in Morrison and Zook, *Revolutionary Currents*, 109–12; David Brion Davis, "Impact of the French and Haitian Revolutions," in Geggus, *The Impact of the Haitian Revolution in the Atlantic World*, 3–9; DuBois, *Avengers of the New World*, 1–91.
8. Jones, *Abraham Lincoln and a New Birth of Freedom*, 83–85; Clavin, *Toussaint Louverture and the American Civil War*, 98–121, 144–62; Jefferson Davis quoted in McPherson, *Battle Cry of Freedom*, 566.
9. Clavin, *Toussaint Louverture and the American Civil War*, 162–81; Rugemer, *The Problem of Emancipation*; Bigelow, *Jamaica in 1850*, 71–78; "What to Do with the Negroes," *Harper's Weekly*, April 5, 1862, HW; Slocum, *The War, and How to End It*, 5–6; Daniel A. P. Murray Pamphlet Collection, AM; Goodloe, *Emancipation and the War*, AM. American Memory is an online archive of pamphlets housed at the Library of Congress.
10. "What to Do with the Negroes," *Harper's Weekly*, April 5, 1862, HW; Pelletan, *An Address to King Cotton*, 1.
11. David Potter, "The Civil War in the History of the Modern World," in Potter, *The South and the Sectional Conflict*, 290–98; McPherson, "'The Whole Family of Man,'" 132–48; Bender, *A Nation among Nations*, 122–30, 164–75; Laboulaye, *Separation*, 12, 15; Pelletan, *An Address to King Cotton*, 1, 19.
12. "Colored Jubilee in Brooklyn," *New York Times*, January 4, 1863; "Washington Correspondence," *Christian Recorder*, January 10, 1863; "Proclamation of Emancipation," *Christian Recorder*, January 31, 1863; "From the Youth's Evangelist: Letter from a Young Soldier in the Army of the Potomac," *Christian Recorder*, February 7, 1863; *Celebration by the Colored People's Educational Monument Association in Memory of Abraham Lincoln*, 13–15, Daniel A. P. Murray Pamphlet Collection, Library of Congress, AM.

13. Benjamin F. Butler to William Henry Seward, November 14, 1862, *OR*, ser. 3, vol. 2, 780–82; Thomas W. Conway to General S. A. Hurlbut, February 1, 1865, *OR*, ser. 1, vol. 48, pt. 1, 706.

14. Blackett, *Divided Hearts*, 48–212; Gavronsky, *The French Liberal Opposition and the American Civil War*, 95–96. Fierce debate surrounds the extent of British working-class support for the Union. For those in agreement with Blackett, see Adams, *Great Britain and the American Civil War*; Pelling, *America and the British Left*; Foner, *British Labor and the American Civil War*. A growing body of revisionist scholarship has pointed out that some working-class groups supported the Confederacy and many British aristocrats opposed slavery. While these studies have done much to point out the complexities of class and race in shaping attitudes toward foreign policy, Foner and Blackett have established the basic class divisions on ideological issues. For the revisionists, see Campbell, *English Public Opinion and the American Civil War*; Ellison, *Support for Secession*; Crook, *American Democracy in English Politics*; Jones, "British Conservatives and the American Civil War"; Harrison, "British Labour and the Confederacy." For works on France that generally agree with Gavronsky, *The French Liberal Opposition and the American Civil War*, see Blackburn, *French Newspaper Opinion on the American Civil War*; West, *Contemporary French Opinion on the American Civil War*.

15. The Working Men of Manchester to President Lincoln, December 31, 1862; Richard Cobden to Charles Sumner, February 13, 1863; Eugene Forcade column on textile workers, February 1, 1863; Letter of Italian liberals to Abraham Lincoln; Barcelona Declaration, December 6, 1864, in Sideman and Friedman, *Europe Looks at the Civil War*, 201, 206, 212, 221, 267; Henry Adams to Charles Francis Adams Jr., January 27, 1863, in Ford, *A Cycle of Adams Letters*, 1:244–46. For more testimony, see *Letters from Europe Touching the American Contest*, 7, 8, 18, 19.

16. Charles Sumner to Abraham Lincoln, November 30, 1863, in Palmer, *The Selected Letters of Charles Sumner*, 2:212.

17. "Our Relations with England," *Harper's Weekly*, May 16, 1863, HW; Hamilton, *Letter of Gen. A. J. Hamilton of Texas to the President of the United States*, 9.

18. Welles, *The Diary of Gideon Welles*, 1:251; John Bigelow to Hargreaves, September 7, 1863, in Bigelow, *Retrospections of an Active Life*, 2:54; Parke Godwin to John Bigelow, December 24, 1861, in Bigelow, *Retrospections of an Active Life*, 1:424; "Why England Keeps Still," *Harper's Weekly*, December 5, 1863, HW; "Why Immigration Increases," *Harper's Weekly*, May 23, 1863, HW; "The Situation," *Harper's Weekly*, May 14, 1863, HW; "English Opinion," *Chicago Daily Tribune*, January 13, 1862; "The War—What Must Be Done," *Independent*, February 22, 1862, CA; "A War with England," *Independent*, January 25, 1862, CA; "The Future," *Independent*, March 15, 1862, CA; "A Monarchical Alliance," *Independent*, April 19, 1862, CA.

19. "Garibaldi and the Liberation of Italy," *Big Blue Union*, September 2, 1862, CA; "Foreign War," *Harper's Weekly*, August 8, 1863, HW; Henry Raymond to William Lowndes Yancey, December 10, 1860, in Raymond, *Disunion and Slavery*, 20, CWLD; Henry Adams to Charles Francis Adams Jr., September 25, 1863, in Ford, *A Cycle of Adams Letters*, 2:87–88. American relations with France are covered in Case and Spencer, *The United States and France*.

20. Palmer, *The Age of the Democratic Revolution*, 2:v, 4–5; Wood, *The Radicalism of the American Revolution*, 5–8; Wood, *Empire of Liberty*, 174–81, 253–56.

21. See Onuf and Onuf, *Nations, Markets, and War*, 144–49; Sewell, "The French Revolution and the Emergence of the Modern Nation Form," 109–12; Grant, *North over South*, 21, 77, 140.

22. Nevins and Thomas, *The Diary of George Templeton Strong*, 3:112–13, 126.

23. Holt, *The Political Crisis of the 1850s*, 51, 151–54, 184–85, 191–98, 202–3, 257–58; Davis, *The Slave Power and the Paranoid Style*.

24. Cairnes, *The Slave Power*, 25–27, 60–63, 100–101.

25. Richard Henry Dana to John Bigelow, December 7, 1861; John Lothrop Motely to John Bigelow, April 24, 1863, and Bigelow quoted in Bigelow, *Retrospections of an Active Life*, 1:329, 332–34, 409, 629.

26. Marx and Engels, *The Civil War in the United States*, 19, 22–23, 23–24, 227; *Waynesboro Village Record*, May 29, 1863, VS; "A New Reign of Terror," *Harper's Weekly*, March 22, 1862, HW; "The Irrepressible Conflict Again," *Harper's Weekly*, February 21, 1863, HW; "The Situation," *New York Herald*, January 5, 1863, CW. For a similar treatment of Bright's speech, see "Foreign News," *Harper's Weekly*, January 17, 1863, HW.

27. John Murray Forbes to William Curtis Noyes, July 28, 1862, in Hughes, *Letters and Recollections of John Murray Forbes*, 1:324–25, CWLD.

28. Welles, *The Diary of Gideon Welles*, 2:141–42; John Murray Forbes to Abraham Lincoln, September 8, 1863, in Hughes, *Letters and Recollections of John Murray Forbes*, 2:73–75, CWLD.

29. Freidel, "The Loyal Publication Society"; Freidel, *Union Pamphlets of the Civil War*, 1:12.

30. Freidel, "The Loyal Publication Society," 361.

31. Meagher, *Letters on Our National Struggle*, 2; Lieber, *Slavery, Plantations, and the Yeomanry*, 2, 3, 5. Meagher's letters were designed to counteract Irish sympathy for the principles of self-determination. For another pamphlet that addressed similar issues in France, see *Reply of Messrs. Agenor de Gasparin, Edouard Laboulaye, Henri Martin, Augustin Cochin, to the Loyal National League of New York*, 7, 8, 14.

32. *Rebel Conditions of Peace and the Mechanics of the South*, 1; Foner, *Free Soil, Free Labor, Free Men*, 40–72. Enrico Dal Lago points out that, during the Age of Revolutions, thinkers often compared plantations to European latifundia. See Dal Lago, *Agrarian Elites*, 54.

33. *The Preservation of the Union*, 5, 6. Adam-Max Tuchinsky demonstrates the degree to which the French Revolution of 1848 influenced American conceptions of free labor and the right to work. See Tuchinsky, "'The Bourgeoisie Will Fall and Fall Forever.'"

34. "Why England Keeps Still," *Harper's Weekly*, December 5, 1863, HW.

35. *The Preservation of the Union*, 6, 7; Meagher, *Letters on Our National Struggle*, 14; Laboulaye, *Separation*, 17.

36. "Shall We Cut Off Our Noses," *Harper's Weekly*, June 28, 1862, HW; "The Real Contest," *Harper's Weekly*, September 6, 1862, HW; Beecher quoted in *New York Herald*, January 19, 1861, CW.

37. J. W. Phelps to Capt. R. S. Davis, June 16, 1862, in *OR*, ser. 1, vol. 15, 488; Anderson, *The Cause of the War*, 12; Anderson, *Letter Addressed to the Opera House Meeting, Cincinnati*, 5, 7, 8, 15; Hamilton, *Letter of Gen. A. J. Hamilton of Texas to the President of the United States*, 14, 16; Owen, *The Conditions of Reconstruction*, 12. For a similar take, see *Elements of Discord in Secessia*, 5.

38. "Free Against Servile Labor," *Waynesboro Village Record*, June 5, 1863, VS,; "The Cause of the War," *Independent*, June 14, 1862, CA; A. L. Gilstrap to William S. Rosecrans, February 27, 1864, in *OR*, ser. 1, vol. 34, pt. 3, 443; McKaye quoted in *Reply of Messrs. Agenor de Gasparin, Edouard Laboulaye, Henri Martin, Augustin Cochin, to the Loyal National League of New York*, 24, 25; "The Irrepressible Conflict Again," *Harper's Weekly*, February 21, 1863, HW. For the clear but sometimes uneasy relationship between antislavery advocates and advocates for worker's rights in Europe, see Cunliffe, *Chattel Slavery and Wage Slavery*.

39. Henry W. Halleck to Ulysses S. Grant, March 31, 1863, in *OR*, ser. 1, vol. 24, pt. 3, 157.

40. Samuel B. Shepard to "Friend Thomas," July 30, 1862, in Silber and Sievens, *Yankee Correspondence*, 67; Hiram Berry to unidentified recipient, March 23, 1862, in Gould, *Major General Hiram G. Berry*, 104, CWLD; Gilpin, *The Last Campaign*, 635, CWLD; Hallock Armstrong to Mary Armstrong, April 8, 1865, in Armstrong, *Letters from a Pennsylvania Chaplain*, 21, CWLD; Chauncey Herbert Cooke to father, August 3, 1863, in Cooke, *Soldier Boy's Letters to His Father and Mother*, 53, CWLD; Day, *My Diary of Rambles with the 25th Massachusetts Volunteer Infantry*, 76, CWLD. Chandra Manning has recently demonstrated that a variety of political viewpoints influenced northern soldiers to link the end of slavery with the defeat of the Confederacy. This study does not seek to challenge those findings, but to show how important a role an international perspective could play in that process, a perspective of which Manning also found evidence. For Manning's interpretation, and evidence of the importance of a global outlook, see Manning, *What This Cruel War Was Over*, 39–43, 216. For a discussion of the North's shift to "hard war," see Grimsley, *The Hard Hand of War*, 96–170.

41. Bradley, *The Star Corps*, 256, CWLD; Charles Fessenden Morse to unidentified recipient, January 31, 1865, in Morse, *Letters Written during the Civil War*, 210, 211, CWLD. For a discussion of the hard war taking place during Sherman's March, see Grimsley, *The Hard Hand of War*, 190–204.

42. Myers, *A Daily Journal of the 192d Regiment Pennsylvania Volunteers*, 155, CWLD; *The Echo from the Army*, 4; Union private quoted in McPherson, *What They Fought For*, 31. McPherson also presents a number of similar quotations.

Chapter 6

1. See, for example, A. Dudley Mann to Judah P. Benjamin, November 14, 1863, James Mason to Judah P. Benjamin, March 31, 1865, in Richardson, *The Messages and Papers of Jefferson Davis and the Confederacy*, 2:591, 710, 717. See also Jones, *Abraham Lincoln and a New Birth of Freedom*, 146–63; Hubbard, *The Burden of Confederate Diplomacy*, 170–80.

2. "A Cool Proposal," *Richmond Enquirer*, June 30, 1863.

3. Ibid.

4. Bledsoe, *An Essay on Liberty and Slavery*, 34, 41. For a discussion of the southern defense of slavery, including the work of George Fitzhugh, see Onuf and Onuf, *Nations, Markets, and War*, 333–38; Fox-Genovese and Genovese, *The Mind of the Master Class*, 223–24; O'Brien, *Conjectures of Order*, 2:972–92; Faust, *The Ideology of Slavery*, 273–78; Cunliffe, *Chattel Slavery and Wage Slavery*, xiv, 11–18. For a detailed discussion of Bledsoe's thought in general, see Genovese, *The Slaveholders' Dilemma*, 49–54.

5. Hall, *The Historic Significance of the Southern Revolution*, 3. For the relationship between slavery and southern nationalism, see Onuf and Onuf, *Nations, Markets, and War*, 333–38.

6. Hall, *The Historic Significance of the Southern Revolution*, 4, 5, 37.

7. Fox-Genovese and Genovese, *The Mind of the Master Class*, 42.

8. Hall, *The Historic Significance of the Southern Revolution*, 37; *North and South*, 111. See also Faust, *The Creation of Confederate Nationalism*, 14–15; McPherson, *What They Fought For*, 9–12.

9. Americus Featherman, "Our Position and That of Our Enemies," *DeBow's Review* 31, no. 1 (July 1861): 29, MOAM; "National Characteristics—The Issue of the Day," *DeBow's Review* 30, no. 1 (January 1861): 44, MOAM; Frank H. Alfriend, "The Great Danger of the Confederacy," *Southern Literary Messenger* 37, no. 1 (January 1863): 39, MOAM; Bledsoe, *An Essay on Liberty and Slavery*, 34, 274; Fox-Genovese and Genovese, *The Mind of the Master Class*, 20–39.

10. Bledsoe, *An Essay on Liberty and Slavery*, 274, 284.

11. Americus Featherman, "Our Position and That of Our Enemies," *DeBow's Review* 31, no. 1 (July 1861): 29, MOAM; "E. Y.," *Richmond Enquirer*, June 4, 1861; Hall, *The Historic Significance of the Southern Revolution*, 15, 37, 40. For similar testimony, see also "Our True Policy, Our True Position," *DeBow's Review* 31, no. 4 and 5 (October and November 1861): 401–2, MOAM.

12. Fox-Genovese and Genovese, *The Mind of the Master Class*, 680; George Fitzhugh, "Society, Labor, Capital, Etc.," *DeBow's Review* 32, no. 1 and 2 (January and February 1862): 134–38, MOAM; *Richmond Daily Examiner*, October 4, 1861.

13. Crabtree and Patton, *Journal of a Secesh Lady*, 715; *New York Herald*, January 19, 1861, CW.

14. Bledsoe, *An Essay on Liberty and Slavery*, 129.

15. *Richmond Daily Examiner*, October 14, 1861; Edward Alfred Pollard, "Hints on Southern Civilization," *Southern Literary Messenger* 32, no. 4 (April 1861): 310, MOAM; "An Alabamian," "The One Great Cause of the Failure of the Federal Government," *Southern Literary Messenger* 32, no. 5 (May 1861): 334, MOAM; Hall, *The Historic Significance of the Southern Revolution*, 15, 17, 19, 35; "From an Englishman in the South," *Index*, June 26, 1862.

16. Fox-Genovese and Genovese, *The Mind of the Master Class*, 297–98; Featherman, "Our Position and That of Our Enemies," 28, MOAM; Frank Alfriend, "A Southern Republic and a Northern Democracy," *Southern Literary Messenger* 37,

no. 5 (May 1863): 284–85, MOAM; Alfriend, "The Great Danger of the Confederacy," 41, MOAM; *Charleston Mercury*, February 26, 1863, CW.

17. *Richmond Enquirer*, November 15, 1864; "The Advocacy of the Southern Cause," *Index*, November 26, 1863.

18. *North and South*, 163. For a glowing review of the work of "White Republican," the author of *North and South*, see "Two Books on America," *Index*, January 29, 1863.

19. *Index*, November 17, 1864; A. Dudley Mann to Judah P. Benjamin, January 5, 1863, in Richardson, *The Messages and Papers of Jefferson Davis and the Confederacy*, 2:388; *Charleston Mercury*, May 7, 1861, CW.

20. Dr. Cartwright, "Abolitionism: A Curse to the North and a Blessing to the South," *DeBow's Review* 32, no. 3 and 4 (March and April 1862): 300, MOAM; "Private Letters," *Index*, May 29, 1862; Henry Hotze to George Witt, August 11, 1864, Henry Hotze Papers.

21. "Monarchy in the New World," *Index*, May 12, 1864; *Richmond Enquirer*, February 13, 1862; "France and Slavery," *Richmond Enquirer*, November 17, 1863; Robert R. Howison, "History of the War," *Southern Literary Messenger* 34, no. 4 (April 1862): 209, MOAM.

22. *New York Herald*, January 19, 1861, CW; Featherman, "Our Position and That of Our Enemies," 30, MOAM; "The Future of the North," *Richmond Enquirer*, May 10, 1861.

23. "Paris Topics," *Index*, July 30, 1863; "First Lessons in Revolution," *Richmond Enquirer*, July 24, 1863; "Paris Topics," *Index*, August 6, 1863; "The New York Riots," *Index*, July 30, 1863.

24. A. Jeffery, "European Emigration and New England Puritanism," *Southern Literary Messenger* 37, no. 8 (August 1863): 466, 469, MOAM; "Fowler," "The True Basis of Political Prosperity," *Southern Literary Messenger* 37, no. 3 (March 1863): 154, MOAM; *North and South*, 6; "The Perils of Peace," *DeBow's Review* 31, no. 4 and 5 (October and November 1861): 397–98, MOAM; "Signa," "Southern Individuality," *Southern Literary Messenger* 38, no. 6 (June 1864): 370, 371, MOAM; "The Last Presidential Election in the United States," *Index*, July 10, 1862; "Monarchy in the New World," *Index*, May 12, 1864.

25. *North and South*, 125; A. Dudley Mann to Judah P. Benjamin, January 5, 1863, in Richardson, *The Messages and Papers of Jefferson Davis and the Confederacy*, 2:388; "Ingredients of the Contending Armies," *Index*, July 3, 1862; Harwell, *Cities and Camps of the Confederate States*, 37, 178; Briggs, *Soldier and Scholar*, 259–60.

26. "A War of Extermination," *Index*, August 27, 1863; "Letter of Hon. Robert J. Walker," *Index*, November 26, 1863; *North and South*, 253, 282. For similar complaints about confiscation, see *Richmond Daily Examiner*, January 28, 1862.

27. "Letter from New Orleans," *Index*, March 3, 1864; "Europe: France," *Index*, October 30, 1862; "The Reviews for July," *Index*, July 9, 1863; *Richmond Daily Examiner*, October 3, 1861; "The Appeal of the Confederate Clergy," *Index*, June 18, 1863.

28. George Fitzhugh, "History of the Origin of Representative Government in Europe," *DeBow's Review* 32, no. 3 and 4 (March and April, 1862): 206, MOAM;

North and South, 214; "Secession from a Northern Point of View," *Index*, May 15, 1862; "Letter from Halifax," *Index*, April 14, 1864; "Letter from New York," *Index*, January 21, 1864; "Southern Prospects," *Index*, May 29, 1862.

29. "The Confederacy in France," *Richmond Enquirer*, July 17, 1863; "France and Slavery," *Richmond Enquirer*, November 17, 1863; "The German View of American Affairs," *Index*, May 1, 1862; "The Imperial Speech," *Index*, November 12, 1863; "Mr. Bright's Platform," *Index*, February 4, 1864; "The Cloven Foot," *Index*, December 3, 1863. For similar arguments, see "Two Writers in the War," *Index*, July 9, 1863; "Foreign Correspondence, Paris," *Index*, September 11, 1862; "Dropping the Mask," *Index*, September 17, 1863; *Index*, November 6, 1862.

30. "E. Y.," *Richmond Enquirer*, June 4, 1861; *North and South*, 240.

31. Henry Hotze to B. Wood, April 21, 1865, Henry Hotze Papers, Library of Congress, Washington, D.C.

32. Ibid.

33. Ibid.

Conclusion

1. Bowen, *A Frenchman in Lincoln's America*, 1:xlvi, xlvii-xlviii.

2. Ibid., 2:282.

3. Ibid., 1:125.

4. Ibid., 1:110, 2:279, 280.

5. For an account of this episode, see Hanna and Hanna, *Napoleon III and Mexico*.

6. "The Fall of Puebla," *Index*, June 18, 1863. The Confederate press printed scores of similar articles during the war.

7. William Henry Seward to John Bigelow, March 17, 1865, in Bigelow, *Retrospections of an Active Life*, 2:412; "The Situation," *Harper's Weekly*, May 14, 1864, HW; Phillips quoted in "France Threatened," *Index*, January 7, 1864.

8. Charles Francis Adams to Charles Francis Adams Jr., in Ford, *A Cycle of Adams Letters*, 2:123-24.

9. For a discussion of this process, see Blum, *Reforging the White Republic*, 209-43.

10. Bowen, *A Frenchman in Lincoln's America*, 1:114.

Bibliography

Manuscript Collections

Charlottesville, Virginia
  Harrison-Small Special Collections Library, University of Virginia
    Balch Family Papers
    Letters of Albert Taylor Bledsoe
    Notebooks of Albert Taylor Bledsoe
    Carter-Blackford Papers
    Gail Hamilton Papers
    J. Theodore Heard Letters
    Henry Hotze Papers
    Robert Mercer Taliaferro Hunter Papers
    Papers of the Kendrick, Smith, Currier, and Owen Families
    Biographical Notes on Professor Charles Kraitsir
    Papers of James Russell Lowell
    Papers of the Minor and Venable Families
    John Reuben Thompson Papers
Columbia, South Carolina
  South Caroliniana Library, University of South Carolina
    John Bannon Papers
Washington, D.C.
  The Library of Congress
    Henry Hotze Papers
    Abraham Lincoln Papers
    Carl Schurz Papers

Government Reports and Publications

U.S. Congress. *The Congressional Globe*. Washington, D.C.: Blair and Rives, 1834–1873.

U.S. Naval War Records Office. *Official Records of the Union and Confederate Navies in the War of the Rebellion*. Washington, D.C.: Government Printing Office, 1894–1922.

U.S. State Department. *Diplomatic Correspondence of the United States.*
Washington, D.C.: Government Printing Office, 1861.

———. *Papers Relating to Foreign Affairs, Part I. Communicated to Congress
December 1, 1862.* Washington, D.C.: Government Printing Office, 1862.

U.S. War Department. *The War of the Rebellion: A Compilation of the Official
Records of the Union and Confederate Armies.* 127 vols. Washington, D.C.:
Government Printing Office, 1880–1901.

Digital Databases and Internet Resources

The American Civil War: Letters and Diaries. Alexandria: Alexander Street Press,
2004.

American Memory. The Library of Congress. http://memory.loc.gov/ammem/
index. html. 22 February 2011.

Chronicling America. The Library of Congress. http://chroniclingamerica.loc.
gov/. 22 February 2011.

The Civil War: A Newspaper Perspective. Malvern, Pa.: Accessible Archives, 1999.

HarpWeek. Norfolk: HarpWeek, 2000. http://www.harpweek.com/. 22 February
2011.

The Making of America. Cornell University. http://moa.cit.cornell.edu/moa/.
22 February 2011.

———. University of Michigan. http://quod.lib.umich.edu/m/moagrp/.
22 February 2011.

The Valley of the Shadow: Two Communities in the American Civil War. Virginia
Center for Digital History, University of Virginia. http://valley.vcdh.virginia.edu/.
22 February 2011.

Newspapers and Periodicals

Atlantic Monthly
Big Blue Union (Marysville,
   Kansas)
Charleston Mercury
Chicago Daily Tribune
Christian Recorder
The Citizen
Continental Monthly
Daily Missouri Democrat
DeBow's Review
Harper's Weekly
The Independent (Oskaloosa,
   Kansas)
The Index
Missouri Republican

New Englander and Yale Review
New York Daily Tribune
New-Yorker illustrirte Zeitung
   und Familienblätter
New York Herald
New York Times
North American Review
Princeton Review
Richmond Daily Examiner
Richmond Enquirer
Southern Citizen
Southern Literary Messenger
Times (London)
Vanity Fair
Waynesboro Village Record

Adams, Henry. *The Education of Henry Adams*. 1918. Reprint, with an introduction by D. W. Brogan. Boston: Houghton Mifflin, 1961.

Addison, Daniel Dulany, ed. *Lucy Larcom: Life, Letters, and Diary*. Boston: Houghton Mifflin, 1894.

Anderson, Charles. *The Cause of the War: Who Brought It On, and For What Purpose*. New York: William C. Bryant, 1863.

―――. *Letter Addressed to the Opera House Meeting, Cincinnati*. New York: William C. Bryant, 1863.

Anderson, John Q., ed. *Brokenburn: The Journal of Kate Stone, 1861–1868*. 1955. Reprint, Baton Rouge: Louisiana State University Press, 1995.

Anneke, Fritz. *Der Zweite Freiheitskampf der Vereinigten Staaten von Amerika*. Frankfurt am Main: J. D. Sauerlander, 1861.

Armstrong, Mary M. Bronson. *Letters from a Pennsylvania Chaplain at the Siege of Petersburg, 1865*. Kent, Ohio, 1961.

Bancroft, Frederic, ed. *Speeches, Correspondence, and Political Papers of Carl Schurz*. 6 vols. New York: G. P. Putnam's Sons, Knickerbocker Press, 1913.

Barnes, James J., and Patience P. Barnes, eds. *The American Civil War through British Eyes: Dispatches from British Diplomats*. 3 vols. Kent, Ohio: Kent State University Press, 2003.

Basler, Roy P., ed. *Abraham Lincoln: His Speeches and Writings*. New York: World, 1946.

Bevier, Robert S. *History of the First and Second Missouri Confederate Brigades, 1861–1865*. St. Louis: Bryan, Brand, 1879.

Bigelow, John. *Jamaica in 1850: or, The Effects of Sixteen Years of Freedom on a Slave Colony*. New York: George P. Putnam, 1851.

―――. *Retrospections of an Active Life*. 2 vols. New York: Baker and Taylor, 1909.

Bledsoe, Albert Taylor. *An Essay on Liberty and Slavery*. Philadelphia: J. B. Lippincott, 1856.

Bowen, Ralph H., ed. *A Frenchman in Lincoln's America*. 2 vols. Chicago: R. R. Donnelley and Sons, 1974.

Bradley, George S. *The Star Corps: or, Notes of an Army Chaplain, During Sherman's Famous March to the Sea*. Milwaukee: Jermain and Brightman, 1865.

Briggs, Ward W., Jr., ed. *Soldier and Scholar: Basil Lanneau Gildersleeve and the Civil War*. Charlottesville: University of Virginia Press, 1998.

Buck, Irving A. *Cleburne and His Command*. New York: Neale, 1908.

Bulloch, James D. *The Secret Service of the Confederate States in Europe, or How the Confederate Cruisers Were Equipped*. 2 vols. New York: Thomas Yoseloff, 1959.

Burnett, Lonnie A. *Henry Hotze, Confederate Propagandist: Selected Writings on Revolution, Recognition, and Race*. Tuscaloosa: University of Alabama Press, 2008.

Butler, Benjamin F. *Private and Official Correspondence of Gen. Benjamin F. Butler, During the Period of the Civil War*. 5 vols. Springfield, Mass.: Plimpton, 1917.

Byrne, Frank L., and Jean Powers Soman, eds. *Your True Marcus: The Civil War Letters of a Jewish Colonel*. Kent, Ohio: Kent State University Press, 1985.

Cairnes, John Elliott. *The Slave Power, Its Character, Career, and Probable Designs: Being an Attempt to Explain the Real Issues in the American Contest*. New York: Carleton, 1862.

Case, Lynn M. *French Opinion on the United States and Mexico, 1860–1867: Extracts from the Reports of the Procureurs Généraux*. New York: D. Appleton Century, 1936.

Case of General Tochman — Referred to the Committee on Foreign Affairs and Ordered to Be Printed. Richmond: Confederate States' Printing Office, 1863.

Castleman, Alfred Lewis. *The Army of the Potomac, Behind the Scenes: A Diary of Unwritten History*. Milwaukee: Strickland and Co., 1863.

Cavanagh, Michael. *Memoirs of Gen. Thomas Francis Meagher*. Worcester, Mass.: Messenger, 1892.

Celebration by the Colored People's Educational Monument Association in Memory of Abraham Lincoln. Washington, D.C.: McGill and Witherow, 1865.

Claytor, William Quesenbury. *Diary of William Quesenbury Claytor*. 2 vols. Alexandria, Va.: Alexander Street Press, 2002.

Conyngham, D. P. *The Irish Brigade and Its Campaigns*. Boston: Patrick Donahoe, 1869.

Cooke, Chauncey Herbert. *Soldier Boy's Letters to His Father and Mother, 1861–65*. Independence, Wis.: News Office, 1915.

Crabtree, Beth Gilbert, and James W. Patton, eds. *Journal of a Secesh Lady: The Diary of Catherine Ann Devereux Edmondston, 1860–1866*. Raleigh: North Carolina Division of Archives and History, 1979.

Day, David L. *My Diary of Rambles with the 25th Massachusetts Volunteer Infantry*. Milford, Mass.: King and Billings, 1884.

Devens, R. M. *Our First Century*. Springfield, Mass.: C. A. Nichols, 1881.

The Echo from the Army: What Our Soldiers Say about the Copperheads. New York: Loyal Publication Society, 1865.

Elements of Discord in Secessia. New York: William C. Bryant, 1863.

Everett, Lloyd T. *Living Confederate Principles: A Heritage for All Time*. Ballston, Va.: Yexid, 1917.

Faust, Drew Gilpin, ed. *The Ideology of Slavery*. Baton Rouge: Louisiana State University Press, 1981.

Foner, Philip S., ed. *Frederick Douglass: Selected Speeches and Writings*. Chicago: Lawrence Hill Books, 1999.

Ford, Worthington Chauncey, ed. *A Cycle of Adams Letters, 1861–1865*. 2 vols. Boston: Houghton Mifflin, 1920.

Freidel, Frank, ed. *Union Pamphlets of the Civil War, 1861–1865*. 2 vols. Cambridge, Mass.: Belknap, 1967.

Gasparin, Agénor de. *The Uprising of a Great People: The United States in 1861*. New York: Charles Scribner, 1862.

Gen. Tochman's Case: To the Honorable Senate and House of Representatives of the Confederate States of America, in Congress Assembled. Richmond: Confederate States' Printing Office, 1864.

Gilpin, Ebenezer Nelson. *The Last Campaign: A Cavalryman's Journal*. Leavenworth, Kans.: Press of Ketcheson, 1908.

Goodloe, Daniel. *Emancipation and the War*. Washington, D.C., 1861.

Gould, David, and James B. Kennedy, eds. *Memoirs of a Dutch Mudsill: The 'War Memories' of John Henry Otto, Captain, Company D, 21st Regiment Wisconsin Volunteer Infantry*. Kent, Ohio: Kent State University Press, 2004.

Gould, Edward Kalloch. *Major General Hiram G. Berry: His Career as a Contractor, Bank President, Politician, and Major-General of Volunteers in the Civil War, Together with his War Correspondence, Embracing the Period from Bull Run to Chancellorsville*. Rockland, Maine: Press of the Courier-Gazette, 1899.

Goyne, Minetta Altgelt, ed. *Lone Star and Double Eagle: Civil War Letters of a German-Texas Family*. Fort Worth: Texas Christian University Press, 1982.

The Great Mass Meeting of Loyal Citizens at Cooper Institute, Friday Evening, March 6, 1863. New York: Loyal Reprints, 1863.

Hall, Rev. William A. *The Historic Significance of the Southern Revolution*. Petersburg, Va.: A. F. Crutchfield, 1864.

Hamilton, A. J. *Letter of Gen. A. J. Hamilton of Texas to the President of the United States*. New York: Loyal Publication Society, 1865.

Hamilton, Joseph Grégorie de Roulhac, ed. *The Correspondence of Jonathan Worth*. Raleigh, N.C.: Edwards and Broughton, 1909.

Harwell, Richard Barksdale, ed. *Cities and Camps of the Confederate States*. Urbana: University of Illinois Press, 1958.

Helbich, Wolfgang, and Walter D. Kamphöfner, eds. *Deutsche im Amerikanischen Bürgerkrieg: Briefe von Front und Farm, 1861–1865*. Paderborn: Ferdinand Schöningh, 2002.

———. *Germans in the Civil War: The Letters They Wrote Home*. Translated by Susan Carter Vogel. Chapel Hill: University of North Carolina Press, 2006.

Helbich, Wolfgang, Walter D. Kamphöfner, and Ulrike Sommer, eds. *News from the Land of Freedom: German Immigrants Write Home*. Ithaca, N.Y.: Cornell University Press, 1988.

Higginson, Thomas Wentworth. *Army Life in a Black Regiment*. Boston: Fields, Osgood, 1870.

Hughes, Sarah Forbes, ed. *Letters and Recollections of John Murray Forbes*. 2 vols. Boston: Houghton Mifflin, 1899.

Ingersoll, Charles. *A Letter to a Friend in a Slave State*. Philadelphia: J. Campbell, 1862.

Jones, John Beauchamp. *A Rebel War Clerk's Diary at the Confederate States Capital*. 2 vols. Philadelphia: J. B. Lippincott, 1866.

Kapp, Friedrich. *Vom radikalen Frühsozialisten des Vormärz zum liberalen Parteipolitiker des Bismarckreichs: Briefe, 1843–1884*. Edited by Hans-Ulrich Wehler. Frankfurt am Main: Sammlung Insel, 1969.

Kennedy, John Pendleton, ed. *Mr. Ambrose's Letters on the Rebellion.* New York: Hurd and Houghton, 1865.

Kohl, Lawrence Frederick, ed. *The Story of the 116th Pennsylvania Volunteers in the War of the Rebellion.* New York: Fordham University Press, 1996.

Kohl, Lawrence Frederick, and Margaret Clossé Richard, eds. *Irish Green and Union Blue: The Civil War Letters of Peter Welsh, Color Sergeant, 28th Regiment Massachusetts Volunteers.* New York: Fordham University Press, 1986.

Laboulaye, Édouard. *Separation: War without End.* New York: Loyal Publication Society, 1864.

Law, E. M. *The Confederate Revolution: An Address Delivered before the Association of the Army of Northern Virginia, at the Meeting Held in Richmond, VA., May 28th, 1890.* Richmond, Va.: William Elllis Jones, 1890.

Letters from Europe Touching the American Contest, and Acknowledging the Receipt, from Citizens of New York, of Presentation Sets of the "Rebellion Record," and "Loyal Publication Society" Publications. New York: Loyal Publication Society, 1864.

Lieber, Francis. *The Arguments of Secessionists: A Letter to the Union Meeting, Held in New York, September 30, 1863.* New York: Holmann, 1863.

———. *No Party Now but All for Our Country.* New York: C. S. Westcott, 1863.

———. *Slavery, Plantations, and the Yeomanry.* New York: Loyal Publication Society, 1863.

The Life of Governor Louis Kossuth with His Public Speeches in the United States, and a Brief History of the Hungarian War of Independence. 1852. Reprint, Budapest: Osiris Kiado, 2001.

Lohmann, Christoph, ed. *Radical Passion: Ottilie Assing's Reports from America and Letters to Frederick Douglass.* New York: Peter Lang, 1999.

Lounsbury, Richard C., ed. *Louisa S. McCord: Political and Social Essays.* Charlottesville: University of Virginia Press, 1995.

Marx, Karl, and Friedrich Engels. *The Civil War in the United States.* Edited by Richard Enmale. New York: International Publishers, 1937.

———. *The Communist Manifesto.* 1848. Reprint, New York: Penguin, 1985.

Mason, Virginia. *The Public Life and Diplomatic Correspondence of James M. Mason with Some Personal History by His Daughter.* Roanoke, Va.: Stone, 1903.

McClelland, Robert. *Letter on the Crisis.* Detroit, 1861.

Meagher, Thomas Francis. *Letters on Our National Struggle.* New York: Loyal Publication Society, 1863.

Mitchel, John. *Jail Journal; or Five Years in British Prisons.* New York: Citizen Printing Office, 1854.

Morse, Charles Fessenden. *Letters Written during the Civil War, 1861–1865.* Boston, 1898.

Myers, John C. *A Daily Journal of the 192d Regiment Pennsylvania Volunteers, Commanded by Col. William B. Thomas: In the Service of the United States for 100 Days.* Philadelphia: Crissy and Markley, 1864.

Nevins, Allan, and Milton Halsey Thomas, eds. *The Diary of George Templeton Strong*. 3 vols. New York: Macmillan, 1952.

North and South. London: Chapman and Hall, 1864.

Owen, Robert Dale. *The Conditions of Reconstruction; in a letter From Robert Dale Owen to the Secretary of State*. New York: William C. Bryant, 1863.

Palmer, Beverly Wilson, ed. *The Selected Letters of Charles Sumner*. 2 vols. Boston: Northeastern University Press, 1990.

Pelletan, Eugène. *An Address to King Cotton*. New York: H. De Mareil, 1863.

The Preservation of the Union, a National Economic Necessity. New York: William C. Bryant, 1863.

Raines, C. W., ed. *Six Decades in Texas; or Memoirs of Francis Richard Lubbock, Governor of Texas in War Time, 1861–1863*. Austin: B. C. Jones, 1900.

Raymond, Henry Jarvis. *Disunion and Slavery: A Series of Letters to Hon. W. L. Yancey of Alabama*. New York, 1861.

Rebel Conditions of Peace and the Mechanics of the South. New York: Loyal Publication Society, 1863.

Reinhart, Joseph R., ed. *Two Germans in the Civil War: The Diary of John Daeuble and the Letters of Gottfried Rentschler, 6th Kentucky Volunteer Infantry*. Knoxville: University of Tennessee Press, 2004.

Reply of Messrs. Agenor de Gasparin, Edouard Laboulaye, Henri Martin, Augustin Cochin, to the Loyal National League of New York, together with the Address of the League. New York: William G. Bryant, 1864.

Reynolds, Larry J., and Susan Belasco Smith, eds. *"These Sad but Glorious Days": Dispatches from Europe, 1846–1850*. New Haven: Yale University Press, 1991.

Richardson, James D., ed. *The Messages and Papers of Jefferson Davis and the Confederacy, Including Diplomatic Correspondence, 1861–1865*. 2 vols. New York: Chelsea House, 1966.

Robinson, Sara Tappan Doolittle Lawrence. *Kansas: Its Interior and Exterior Life*. Boston: Crosby, Nichols, 1856.

Rowan, Steven, ed. and trans. *Germans for a Free Missouri: Translations from the St. Louis Radical Press, 1857–1862*. Columbia: University of Missouri Press, 1983.

———, ed. *Memoirs of a Nobody: The Missouri Years of an Austrian Radical*. St. Louis: Missouri Historical Society Press, 1997.

Russell, William Howard. *My Diary, North and South*. Boston: T. O. H. P. Burnham, 1863.

Schafer, Joseph, ed. *Intimate Letters of Carl Schurz*. New York: Da Capo, 1929.

Schoonover, Thomas D., ed. *Mexican Lobby: Matías Romero in Washington, 1861–1867*. Lexington: University Press of Kentucky, 1986.

Schurz, Carl. *The Reminiscences of Carl Schurz*. 3 vols. New York: McClure, 1907.

Seward, William Henry. *The Papers of William H. Seward*. Woodbridge, Conn.: Research Publications, 1981.

———. *The Works of William H. Seward*. Edited by George E. Baker. 5 vols. Boston: Houghton Mifflin, 1884.

Sideman, Belle Becker, and Lillian Friedman, eds. *Europe Looks at the Civil War*. New York: Orion, 1960.

Silber, Nina, and Mary Beth Sievens, eds. *Yankee Correspondence: Civil War Letters between New England Soldiers and the Home Front*. Charlottesville: University of Virginia Press, 1996.

Slocum, William N. *The War, and How to End It*. San Francisco, 1861.

Some Lincoln Correspondence with Southern Leaders before the Outbreak of the Civil War, from the Collection of Judd Stewart. New York: J. Stewart, 1909.

Southern Historical Society Papers. 52 vols. 1876–1959. Reprint, Wilmington, N.C.: Broadfoot, 1990.

Thorndike, Rachel Sherman, ed. *The Sherman Letters: Correspondence between General and Senator from 1837–1891*. New York: Charles Scribner's and Sons, 1894.

The Three Voices: The Soldier, Farmer, and Poet, to the Copperheads. New York: William C. Bryant, 1863.

Tochman, Gaspar. *Poland, Russia, and the Policy of the Latter towards the United States*. Baltimore: John D. Toy, 1844.

Trautmann, Frederic, ed. *A Prussian Observes the American Civil War: The Military Studies of Justus Scheibert*. Columbia: University of Missouri Press, 2001.

Turchin, John B. *Chickamauga*. Chicago: Fergus, 1888.

Von Borcke, Heros. *Memoirs of the Confederate War for Independence*. 2 vols. 1866. Reprint, New York: Peter Smith, 1938.

Welles, Gideon. *The Diary of Gideon Welles, Secretary of the Navy under Lincoln and Johnson*. 3 vols. Boston: Houghton Mifflin, 1909.

Secondary Sources

Adams, Ephraim. *Great Britain and the American Civil War*. London: Longman's, Green, 1925.

Anbinder, Tyler. *Five Points*. New York: Free Press, 2001.

Anderson, Benedict. *Imagined Communities: Reflections on the Origin and Spread of Nationalism*. 1983. Reprint, London: Verso, 1990.

Arenson, Adam. *The Great Heart of the Republic: St. Louis and the Cultural Civil War*. Cambridge, Mass.: Harvard University Press, 2011.

Ashworth, John. *Slavery, Capitalism, and Politics in the Antebellum Republic*. Cambridge: Cambridge University Press, 1995.

Athearn, Robert G. *Thomas Francis Meagher: An Irish Revolutionary in America*. New York: Arno, 1976.

Ayers, Edward L. *In the Presence of Mine Enemies: War in the Heart of America, 1859–1863*. New York: W. W. Norton, 2003.

Bayly, C. A. *The Birth of the Modern World, 1780–1914: Global Connections and Comparisons*. Oxford: Blackwell, 2004.

Beard, Charles A., and Mary R. Beard. *The Rise of American Civilization*. 2 vols. New York: Macmillan, 1927.

Bender, Thomas. *A Nation among Nations: America's Place in World History.* New York: Hill and Wang, 2006.

———, ed. *Rethinking American History in a Global Age.* Berkeley: University of California Press, 2002.

Beringer, Richard E., Herman Hattaway, Archer Jones, and William N. Still Jr. *Why the South Lost the Civil War.* Athens: University of Georgia Press, 1986.

Berwanger, Eugene H. *The British Foreign Service and the American Civil War.* Lexington: University Press of Kentucky, 1994.

Blackburn, George M. *French Newspaper Opinion on the American Civil War.* Westport, Conn.: Greenwood, 1997.

Blackett, R. J. M. *Divided Hearts: Britain and the American Civil War.* Baton Rouge: Louisiana State University Press, 2001.

Blum, Edward J. *Reforging the White Republic: Race, Religion, and American Nationalism, 1865–1898.* Baton Rouge: Louisiana State University Press, 2005.

Bolt, Christine. *The Anti-Slavery Movement and Reconstruction: A Study in Anglo-American Co-operation, 1833–77.* London: Oxford University Press, 1969.

Bonner, Robert E. *Mastering America: Southern Slaveholders and the Crisis of American Nationhood.* Cambridge: Cambridge University Press, 2009.

———. "Slavery, Confederate Diplomacy, and the Racialist Mission of Henry Hotze." *Civil War History* 51, no. 3 (2005): 288–316.

Boritt, Gabor S., ed. *Why the Confederacy Lost.* New York: Oxford University Press, 1992.

Boston, Ray. *British Chartists in America, 1839–1900.* Totowa, N.J.: Rowman and Littlefield, 1971.

Bowman, Shearer Davis. *Masters and Lords: Mid-19th-Century U. S. Planters and Prussian Junkers.* New York: Oxford University Press, 1993.

Brancaforte, Charlotte L., ed. *The German Forty-Eighters in the United States.* New York: Peter Lang, 1989.

Browne, Paul Leduc, and Douglas Moggach, eds. *The Social Question and the Democratic Revolution: Marx and the Legacy of 1848.* Ottawa: University of Ottawa Press, 2000.

Burton, William L. *Melting Pot Soldiers: The Union's Ethnic Regiments.* Ames: Iowa State University Press, 1988.

Campbell, Duncan Andrew. *English Public Opinion and the American Civil War.* Suffolk: Baydell, 2003.

Carroll, Daniel B. *Henri Mercier and the American Civil War.* Princeton, N.J.: Princeton University Press, 1971.

Carton, Evan. *Patriotic Treason: John Brown and the Soul of America.* New York: Free Press, 2006.

Case, Lynn M., and Warren F. Spencer. *The United States and France: Civil War Diplomacy.* Philadelphia: University of Pennsylvania Press, 1970.

Claeys, Gregory. "Mazzini, Kossuth, and British Radicalism, 1848–1854." *Journal of British Studies* 28 (1989): 225–61.

Clavin, Matthew J. *Toussaint Louverture and the American Civil War: The Promise and Peril of a Second Haitian Revolution*. Philadelphia: University of Pennsylvania Press, 2009.

Crook, D. P. *American Democracy in English Politics, 1815–1850*. Oxford: Oxford University Press, 1965.

———. *The North, the South, and the Powers, 1861–1865*. New York: John Wiley and Sons, 1974.

Cullop, Charles P. *Confederate Propaganda in Europe, 1861–1865*. Coral Gables, Fla.: University of Miami Press, 1969.

———. "An Unequal Duel: Union Recruiting in Ireland, 1863–1864." *Civil War History* 13 (1967): 101–13.

Cunliffe, Marcus. *Chattel Slavery and Wage Slavery: The Anglo-American Context, 1830–1860*. Athens: University of Georgia Press, 1979.

Curti, Merle. "Austria and the United States, 1848–1852." *Smith College Studies in History* 11 (1926): 141–42.

———. "The Impact of the Revolutions of 1848 on American Thought." *Proceedings of the American Philosophical Society* 93 (1949): 209–15.

Curtis, Eugene M. "American Opinion of the French Nineteenth Century Revolutions." *American Historical Review* 29 (January 1924): 25–60.

Daddysman, James W. *The Matamoros Trade: Confederate Commerce, Diplomacy, and Intrigue*. Newark: University of Delaware Press, 1984.

Dal Lago, Enrico. *Agrarian Elites: American Slaveholders and Southern Italian Landowners, 1815–1861*. Baton Rouge: Louisiana State University Press, 2005.

Davis, David Brion. *The Problem of Slavery in the Age of Revolution, 1770–1823*. Ithaca, N.Y.: Cornell University Press, 1975.

———. *The Slave Power and the Paranoid Style*. Baton Rouge: Louisiana State University Press, 1969.

Deak, Istvan. *The Lawful Revolution: Louis Kossuth and the Hungarians, 1848–1849*. New York: Columbia University Press, 1979.

Diedrich, Maria. *Love across Color Lines: Ottilie Assing and Frederick Douglass*. New York: Hill and Wang, 1999.

Dowe, Dieter, Heinz-Gerhard Haupt, Dieter Langewiesche, and Jonathan Sperber, eds. *Europe in 1848: Revolution and Reform*. New York: Berghahn Books, 2001.

Doyle, Don H. *Nations Divided: America, Italy, and the Southern Question*. Athens: University of Georgia Press, 2002.

———, ed. *Secession as an International Phenomenon: From America's Civil War to Contemporary Separatist Movements*. Athens: University of Georgia Press, 2010.

Doyle, Don H., and Marco Antonio Pamplona, eds. *Nationalism in the New World*. Athens: University of Georgia Press, 2006.

Duberman, Martin. *Charles Francis Adams, 1807–1886*. Stanford, Calif.: Stanford University Press, 1960.

DuBois, Laurent. *Avengers of the New World: The Story of the Haitian Revolution*. Cambridge, Mass.: Harvard University Press, 2005.

Eaton, Clement. *A History of the Southern Confederacy.* New York: Free Press, 1954.

Egnal, Marc. "The Beards Were Right: Parties in the North, 1840–1860." *Civil War History* 47 (March 2001): 30–56.

Ellison, Mary. *Support for Secession: Lancashire and the American Civil War.* Chicago: University of Chicago Press, 1972.

Engle, Stephen D. *Yankee Dutchman: The Life of Franz Sigel.* Fayetteville: University of Arkansas Press, 1993.

Evans, R. J. W., and Hartmut Pogge von Strandmann, eds. *The Revolutions in Europe, 1848–1849: From Reform to Reaction.* Oxford: Oxford University Press, 2000.

Faherty, William Barnaby. *Exile in Erin: A Confederate Chaplain's Story, the Life of Father John B. Bannon.* Saint Louis: Missouri Historical Society Press, 2002.

Faust, Drew Gilpin. *The Creation of Confederate Nationalism: Ideology and Identity in the Civil War South.* Baton Rouge: Louisiana State University Press, 1988.

Foner, Eric. *Free Soil, Free Labor, Free Men: The Ideology of the Republican Party before the Civil War.* New York: Oxford University Press, 1970.

Foner, Philip S. *British Labor and the American Civil War.* New York: Holmes and Meier, 1981.

Fox-Genovese, Elizabeth, and Eugene D. Genovese. *The Mind of the Master Class: History and Faith in the Southern Slaveholders' Worldview.* Cambridge: Cambridge University Press, 2005.

Freehling, William W. *The South vs. the South.* Oxford: Oxford University Press, 2001.

Freidel, Frank. "The Loyal Publication Society: A Pro-Union Propaganda Agency." *Mississippi Valley Historical Review* 26 (December 1939): 359–63.

Freitag, Sabine. *Friedrich Hecker: Two Lives for Liberty.* Edited and translated by Steven Rowan. St. Louis: St. Louis Mercantile Library, 2006.

Fuess, Claude Moore. *Carl Schurz, Reformer, 1829–1906.* New York: Dodd, Mead, 1932.

Gallagher, Gary W. *The Confederate War.* Cambridge, Mass.: Harvard University Press, 1997.

———, ed. *The Antietam Campaign.* Chapel Hill: University of North Carolina Press, 1999.

Gavronsky, Serge. *The French Liberal Opposition and the American Civil War.* New York: Humanities Press, 1968.

Gay, H. Nelson. "Garibaldi's Sicilian Campaign as Reported by an American Diplomat." *American Historical Review* 27 (January 1922): 219–44.

Gazely, John Gerow. *American Opinion of German Unification.* New York: Columbia University Press, 1926.

Geggus, David P., ed. *The Impact of the Haitian Revolution in the Atlantic World.* Columbia: University of South Carolina Press, 2002.

Gellner, Ernest. *Nations and Nationalism.* Oxford: Blackwell, 1983.

Gemme, Paola. *Domesticating Foreign Struggles: The Italian Risorgimento and Antebellum American Identity.* Athens: University of Georgia Press, 2005.

Genovese, Eugene D. *The Slaveholders' Dilemma: Freedom and Progress in Southern Conservative Thought, 1820–1860*. Columbia: University of South Carolina Press, 1992.

Gerteis, Louis S. *Civil War St. Louis*. Lawrence: University of Kansas Press, 2001.

Glicksberg, Charles I. "Henry Adams Reports on a Trades-Union Meeting." *New England Quarterly* 15 (1942): 724–28.

Golder, Frank A. "The American Civil War through the Eyes of a Russian Diplomat." *American Historical Review* 26 (April 1921): 454–63.

Grant, Susan-Mary. *North over South: Northern Nationalism and American Identity in the Antebellum Era*. Lawrence: University Press of Kansas, 2000.

Grimsley, Mark. *The Hard Hand of War*. Cambridge: Cambridge University Press, 1995.

Guterl, Matthew Pratt. *American Mediterranean: Southern Slaveholders in the Age of Emancipation*. Cambridge, Mass.: Harvard University Press, 2008.

Hanna, Alfred Jackson, and Kathryn Abbey Hanna. *Napoleon III and Mexico: American Triumph over Monarchy*. Chapel Hill: University of North Carolina Press, 1971.

Harrison, Royden, "British Labor and American Slavery." *Science and Society* 25 (December 1961): 291–319.

————. "British Labor and the Confederacy." *International Review of Social History* 2 (1957): 78–105.

————, ed. *The English Defence of the Commune, 1871*. London: Merlin, 1971.

Hartz, Louis. *The Liberal Tradition in America: An Interpretation of American Political Thought since the Revolution*. New York: Harcourt, Brace, 1955.

Hernon, Joseph M., Jr. *Celts, Catholics, and Copperheads: Ireland Views the American Civil War*. Columbus: Ohio State University Press, 1968.

————. "The Irish Nationalists and Southern Secession." *Civil War History* 12 (March 1966): 43–53.

Hess, Earl J. *Liberty, Virtue, and Progress: Northerners and Their War for Union*. New York: New York University Press, 1988.

Hobsbawm, Eric J. *The Age of Capital, 1848–1875*. London: Weidenfeld and Nicolson, 1975.

————. *The Age of Revolution, 1789–1848*. New York: World, 1962.

————. *Nations and Nationalism since 1780: Programme, Myth, Reality*. Cambridge: Cambridge University Press, 1990.

Holt, Michael F. *The Political Crisis of the 1850s*. New York: W. W. Norton, 1978.

————. *The Rise and Fall of the American Whig Party: Jacksonian Politics and the Onset of the Civil War*. New York: Oxford University Press, 1999.

Hubbard, Charles M. *The Burden of Confederate Diplomacy*. Knoxville: University of Tennessee Press, 1998.

Huston, James. *Calculating the Value of Union: Slavery, Property Rights, and the Economic Origins of the Civil War*. Chapel Hill: University of North Carolina Press, 2003.

Hyman, Harold, ed. *Heard round the World: The Impact Abroad of the Civil War*. New York: Alfred A. Knopf, 1969.

Ignatiev, Noel. *How the Irish Became White.* New York: Routledge, 1995.

Jenkins, Brian. *Britain and the War for the Union.* Montreal: McGill-Queens University Press, 1974.

Jones, Howard. *Abraham Lincoln and a New Birth of Freedom: The Union and Slavery in the Diplomacy of the Civil War.* Lincoln: University of Nebraska Press, 1999.

———. *Union in Peril: The Crisis over British Intervention in the Civil War.* Chapel Hill: University of North Carolina Press, 1992.

Jones, Peter. *The 1848 Revolutions.* New York: Longman, 1991.

Jones, W. D. "British Conservatives and the American Civil War." *American Historical Review* 8 (1953): 527–43.

Jordan, Donald, and Edwin J. Pratt. *Europe and the American Civil War.* Boston: Houghton Mifflin, 1931.

Katz, Philip. *From Appomattox to Montmartre: Americans and the Paris Commune.* Cambridge, Mass.: Harvard University Press, 1998.

Körner, Axel, ed. *1848: A European Revolution? International Ideas and National Memories of 1848.* London: Macmillan, 2000.

Lawson, Melinda. *Patriot Fires: Forging a New American Nationalism in the Civil War North.* Lawrence: University Press of Kansas, 2002.

Levine, Bruce. *The Spirit of 1848: German Immigrants, Labor Conflict, and the Coming of the Civil War.* Chicago: University of Illinois Press, 1992.

Lillibridge, G. D. *Beacon of Freedom: The Impact of American Democracy upon Great Britain, 1830–1870.* Philadelphia: University of Pennsylvania Press, 1955.

Lonn, Ella. *Foreigners in the Confederacy.* 1940. Reprint, Gloucester, Mass.: Peter Smith, 1965.

———. *Foreigners in the Union Army and Navy.* Baton Rouge: Louisiana State University Press, 1951.

Luebke, Frederick C., ed. *Ethnic Voters and the Election of Lincoln.* Lincoln: University of Nebraska Press, 1971.

Mahin, Dean. *One War at a Time: The International Dimensions of the American Civil War.* Washington, D.C.: Brassey's, 1999.

Manning, Chandra. *What This Cruel War Was Over: Soldiers, Slavery, and the Civil War.* New York: Alfred A. Knopf, 2007.

Marten, James. *Texas Divided: Loyalty and Dissent in the Lone Star State, 1856–1874.* Lexington: University Press of Kentucky, 1990.

May, Robert E., ed. *The Union, the Confederacy, and the Atlantic Rim.* West Lafayette, Ind.: Purdue University Press, 1995.

McCardell, John. *The Idea of a Southern Nation: Southern Nationalists and Southern Nationalism, 1830–1860.* New York: Norton, 1979.

McGovern, Bryan P. *John Mitchel: Irish Nationalist, Southern Secessionist.* Knoxville: University of Tennessee Press, 2009.

McGrane, Reginald C. "The American Position on the Revolution of 1848 in Germany." *Historical Outlook* 11 (1920): 333–39.

McPherson, James M. *Abraham Lincoln and the Second American Revolution.* New York: Oxford University Press, 1991.

———. *Battle Cry of Freedom: The Civil War Era*. New York: Oxford University Press, 1988.

———. *Is Blood Thicker Than Water? Crises of Nationalism in the Modern World*. New York: Vintage, 1998.

———. *What They Fought For, 1861–1865*. Baton Rouge: Louisiana State University Press, 1994.

Merli, Frank J. *Great Britain and the Confederate Navy, 1861–1865*. Bloomington: Indiana University Press, 1965.

Miller, Randall M., Harry S. Stout, and Charles Reagan Wilson, eds. *Religion and the American Civil War*. New York: Oxford University Press, 1998.

Moore, Barrington, Jr. *Social Origins of Dictatorship and Democracy: Lord and Peasant in the Making of the Modern World*. Boston: Beacon Press, 1966.

Morrison, Michael A. "American Reaction to European Revolutions, 1848–1852: Sectionalism, Memory, and the Revolutionary Heritage." *Civil War History* 49, no. 2 (June 2003): 111–32.

Morrison, Michael A., and Melinda Zook, eds. *Revolutionary Currents: Nation Building in the Transatlantic World*. New York: Rowman and Littlefield, 2004.

Nadel, Stanley. *Little Germany: Ethnicity, Religion, and Class in New York City, 1845–80*. Urbana: University of Illinois Press, 1990.

Nash, Gary B. *Race and Revolution*. Madison: University of Wisconsin Press, 1990.

Oates, Stephen B. "Henry Hotze: Confederate Agent Abroad." *Historian* 27 (1965): 131–54.

O'Brien, Michael. *Conjectures of Order: Intellectual Life and the American South, 1810–1860*. 2 vols. Chapel Hill: University of North Carolina Press, 2004.

Öfele, Martin W. *German-Speaking Officers in the U. S. Colored Troops, 1863–1867*. Gainesville: University Press of Florida, 2004.

Oliver, John W. "Louis Kossuth's Appeal to the Middle West." *Mississippi Valley Historical Review* 14 (March 1928): 481–95.

Onuf, Nicholas, and Peter Onuf. *Federal Union, Modern World: The Law of Nations in an Age of Revolutions, 1776–1814*. Madison, Wis.: Madison House, 1993.

———. *Nations, Markets, and War: Modern History and the American Civil War*. Charlottesville: University of Virginia Press, 2006.

Owsley, Frank L. *King Cotton Diplomacy: Foreign Relations of the Confederate States of America*. Chicago: University of Chicago Press, 1931.

Palmer, R. R. *The Age of the Democratic Revolution: A Political History of Europe and America, 1760–1800*. 2 vols. Princeton, N.J.: Princeton University Press, 1959, 1964.

Paludan, Phillip Shaw. *A People's Contest: The Union and the Civil War, 1861–1865*. 2nd ed. Lawrence: University Press of Kansas, 1996.

Pelling, Henry. *America and the British Left: From Bright to Beven*. New York: New York University Press, 1957.

Potter, David. *The Impending Crisis, 1848–1861*. New York: Harper and Row, 1976.

———. *The South and the Sectional Conflict*. Baton Rouge: Louisiana State University Press, 1968.

Price, Roger. *The Revolutions of 1848*. London: Macmillan, 1988.

Rable, George C. *The Confederate Republic: A Revolution against Politics*. Chapel Hill: University of North Carolina Press, 1994.

Randall, J. G. *Lincoln the Liberal Statesman*. New York: Dodd, Mead, 1947.

Rawley, James A. "The American Civil War and the Atlantic Community." *Georgia Review* 21 (Summer 1967): 185–94.

Reynolds, Larry J. *European Revolutions and the American Literary Renaissance*. New Haven, Conn.: Yale University Press, 1988.

Roberts, Timothy Mason. *Distant Revolutions: 1848 and the Challenge of American Exceptionalism*. Charlottesville: University of Virginia Press, 2009.

Roediger, David R. *The Wages of Whiteness: Race and the Making of the American Working Class*. New York: Verso, 1991.

Royster, Charles. *The Destructive War: William Tecumseh Sherman, Stonewall Jackson, and the Americans*. New York: Vintage, 1991.

Rubin, Anne Sarah. *A Shattered Nation: The Rise and Fall of the Confederacy, 1861–1868*. Chapel Hill: University of North Carolina Press, 2005.

Rugemer, Edward Bartlett. *The Problem of Emancipation: The Caribbean Roots of the American Civil War*. Baton Rouge: Louisiana State University Press, 2008.

Runkle, Gerald. "Karl Marx and the American Civil War." *Comparative Studies in Society and History* 6 (January 1964): 117–41.

Schafer, Joseph. *Carl Schurz: Militant Liberal*. Evansville, Wis.: Antes, 1930.

———. "Who Elected Lincoln?" *American Historical Review* 47 (October 1941): 51–53.

Schoen, Brian. *The Fragile Fabric of Union: Cotton, Federal Politics, and the Global Origins of the Civil War*. Baltimore: Johns Hopkins University Press, 2009.

Sears, Louis Martin. "A Confederate Diplomat at the Court of Napoleon III." *American Historical Review* 26 (January 1921): 255–81.

Shepperson, Wilbur S. *Emigration and Disenchantment: Portraits of Englishmen Repatriated from the United States*. Norman: University of Oklahoma Press, 1965.

Sklar, Kathryn Kish, and James Brewer Stewart, eds. *Women's Rights and Transatlantic Antislavery in the Era of Emancipation*. New Haven: Yale University Press, 2007.

Spencer, Donald S. *Louis Kossuth and Young America: A Study of Sectionalism and Foreign Policy, 1848–1852*. Columbia: University of Missouri Press, 1977.

Sperber, Jonathan. *The European Revolutions, 1848–1851*. Cambridge: Cambridge University Press, 1994.

Stearns, Peter N. *1848: The Revolutionary Tide in Europe*. New York: Norton, 1974.

Stern, Philip Van Doren. *When the Guns Roared: World Aspects of the American Civil War*. New York: Doubleday, 1965.

Stock, Leo Francis. "Catholic Participation in the Diplomacy of the Southern Confederacy." *Catholic Historical Review* 26 (April 1930): 1–18.

Szilassy, Sander. "America and the Hungarian Revolution of 1848–1849." *Slavonic and East European Review* 44 (April 1966): 192–94.

Tacke, Charlotte, ed. *1848: Memory and Oblivion in Europe*. New York: Peter Lang, 2000.

Taylor, John M. *William Henry Seward: Lincoln's Right Hand*. New York: Harper Collins, 1991.

Thomas, Emory M. *The Confederacy as a Revolutionary Experience*. Englewood Cliffs, N.J.: Prentice Hall, 1971.

———. *The Confederate Nation, 1861–1865*. New York: Harper and Row, 1979.

Thomas, John L., ed. *Abraham Lincoln and the American Political Tradition*. Amherst: University of Massachusetts Press, 1986.

Thomson, Guy, ed. *The European Revolutions of 1848 and the Americas*. London: Institute of Latin American Studies, 2002.

Towers, Frank. *The Urban South and the Coming of the Civil War*. Charlottesville: University of Virginia Press, 2004.

Trefousse, Hans. *Carl Schurz*. Knoxville: University of Tennessee Press, 1982.

Tuchinsky, Adam-Max. "'The Bourgeoisie Will Fall and Fall Forever': The *New-York Tribune*, the 1848 French Revolution, and American Social Democratic Discourse." *Journal of American History* 92 (September 2005): 470–97.

Tucker, Phillip Thomas. *The Confederacy's Fighting Chaplain: Father John B. Bannon*. Tuscaloosa: University of Alabama Press, 1992.

———. "Confederate Secret Agent in Ireland: Father John B. Bannon and the Irish Mission, 1863–1864." *Journal of Confederate History* 5 (1990): 55–85.

Tyler, Ronnie C. *Santiago Vidaurri and the Southern Confederacy*. Austin: Texas State Historical Association, 1973.

Tyrner-Tyrnauer, A. R. *Lincoln and the Emperors*. New York: Harcourt, Brace and World, 1962.

Van Deusen, Glyndon G. *Horace Greeley: Nineteenth-Century Crusader*. New York: Hill and Wang, 1953.

———. *Thurlow Weed, Wizard of the Lobby*. Boston: Little, Brown, 1947.

———. *William Henry Seward*. New York: Oxford University Press, 1967.

Warren, Craig A. "'Oh, God, What a Pity!': The Irish Brigade at Fredericksburg and the Creation of a Myth." *Civil War History* 47 (September 2001): 193–221.

West, W. Reed. *Contemporary French Opinion on the American Civil War*. Baltimore: Johns Hopkins University Press, 1924.

Whitridge, Arnold. "British Liberals and the American Civil War." *History Today* 12 (1962): 688–95.

Williams, Samuel C. "John Mitchel, the Irish Patriot, Resident of Tennessee." *East Tennessee Historical Society Publications* 10 (1938): 44–56.

Wittke, Carl. *The Irish in America*. Baton Rouge: Louisiana State University Press, 1956.

———. *Refugees of Revolution: The German Forty-Eighters in America*. Westport, Conn.: Greenwood, 1952.

Woldman, Albert A. *Lincoln and the Russians*. Cleveland: World, 1952.

Wood, Gordon S. *Empire of Liberty*. New York: Oxford University Press, 2009.

Young, Robert W. *Senator James Murray Mason: Defender of the Old South*. Knoxville: University of Tennessee Press, 1998.

Zucker, A. E., ed. *The Forty-Eighters: Political Refugees of the German Revolution of 1848*. New York: Columbia University Press, 1950.

Index

tion from, 29–30; and diplomatic relations with Confederacy, 89, 94. *See also* Great Britain; Revolutions of 1848

Irish Brigade, 52, 53

Irish Confederation, 25

Italian states, 65, 82, 100, 103; and revolutions of 1848, 7, 15–17, 26, 36–37, 48, 64, 72, 75–76, 88, 96, 104, 112, 153; unification of, 8, 50–51, 64, 68–69, 76, 80, 82–83, 96–97, 112, 116; and French Revolution, 13; and diplomatic relations with Union, 74. *See also* Kingdom of the Two Sicilies; Papal States; Revolutions of 1848; Risorgimento; Roman Republic

Italy. See Italian states

Jackson, Claiborne Fox, 41, 43
Jackson, Thomas Jonathan, 97
Jamaica, emancipation in, 111
Jefferson, Thomas, 12
Jeffersonian Republican Party, 117
Johnson, Andrew, 155–56
Judd, Norman B., 72

Kansas, violence in, 34, 119
Kansas-Nebraska Act, 28–29, 119; Irish reactions to, 30–31, 33–34; German reactions to, 31–34
Kapp, Friedrich, 23, 27, 32, 34, 49
Kennedy, John Pendleton, 75
Kenrick, Peter Richard (archbishop of St. Louis), 47
King, Rufus, 72
Kingdom of the Two Sicilies, 15, 97, 103
Kinkel, Gottfried, 22, 32–34, 51
Know Nothing Party, 43
Kossuth, Louis, 16, 19–23, 34, 45, 48–49, 61, 67, 94–96, 121, 141–42

Laboulaye, Édouard, 112, 125
Lamar, Lucius Quintus Cincinnatus, 103–4

Lamartine, Alphonse de, 15, 16, 138, 148

Latin America, wars of independence in, 3, 12, 13, 69–70, 82, 150, 153

Ledru-Rollin, Alexandre Auguste, 15, 45

Leopold I (king of Belgium), 149

Lieber, Francis, 122–23

Lincoln, Abraham, 37, 39, 51, 61–63, 65–67, 75, 76–77, 82, 95–96, 101–3, 105, 107–10, 112–15, 121–22, 143, 146

Louis Philippe (king of France), 13, 15

Loyal Publication Society, 122–24

Lubbock, Francis Richard, 57

Lucas, Edward, 86

Lyon, Nathaniel, 44, 46

Mahler, Franz, 51

Manassas, Battle of. *See* Bull Run, Battle of

Manetta, Fillip, 86

Mann, A. Dudley, 17, 19, 80–81, 84, 95, 141, 145–46, 149

Marsh, George Perkins, 74

Martin, John, 56–57, 94

Marx, Karl, 4–5, 7, 23, 39, 120, 138

Mason, James M., 82–84, 105, 149

Mazzini, Giuseppe, 23, 45, 141–42

McClellan, George B., 8, 109

McClelland, Robert, 70–71

McCord, Louisa, 18–19

McKaye, James, 128

Meagher, Thomas Francis, 16, 22, 25–26, 52, 57, 94, 123, 125

Metternich, Clemens von, 15

Mexican-American War, 11, 17

Mexico, 70, 154–56; and Mexican-American War, 11, 17; and diplomatic relations with U.S., 82. *See also* Latin America, wars of independence in

Mill, John Stuart, 75–76

Milroy, Robert H., 101, 130–31

Mitchel, John, 16, 22–23, 25–26, 30–31, 33–34, 36, 56–57, 84, 94

Monroe Doctrine, 13, 19, 53